Chinese Cyberspaces

Chinese Cyberspaces provides a multi-disciplinary study on the recent development and consequences of Internet expansion in China taken from social, political, cultural and economic perspectives. The book provides critical analysis of the effects of Internet technology on China's information policy and overall political stability as well as the political implications.

Original fieldwork from a leading group of international scholars carried out over the last two years suggests that although the digital divide has developed along typical lines of gender, urban versus rural, and income, it has also been greatly influenced by the Communist Party's attempts to exert efficient control. This compelling overview of the current situation regarding Internet development in China and its potential future trends will appeal to social science academics and decision makers in politics, business and international organizations.

Jens Damm is Research Associate at the Seminar of East Asian Studies, at Freie Universität, Berlin, Germany.

Simona Thomas was Research Associate at the Centre for Chinese and East Asian Politics at Freie Universität, Berlin, Germany, and works as a Scientific Author in Berlin.

Asia's transformations
Edited by Mark Selden
Binghamton and Cornell Universities, USA

The books in this series explore the political, social, economic, and cultural consequences of Asia's transformations in the twentieth and twenty-first centuries. The series emphasizes the tumultuous interplay of local, national, regional and global forces as Asia bids to become the hub of the world economy. While focusing on the contemporary, it also looks back to analyze the antecedents of Asia's contested rise.

This series comprises several strands:

Asia's Transformations aims to address the needs of students and teachers, and the titles will be published in hardback and paperback. Titles include:

Debating Human Rights
Critical essays from the United States and Asia
Edited by Peter Van Ness

Hong Kong's History
State and society under colonial rule
Edited by Tak-Wing Ngo

Japan's Comfort Women
Sexual slavery and prostitution during World War II and the US occupation
Yuki Tanaka

Opium, Empire and the Global Political Economy
Carl A. Trocki

Chinese Society
Change, conflict and resistance
Edited by Elizabeth J. Perry and Mark Selden

Mao's Children in the New China
Voices from the Red Guard generation
Yarong Jiang and David Ashley

Remaking the Chinese State
Strategies, society and security
Edited by Chien-min Chao and Bruce J. Dickson

Korean Society
Civil society, democracy and the state
Edited by Charles K. Armstrong

The Making of Modern Korea
Adrian Buzo

The Resurgence of East Asia
500, 150 and 50 year perspectives
Edited by Giovanni Arrighi, Takeshi Hamashita and Mark Selden

Chinese Society, second edition
Change, conflict and resistance
*Edited by Elizabeth J. Perry and
Mark Selden*

Ethnicity in Asia
Edited by Colin Mackerras

The Battle for Asia
From decolonization to
globalization
Mark T. Berger

**State and Society in 21st
century China**
*Edited by Peter Hays Gries and
Stanley Rosen*

Japan's Quiet Transformation
Social change and civil
society in the 21st century
Jeff Kingston

Confronting the Bush Doctrine
Critical views from the
Asia-Pacific
*Edited by Mel Gurtov and
Peter Van Ness*

**China in War and Revolution,
1895–1949**
Peter Zarrow

**The Future of US–Korean
Relations**
The Imbalance of Power
Edited by John Feffer

Asia's Great Cities
Each volume aims to capture the heartbeat of the contemporary city from
multiple perspectives emblematic of the authors' own deep familiarity with
the distinctive faces of the city, its history, society, culture, politics and
economics, and its evolving position in national, regional and global frameworks. While most volumes emphasize urban developments since the
Second World War, some pay close attention to the legacy of the longue
durée in shaping the contemporary. Thematic and comparative volumes
address such themes as urbanization, economic and financial linkages,
architecture and space, wealth and power, gendered relationships, planning
and anarchy, and ethnographies in national and regional perspective.

Titles include:

Bangkok
Place, practice and representation
Marc Askew

Beijing in the Modern World
*David Strand and Madeline Yue
Dong*

Shanghai
Global city
Jeff Wasserstrom

Hong Kong
Global city
Stephen Chiu and Tai-Lok Lui

Representing Calcutta
Modernity, nationalism, and the
colonial uncanny
Swati Chattopadhyay

Singapore
Wealth, power and the culture of
control
Carl A. Trocki

Asia.com is a series which focuses on the ways in which new information and communication technologies are influencing politics, society and culture in Asia. Titles include:

Japanese Cybercultures
Edited by Mark McLelland and Nanette Gottlieb

Asia.com
Asia encounters the Internet
Edited by K.C. Ho, Randolph Kluver and Kenneth C.C. Yang

The Internet in Indonesia's New Democracy
David T. Hill and Krishna Sen

Chinese Cyberspaces
Technological changes and political effects
Edited by Jens Damm and Simona Thomas

Literature and Society is a series that seeks to demonstrate the ways in which Asian literature is influenced by the politics, society and culture in which it is produced. Titles include:

The Body in Postwar Japanese Fiction
Edited by Douglas N. Slaymaker

Chinese Women Writers and the Feminist Imagination (1905–1945)
Haiping Yan

Routledge Studies in Asia's Transformations is a forum for innovative new research intended for a high-level specialist readership, and the titles will be available in hardback only. Titles include:

1. The American Occupation of Japan and Okinawa*
Literature and memory
Michael Molasky

2. Koreans in Japan*
Critical voices from the margin
Edited by Sonia Ryang

3. Internationalizing the Pacific
The United States, Japan and the Institute of Pacific Relations in war and peace, 1919–1945
Tomoko Akami

4. Imperialism in South East Asia
'A fleeting, passing phase'
Nicholas Tarling

5. Chinese Media, Global Contexts
Edited by Chin-Chuan Lee

6. Remaking Citizenship in Hong Kong
Community, nation and the global city
Edited by Agnes S. Ku and Ngai Pun

7. Japanese Industrial Governance
Protectionism and the licensing state
Yul Sohn

Critical Asian Scholarship is a series intended to showcase the most important individual contributions to scholarship in Asian Studies. Each of the volumes presents a leading Asian scholar addressing themes that are central to his or her most significant and lasting contribution to Asian studies. The series is committed to the rich variety of research and writing on Asia, and is not restricted to any particular discipline, theoretical approach or geographical expertise.

Chinese Cyberspaces

Technological changes
and political effects

**Edited by Jens Damm
and Simona Thomas**

Routledge
Taylor & Francis Group

LONDON AND NEW YORK

First published 2006
by Routledge
2 Park Square, Milton Park, Abingdon, Oxon OX14 4RN

Simultaneously published in the USA and Canada
by Routledge
270 Madison Ave, New York, NY 10016

Routledge is an imprint of the Taylor & Francis Group

Typeset in Times New Roman by
Florence Production Ltd, Stoodleigh, Devon

Printed and bound in Great Britain by
Biddles Ltd, Kings Lynn, Norfolk

British Library Cataloguing in Publication Data
A catalogue record for this book is available from the British Library

Library of Congress Cataloging in Publication Data
Chinese cyberspaces: technological changes and political
effects/edited by Jens Damm and Simona Thomas.
    p. cm. – (Asia's transformations)
  Includes bibliographical references and index.
1 Internet – Social aspects – China. 2. Internet – Political aspects
– China. 3. Information policy – China. 4. Digital divide –
China. 5. Internet in public administration – China. I. Damm,
Jens. II. Thomas, Simona. III. Series.
HN740.Z9I565 2006
303.48′33′0951 – dc22   2005018143

ISBN10: 0–415–33208–7

ISBN13: 9–78–0–415–33208–8

Contents

Figures

Tables

Contributors

Michael Chase is an Associate International Policy Analyst at the RAND Corporation and a PhD candidate at the Johns Hopkins University School of Advanced International Studies (SAIS). His research interests include East Asian security issues and the social and political influence of the Internet in China. He received his BA in politics from Brandeis University in 1998 and his MA in international relations from SAIS in 2001.

Duncan Clark is the Managing Director, BDA China Ltd; he founded BDA in Hong Kong and set up BDA's Beijing Representative Office in 1994. He has over ten years' experience in telecom and technology financing and consulting, including four years as an investment banker with Morgan Stanley. He has seven years' experience in China's telecom and technology sectors and has been involved in the Internet in China since its commercial inception in 1995. He has leveraged this experience to guide BDA towards becoming the leading telecom and technology consultancy in China.

Prior to founding BDA, Duncan worked as an investment banker at Morgan Stanley & Co., in the firm's London and Hong Kong offices. He specialized in telecom and high-technology corporate finance advisory, M&A and equity financing assignments including telecom carrier privatization.

Duncan Clark graduated from the London School of Economics with a BSc (Hons) in Economics in 1990. He is bilingual in English and French, and has a working knowledge of Mandarin.

Jens Damm is a Research Associate at the Seminar of East Asian Studies, Sinology, at Freie Universität Berlin. His research interests include China's Internet policy, gender studies, and identity politics in Chinese societies. He is the author of *Homosexualität und Gesellschaft in Taiwan* (Münster: Lit, 2003) and co-editor of *Chinesische Literatur. Zum siebzigsten Geburtstag von Eva Müller* (Münster: Lit, 2005). He has published many articles on gender questions, Chinese cyberspaces and Taiwan-related questions. He graduated from the University of Trier in 1994 with an MA in Sinology and Economics and gained his PhD at Freie Universität Berlin in 2002. He has studied and carried out research in both China and Taiwan.

Nina Hachigian is a Senior Political Scientist at the RAND Corporation and the Director of the RAND Center for Asia Pacific Policy where her research focuses on security and technology issues in Asia. She is the co-author of *The Information Revolution in Asia* (Santa Monica: RAND, 2003). Before joining RAND, she was a Senior Fellow at the Pacific Council on International Policy. Prior to this, she served at the White House as an assistant to the Deputy National Security Advisor, Jim Steinberg, a former RAND researcher, and the National Security Advisor, Samuel R. "Sandy" Berger. Nina Hachigian received her BS in biology from Yale in 1989, graduating magna cum laude, and her JD from the Stanford University School of Law in 1994, graduating with distinction.

Eric Harwit is Associate Professor of Asian Studies, University of Hawaii, and Lecturer, College of Business Administration, University of Hawaii. He was a Visiting Associate Professor, Stanford University, from 2000 to 2001.

He gained his PhD in political science at University of California, Berkeley in 1992; he also studied in Beijing (University of International Business and Economics) and in Tokyo. He has written a monograph on China's automobile industry (1995), and has published widely on the Internet in China, and on China's telecommunications industry.

Johan Lagerkvist is a PhD candidate at the Department of East Asian languages, Lund University, Sweden. He received his MA in East Asian Studies from Stockholm University in 1997, and a Bachelor's degree in political science from Stockholm University in 2001. He worked as a project coordinator at the Nordic Center, Fudan University, Shanghai, from 1997–2000. His main research interests include the social and political impacts of China's globalization, mass media and Internet development in China and Southeast Asia. He guest-edited the theme issue "Chinese intellectuals' thoughts on the Internet," *Contemporary Chinese Thought* (2003). He has written several articles on communications development in China, including "The techno-cadre's dream: administrative reform by electronic governance in China today?" in *China Information* (2005), and "The rise of online public opinion in the PRC" in *China: An International Journal* (2005).

James Mulvenon is Deputy Director, Advanced Analysis at DGI's Center for Intelligence Research and Analysis. Previously, he was a Political Scientist at the RAND Corporation and Deputy Director of RAND's Center for Asia-Pacific Policy. A specialist on the Chinese military, his current research focuses on Chinese C4ISR, defense research/development/acquisition organizations and policy, strategic weapons doctrines (computer network attack and nuclear warfare), patriotic hackers, and the military and civilian implications of the information revolution in China. His book *Soldiers of Fortune* (Armonk, NY: M.E. Sharpe, 2001), examines the Chinese military's multi-billion dollar business empire. James Mulvenon received his PhD in political science from the University of California, Los Angeles.

Simona Thomas is a Scientific Author and her main research focus is on e-commerce/e-business and its effects on Chinese and foreign companies in the PRC. After working as a Researcher at the Chinese Language Department, Trier University, Germany, she worked as a consultant with the Volkswagen Group China, Beijing, PRC. As Research Associate at the Center for Chinese and East Asian Politics, Department of Political and Social Sciences, Freie Universität Berlin, she took part in the project "Internet Policy in the PRC," funded by the Deutsche Forschungsgemeinschaft (DFG). She also took part in the e-learning project "Chinese History Online" at the Seminar of East Asian Studies, Freie Universität Berlin. She has written several articles on the Chinese Internet, with publications appearing, for example, in *China aktuell.*

Simona Thomas obtained an MA in Chinese Studies in 1999 at the University of Trier after gaining an MA in Business Administration (Diplom-Kauffrau) in 1996. She is a PhD candidate at the Center for Chinese and East Asian Politics, Department of Political and Social Sciences, Freie Universität Berlin.

Xie Kang gained his PhD at Renmin University of China. His research interests and teaching courses include economics of information and economics of e-commerce. At present, Xie Kang is a Professor at the School of Business at Sun Yat-Sen University in Guangzhou City, China. He is Dean of the Center for Information, Economy and Politics at Sun Yat-Sen University, and a standing member of the Council for Information at the Economics Academy of China. He is the author of many academic publications and research papers in Chinese including: *The Principle of Economics of Information* (Changsha: The Publishing Press of Zhongnan Industrial University, 1998), *The Knowledge Advantage: Study on Mechanism for Enterprise Competitiveness – Promoting by Informatization* (Guangzhou: Guangdong People's Publishing House, 1999), *Information Economy in the World and National Knowledge Advantage* (Guangzhou: Guangdong People's Publishing House, 2001) and co-author of *E-Banking* (Changchun Publishing Press, 2000) and *The Competitive Strategy in E-Banking* (Guangzhou: Guangdong People's Publishing House, 2001).

Abbreviations

aadn	administrative area domain name
AAS	Association of Asian Studies
ac	academic
ADSL	Asymmetric Digital Subscriber Line
aka	also known as
AoIR	Association of Internet Researchers
B2B	business-to-business
B2C	business-to-consumer
B2G	business-to-government
BAIC	Beijing Administration of Industry and Commerce
BBS	Bulletin Board Service
CAAC	Civil Aviation Administration of China
CAD	computer-aided design
CAEFI	China Association of Enterprises with Foreign Investment
CAM	computer-aided management
CANet	China Academic Network
CAPP	computer-aided process planning
CAS	Chinese Academy of Sciences
CASS	Chinese Academy of Social Sciences
CCP	Chinese Communist Party
CD	compact disk
CE	communication equipment
CEO	Chief Executive Officer
CERNET	China Education and Research Network
CGI	Common Gateway Interface
CGWNet	China Great Wall Network
ChinaGBN	Golden Bridge Network
CHINAPAC	Packet-data network built by the MPT
CIETNet	Network of the Ministry of Foreign Trade and Economic Cooperation
CMNet	China Mobile Network
CNNIC	China Internet Network Information Center
com	commercial

CRM	customer relationship management
CRnet	China Research Network
CSNet	China Satellite Network
CSTNet	China Science and Technology Network
DDN	Digital Data Network
DDoS	Distributed Denial of Service
DFG	Deutsche Forschungsgemeinschaft
DFN	Digital Freedom Network
DNS	Domain Name Service
EACS	European Association of Chinese Studies
ECCF	E-Commerce China Forum
ECWG	E-Commerce Working Group
EDI	electronic data interchange
edu	educational
ERP	enterprise resource planning
GDP	Gross Domestic Product
GNP	Gross National Product
GOP	Government Online Project
gov	governmental
HTTP	Hyper Text Transfer Protocol
HTTPS	Hyper Text Transfer Protocol Secure
ICA	International Communication Association
ICAS	International Convention of Asia Scholars
ICMP	Internet Control Message Protocol
ICP	Internet Content Provider
ICT	Information and Communication Technology
IHEP	Institute of High Energy Physics
IIF	International Informatization Forum
IPSEC	Internet Protocol Security
IT	Information Technology
JIT	just in time
LP	linear programming
Mbps	megabits per second
MEI	Ministry of Electronics Industry
MOFTEC	Ministry of Foreign Trade and Co-operation
MP3	MPEG1 Layer 3
MPS	Ministry of Public Security
MPT	Ministry of Posts and Telecommunications
MSS	Ministry of State Security
n.a.	not available
net	network
P2P	peer-to-peer
PC	personal computer
PRC	People's Republic of China
PTA	provincial telecommunications administrations

RMB	Renminbi
S/MIME	Secure/Multi-purpose Internet Mail Extension
SARFT	State Administration of Radio, Films, and Television
SARS	Severe Acute Respiratory Syndrome
SCM	supply chain management
SEC	State Education Commission
SEZ	Special Economic Zone
SMS	Short Message Service
SMTP	Simple Mail Transport Protocol
SSH	Secure Shell
SSL	Secure Socket Layer
TCP/IP	Transmission Control Protocol/Internet Protocol
UNCTAD	United Nations Conference on Trade and Development
UNESCO	United Nations Educational, Scientific and Cultural Organization
UniNET	China Unicom Network
UNPAN	United Nations Online Network in Public Administration and Finance
URL	Uniform Resource Locator
VPN	Virtual Private Network
WTO	World Trade Organization

Preface

The chosen title *Chinese Cyberspaces* reflects the multifaceted development of the Internet in China. The editors were involved in an interdisciplinary research project funded by the DFG (Deutsche Forschungsgemeinschaft), May 2001–April 2003, on China's Internet policy at Freie Universität Berlin. The main theme of this volume represents the outcome of the research, which was on China's Internet Policy between Technological Development and Political Reaction. The project was based on the premise that the two main objectives of the Chinese leadership's regulative policy are contradictory: on the one hand, the Chinese state is attempting to exert control over Internet use for political reasons and, on the other hand, the state is attracted by the economic advantages offered by the technological modernization of information and communication. The project focused on three central aspects of Internet development in China: on e-government from a macro-perspective, on a content analysis of e-government from a micro-perspective, analyzing local and regional portals, and on the impact of e-commerce from the perspective of foreign enterprises in China.

In particular, we would like to thank the DFG for funding the project. Prof. Eberhard Sandschneider and Zhang Junhua developed the project and we would like to offer them our special thanks. Prof. Sandschneider, as the director of the project, introduced us to the concepts of the political impact of the Internet on the transformation of China today. Zhang Junhua shaped our understanding of the complex relationships in the field of governmental reforms. Karin Damman-Börger managed the administration of the project with the greatest enthusiasm; the student assistants supported us in every way and also helped with long and fruitful discussions and comments to shape the project: we would like to name in particular, Horst Schmidt, Eva Knoll, Yeeman Lee and Carola Milbrodt. We also would like to thank all the other staff at the Center for Chinese and East Asian Politics, Otto Suhr Institute of Political Science, Freie Universität Berlin, for their unremitting support.

This volume is the result of an intensive exchange between colleagues "online and offline." A "virtual research community" network of international Internet researchers on China, the Yahoo group "Chineseinternet-research," http://groups.yahoo.com/group/chineseinternetresearch, became the starting point for information exchange and discussions, and supported the introduction of new members to the research community. This group is continuing to develop its international character by bringing together researchers from Asia including China, North America, Australia and Europe and has pushed the research towards interdisciplinary approaches ranging from political sciences, economics, media and communication sciences to sinology.

The editors and authors participated in various conferences focusing on different aspects and belonging to different academic disciplines: first, at the annual meeting of the Association for Asian Studies (AAS) in Washington DC in 2001; second, at the conference "Internet Research 3.0" in Maastricht, the Netherlands, in the following year, which was organized by the international Association of Internet Researchers (AoIR). The international conference "China and the Internet: Technology, Economy, and Society in Transition" in Los Angeles, May 2003, brought together the members of the "Chinainternetresearch" newsgroup. Further conferences have been: the annual meeting of the ICA, the International Communication Association in San Diego, April 2003; the International Convention of Asia Scholars (ICAS3) meeting in Singapore in 2003; and the biannual conference of the European Association of Chinese Studies (EACS), in Heidelberg, Germany, in August 2004. At this point, we should like to offer thanks to all our colleagues for the fruitful discussions that took place at these conferences.

The publication of this volume has only been made possible with the help and support of Ann Mackay, who has worked on the English text with meticulous care in preparing it for printing.

Jens Damm and Simona Thomas
April, 2005

1 Introduction

Chinese cyberspaces: technological changes and political effects

Jens Damm and Simona Thomas

The introduction of the World Wide Web with its user-friendly surface made the Internet potentially accessible to a mass audience in the People's Republic of China (PRC) in the mid-1990s. This triggered the interest of Western analysts and journalists in the future role of this technology with regard to its influence on the media and the political transformation of China.[1] In particular, the Internet boom at the end of the 1990s and during the first years of the new millennium increased speculation about the degree of change that could be expected in Chinese politics, with a technology-deterministic view very often prevailing. The perspective of this volume places a strong focus on the societal and political effects that accompany the technological changes. As a result of this work, we are introducing the term "e-policy" as a concept combining the twin pillars of e-government and e-commerce. The volume is positioned with regard to Internet Studies in general and problems related to the research on China's Internet development in particular.

Articles and works dealing with the Internet in general provided the basic foundations for the research. While, in the beginning, the Internet attracted most attention as a media topic, it has diversified during the last decade into various other academic fields: the definition of the Internet as a new medium among traditional media (Winter 1998, Curran and Park 2000); the complex interaction between technology, economics and politics in the information age (Castells 1996); problems of network infrastructure and identifying the factors that determine the so-called digital divide (Nagy *et al.* 1995, Callon 1996, Norris 2001, Pavlik 2001; for China: Harwit and Clark 2001, Giese 2003a, Fan 2001); the utilization of information and communication technology (ICT) for administrative reforms (Hague and Loader 1999; for China: Hachigian 2001, Zhang 2001); the adaptation of policy and legislation including the production and control of online content (Lessig 1999, Franda 2002, Kalathil and Boas 2003); "the dark-side," that is, hackers and cyber-war (Arquilla and Ronfeldt 1996; for China: Chase and Mulvenon 2002). In the field of the use of ICT for economic purposes, discussions about the potential of a globalized/localized structured e-commerce/e-business have widened since the burst of the "new economy bubble"

(UNCTAD 2003, 2004; for China: Wong and Nah 2001, Zeng 2001, Xie 2001). In the field of political science, the discussion about concepts of good governance in the form of a possible e-government and e-governance has appeared (Center for Democracy and Technology and infoDev 2002, Loader, 1997, United Nations 2004, UNESCO 2002, 2005; for China: Zhang 2001, 2002, Wang 2003). Media and communication science, as well as sociological works, have focused on aspects of the relationship between Internet and society, such as virtual identities and the building of online communities (Lagerkvist 2003, Rheingold 1993, Nie and Erbring 2000, Sunstein 2001; for China: Giese 2003b).

Internet-related research dealing with China is giving rise to an increasing number of works dedicated to this topic (monographs and edited works include, for example, Mueller and Tan 1997, Hughes and Wacker 2003, Ho *et al.* 2003, Zhang and Woesler 2002).[2] While, in the early days, empirical facts along with questions of censorship and control stood at the center of the research (Chu 1994, Chan 1994, Lee 1994, Hong 1998, Lynch 1999, Foster and Goodman 2000), by the end of the 1990s, more and more complex analyses had begun to appear. The predominant focus of the research differed according to the affiliation of the author: many Western publications on the Chinese Internet have stressed two points in particular: the expected "liberating effects" of the new technology and the "counter measures" of the Chinese government, which have been summarized under the term "control and censorship" within a technology-deterministic paradigm (Edelman and Zittrain 2002, see also Fang 2004: 114–23, Tsui 2003). In China itself, a "leapfrogging discourse" has emerged which stresses the economic benefits for development (Wu *et al.* 2002, see also, Dai 2003 and Li and Wong 2001). Technology-oriented "modernization" and the leapfrogging of industrial development have remained at the heart of Chinese research and frequent reference is made to Western works, in particular, to Toffler's "Third Wave."[3] The term *jishu kuayue* (technological leapfrogging) is used in this context to refer to the idea of omitting a stage in economic development with the help of ICT, achieving, through informatization (the third wave), also the foundations of the second wave (industrialization). The public discourse is shaped by these ideas, the protagonists ranging from the government, the mass media and companies to the average users.[4] In 1997, the Chinese Internet Network Information Center (CNNIC) published the first statistical report to provide various data on the development of the Internet in China and, since 1998, these reports, which include information on user demographics, access locations and average online behavior, have been published twice-yearly (CNNIC 10/1997, 7/1998, 1/1999, 7/1999, 1/2000, 7/2000, 1/2001, 7/2001, 1/2002, 7/2002, 1/2003, 7/2003, 1/2004, 7/2004, 1/2005). In addition to these nation-wide developments, a few research projects have been undertaken which also deal with Internet use in the hinterland or the impact of the Internet on "especially vulnerable groups," such as children, women, peasants, migrants and minorities, asking how these groups perceive themselves since they cannot be subsumed under the heading of "mainstream middle class users" (Guo and Bu 2001, see also, Hachigian 2001, Hachigian and Wu 2003).

When the Internet arrived in China in the 1990s, the Chinese government was in the middle of a reform process that was intended to support the process of integration into the global economic system. It is obvious that, at this time, the PRC had not yet developed a coherent strategy for dealing with the phenomena of new and emerging technology, including the Internet. It had a – more or less – "laissez faire" attitude to the development of the Internet, so that different groups and regions were able to pursue their own individual strategies to some extent. Currently, the following groups of protagonists can be distinguished: the government, which itself is divided not only into central and local levels, but also into different responsible authorities; the national and international business community; the administration at different levels; the news media; the citizens and, finally, the technologically enabled users who might now act within the newly formed virtual groups.

Organization of the volume

The volume, *Chinese Cyberspaces*, provides a multidisciplinary perspective on the recent developments and effects of Internet technology in China.[5] The main themes and objectives are concerned with technological developments, with the political consequences from both macro- and micro-perspectives, and with the economic effects of the Internet. It thus offers a comprehensive overview and analysis of the current situation regarding the Chinese Internet and an outline of potential future trends. This is presented by economists, political scientists and sinologists from China, the US and Europe and is based on field work carried out in the PRC.

Chapter 2, "Government policy and political control over China's Internet" by Eric Harwit and Duncan Clark, focuses on the actors responsible for establishing the network outline. Harwit and Clark consider the role of the government, and the implications of governmental and administrative actions for the new data network technology. They examine government control over the physical data pipelines and network content, the management and revenue flows from the information highway, and the political efforts to capture profits generated at various levels of the network system. User demographics are used to compile a profile of the typical Internet user in today's PRC. The authors come to the conclusion that, at least in the short term, the Internet is not an appropriate tool for generating major social or political transformation in the PRC, and they emphasize that the political drive for control over Internet revenue and general network content is muted by a desire to maximize the broader economic and educational features of the network that could benefit the entire nation.

Chapter 3, "In the crossfire of demands: Chinese news portals between propaganda and the public," by Johan Lagerkvist, presents findings from interviews with China's online news industry. It is shown that the delicate relationship between news making and news control is undergoing interesting changes: while self-censorship is practiced in Chinese cyberspace, and the Chinese government is firmly determined to keep news reporting within limits set by the Communist Party, economic logic and changed value orientations among China's Internet surfers equip editors of online news organizations with arguments they can use to negotiate online spatial freedom with government officials. This analysis of the "soft" negotiation processes for China's online news networks, most notably the administration of municipal online news portals, is primarily based on in-depth interviews with editors and journalists of Beijing's *Qianlong Wang* and Shanghai's *Dongfang Wang*. Issues raised in the analysis concern the role the online news genre may play in the development of more independent news making in China. Optimistic assumptions that online news media in a globalizing China will offer less controlled news coverage and follow-up commentaries than offline news outlets such as print media and television, are not altogether wrong. But such forecasts must be qualified against continued government censorship, and self-censorship among online journalists and news consumers.

Chapter 4, "Comrade to comrade networks: the social and political implications of peer-to-peer networks in China," by Michael Chase, Nina Hachigian and James Mulvenon, deals with technological influences and attempts by the Chinese Communist Party (CCP) to exert efficient control. Analyzing the impact on the balance of power between governments and their citizens, the authors present a comprehensively detailed analysis of the seldom-researched influence of technology on society: peer-to-peer (P2P) technology in China is seen as a tool that allows users to exchange information without a centralized point of contact. The problem of technology assessment is addressed, with regard to the possible short- and long-term implications. It is concluded that the average Chinese web users are, without doubt, more interested in the use of the technology for entertainment than politics and that, in the short term, therefore, neither the Internet nor P2P technology will lead to profound shifts in political power.

Chapter 5, "China's e-policy: examples of local e-government in Guangdong and Fujian," by Jens Damm, offers a micro-perspective on local e-government. Based on field work in the two relatively wealthy provinces of Guangdong and Fujian, there is an analysis of the different stages achieved by e-government and various inherent problems. The author arrives at the following conclusions: local e-government lays a strong emphasis on providing people with more convenient access to government information. It is an integral part of the government reforms aimed at increasing efficiency. In giving a more detailed analysis of one example, the Taijiang district in Fuzhou, he describes local e-government as "local portals," offering much more content than just links to the relevant information and government agencies.

Chapter 6, "Industrialization supported by informatization: the economic effects of the Internet in China," by Xie Kang, establishes an academic framework to explain the potentially beneficial effects of the Internet on the Chinese economy from the perspective of an economist based in Guangzhou. Analyzing the spill over effects of the Internet in China, the author considers that the Internet not only offers a way to shorten the distance between China and the developed countries by improving communication generally, but also provides tools that may be implemented to narrow the digital divide between China and the developed countries. He concludes that despite a lack of investment in the Internet in some areas, there is a substantial amount of evidence to show that the Internet has made a positive impact on economic growth in China.

Chapter 7, "Net business: China's potential for a global market change," by Simona Thomas, addresses the developments in China's e-commerce. Analyzing the framework set up by the relevant state protagonists, such as the former Ministry of Foreign Trade and Co-operation (MOFTEC), the author's perspective is directed towards the role of foreign enterprises. Interviews were conducted with two main groups: foreign companies from different industrial sectors (such as information technology, systems and applications, transportation, advertising, law consultancy) and the German Chamber of Commerce and lobby groups. The author concludes that since Chinese companies are benefiting largely from the use of the new media applications, the greatest challenge for foreign companies will be to understand the specifics of the Chinese market.

Conclusion

After a rather slow start in the mid-1990s, the number of Chinese Internet users began to double and triple every year, and today Chinese Cyberspace is regarded to be the second largest in the world, only lagging behind English Cyberspace. Table 1.1 shows this growing role of the Chinese language in the World Wide Web.

Long-term predictions on such a rapidly developing topic as the Internet are very likely to fail. Our research indicates a heterogeneous usage of the new technologies by various and different protagonists. The main trends resulting from the research presented in this volume show that, first, the main beneficiaries of the current stage of Internet development in China are the users themselves who are able to play a self-determined role without conforming to any state curricula. The tremendous increase in local content provided on Chinese portals mirrors the diverging interests of individual users in modern Chinese society. In addition, very specific singular interests are formulated in spheres such as web communities. These developments

Table 1.1 Chinese language in the World Wide Web (2005)

Language used in the World Wide Web by users	
English	295 million
Chinese	110 million
Destination of Chinese users	
PRC	94.00 million
Hong Kong	4.90 million
Singapore	2.14 million
Malaysia	3.00 million
Taiwan	8.80 million
USA	1.50 million
Language version of websites that had been viewed by users in the PRC (Jan. 2005)	
Domestic Chinese websites	82.6 percent
Overseas Chinese websites	7.0 percent
Overseas English websites	5.6 percent
Domestic English websites	4.7 percent

Source: Authors' own compilation based on data from GlobalReach 2005, CNNIC 1/2005.

are characteristic features of an emerging urban post-modern society shaped by a high degree of individualism.

The second group of beneficiaries are the Chinese enterprises. The tremendous investments in the ICT sector within the period of the ninth and tenth Five-Year-Plans are paying off. Whether these companies will really become competitive on a global scale through e-commerce applications remains doubtful at this point in time (see also, Nolan 2001). Regarding the competition within the Chinese domestic market, foreign companies will no longer be able to maintain a leading role by relying solely on the advantageous positioning in the capital-intensive fields which they held in the past.

As mentioned earlier, one result of this work is that we have presented the term "e-policy" as a concept combining the twin pillars of e-government and e-commerce. This policy is a combination of the attempts and strategic plans of the government to guide Internet developments in the desired direction. This constitutes a learning process for different societal and political agents. We would like to stress that we do not assume the existence of a "full-blown blue-print" developed by central government in advance; we see e-policy in terms of an ongoing process. This kind of e-policy is shaped by the two main objectives of the Chinese leadership regarding regulative Internet policy which are sometimes contradictory: although the state wishes, for political reasons, to exert control over Internet use, it is attracted by the potential offered by the Internet for economic gains and for governmental reform. Economic gains can accrue from the modernization of ICT, and governmental reforms can be achieved through the introduction of e-government, which is said to offer greater transparency. We conclude with a quote from Reagle (1999):

> There are in total four things that regulate cyberspace: laws (by government sanction and force), social norms (by expectation, encouragement, or embarrassment), markets (by price and availability), and architecture (what the technology permits, favors, dissuades, or prohibits).[6]

Notes

1 Although the first email was sent from China as early as September 20, 1987, the Internet in China did not begin to develop exponentially until 1995. The first email by Professor Qian Tianbai is said to have contained the message "Beyond the Great Wall, joining the world" (*yueguo changcheng, zouxiang shijie*) (see Qiu 2003: 1).
2 For a further detailed bibliography including various articles, see "Bibliography on the Internet in China," compiled by Randy Kluver. Online. Available HTTP: http://china-wired.com/field/kluver/bibliography-kluver.htm.
3 Alvin Toffler's work *The Third Wave* was translated into Chinese in the 1980s. All his works are said to have become bestsellers in China and many of his phrases have been widely used in China's social, economic and cultural lives. The article "Futurist Toffler: China has Seen 'Astonishing Changes'" was even published on the official website of the Chinese embassy in the US (November 28, 2001. Online. Available HTTP: http://www.china-embassy.org/eng/zt/mgryzdzg/t36523.htm, accessed June 1, 2004). Various articles on "Toffler" and his "Third Wave" can be found at the official Chinese news portal *Renmin Wang*, http://www.people.com.cn, for example, "Tuofule yuyan: 'disici langchao' yi renlei jinru taikong juzhu wei tedian de shidai jijiang dao lai" [Toffler's prediction: "The fourth wave" characterized by human beings residing in outer space] (http://www.people.com.cn/GB/kejiao/42/155/20011128/614385.html, accessed June 3, 2004); "Meiguo zhuming weilaixuejia Tuofule fabiao fanghua guan'gan Zhongguo de bianhua lingren jingyan" [The famous American futurologist, Toffler, expresses his opinion after visiting China – the changes in China are astonishing] (http://www.people.com.cn/GB/paper39/4833/524530.html, accessed June 3, 2004).
4 For a critical evaluation of these approaches, see Hughes and Wacker 2003, and, in particular, Dai 2003.
5 For a complex definition of the dimensions of the term "Cyberspace(s)," see, for example, *An Atlas of Cyberspaces* (September 21, 2004) and Benedikt 1992.
6 See also Lessig 1999.

References

An Atlas of Cyberspaces (September 21, 2004) "Definition cyberspaces." Online. Available HTTP: http://www.geog.ucl.ac.uk/casa/martin/atlas/conceptual.html (accessed September 21, 2004).

Arquilla, John and Ronfeldt, David (1996) *The Advent of Netwar*, Santa Monica, CA: RAND.

Benedikt, Michael (1992) *Cyberspace: First Steps*, Cambridge, MA: MIT Press.

Callon, Jack D. (1996) *Competitive Advantage through Information Technology*, Columbus, OH: McGraw-Hill.

Castells, Manuel (1996) *The Rise of the Network Society*, Malden, MA: Blackwell.

Center for Democracy and Technology and infoDev (2002) *The E-Government Handbook for Developing Countries*. Online. Available HTTP: http://www.cdt.org/egov/handbook/2002-11-14egovhandbook.pdf (accessed March 5, 2003).

Chan, Joseph Man (1994) "Media internationalization in China: processes and tensions," *Journal of Communication (JOC)*, 44: 3, pp. 70–88.

Chase, Michael S. and Mulvenon, James C. (2002) *You've Got Dissent: Chinese Dissident Use of the Internet and Beijing's Counter-Strategies*, Santa Monica, CA: RAND (MR-1543).

Chu, Leonard L. (1994) "Continuity and change in China's media reform," *Journal of Communication (JOC)*, 44: 3, pp. 4–21.

CNNIC (10/1997) *Statistical Report of the Development of China Internet (1997.10)*. Online. Available HTTP: http://www.cnnic.net.cn (accessed February 15, 2003).

CNNIC (7/1998) *Statistical Report of the Development of China Internet (1998.7)*. Online. Available HTTP: http://www.cnnic.net.cn (accessed 15 February 2003).

CNNIC (1/1999) *Statistical Report of the Development of China Internet (1999.1)*. Online. Available HTTP: http://www.cnnic.net.cn (accessed February 15, 2003).

CNNIC (7/1999) *Semi-Annual Survey Report on Internet Development in China (1999.7)*. Online. Available HTTP: http://www.cnnic.net.cn (accessed February 15, 2003).

CNNIC (1/2000) *SemiAnnual Survey Report on Internet Development in China (2000.1)*. Online. Available HTTP: http://www.cnnic.net.cn (accessed February 15, 2003).

CNNIC (7/2000) *Semiannual Survey Report on the Development of China's Internet (2000.7)*. Online. Available HTTP: http://www.cnnic.net.cn (accessed February 15, 2003).

CNNIC (1/2001) *Semiannual Survey Report on the Development of China's Internet (2001.1)*. Online. Available HTTP: http://www.cnnic.net.cn (accessed February 15, 2003).

CNNIC (7/2001) *Semiannual Survey Report on the Development of China's Internet (2001.7)*. Online. Available HTTP: http://www.cnnic.net.cn (accessed February 15, 2003).

CNNIC (1/2002) *Statistical Survey Report on the Development of Internet in China, (2002.1)*. Online. Available HTTP: http://www.cnnic.net.cn (accessed February 15, 2003).

CNNIC (7/2002) *Statistical Survey Report on the Development of Internet in China (2002.7)*. Online. Available HTTP: http://www.cnnic.net.cn (accessed February 15, 2003).

CNNIC (1/2003) *Statistical Survey Report on the Development of Internet in China (2003.1)*. Online. Available HTTP: http://www.cnnic.net.cn (accessed February 15, 2003).

CNNIC (7/2003) *12th Statistical Survey on the Internet Development in China (2003.7)*. Online. Available HTTP: http://www.cnnic.net.cn (accessed August 17, 2003).

CNNIC (1/2004) *13th Statistical Survey on the Internet Development in China (2004.1)*. Online. Available HTTP: http://www.cnnic.net.cn (accessed March 23, 2004).

CNNIC (7/2004) *14th Statistical Survey Report on the Development on Internet in China (2004.7)*. Online. Available HTTP: http://www.cnnic.net.cn (accessed August 21, 2004).

CNNIC (1/2005) *15th Statistical Survey on the Internet Development in China (2005.1)*. Online. Available HTTP: http://www.cnnic.net.cn (accessed March 23, 2005).

Curran, James and Park, Myung-Jin (eds) (2000) *De-Westernizing Media Studies*, London and New York: Routledge.

Dai, Xiudian (2003) "ICTs in China's development strategy," in Hughes/Wacker 2003, pp. 8–29.

Edelman, Benjamin and Zittrain, Jonathan (2005) *Empirical Analysis of Internet Filtering in China*, Berkman Center for Internet & Society, Harvard Law School. Online. Available HTTP: http://cyber.law.harvard.edu/filtering/china/China-highlights.html (accessed February 3, 2005).

Fan, Xing (2001) *Communications and Information in China: Regulatory Issues, Strategic Implications*, Lanham/Oxford: University Press of America.

Fang, Weigui (2004) *Das Internet und China. Digital sein, digitales Sein im Reich der Mitte*, Hannover: Heise.

Foster, William and Goodman, Seymour E. (2000) *The Diffusion of the Internet in China*, A Report of the Center for International Security and Cooperation, Stanford University.

Franda, Marcus (2002) *Launching into Cyberspace: Internet Development and Politics in Five World Regions*, Boulder, CO and London: Lynne Rienner Publishers.

Giese, Karsten (2003a) "Internet growth and the digital divide: implications for spatial development," in Hughes and Wacker 2003, pp. 30–57.

Giese, Karsten (2003b) "Construction and performance of virtual identity in the Chinese Internet," in Ho, Kluver and Yang 2003, pp. 193–210.

Guo, Liang and Bu, Wei (2001) *Hulianwang shiyong zhuangkuang ji yingxiang de diaocha baogao* [Survey report on Internet usage and impact], Beijing: Chinese Academy of Social Sciences, April 2001. Online. Available HTTP: http://www.chinace.org/ce/itre/index.htm (accessed January 5, 2005).

Hachigian, Nina (2001) "China's cyber-strategy," *Foreign Affairs*, 80: 2 (March/April), pp. 118–33.

Hachigian, Nina and Wu, Lily (2003) *The Information Revolution in Asia*, Santa Monica, CA: RAND. Online. Available HTTP: http://www.rand.org/publications/MR/MR1719/ (accessed July 17, 2003).

Hague, Barry N. and Loader, Brian D. (1999) *Digital Democracy: Discourse and Decision Making in the Information Age*, London: Routledge.

Harwit, Eric and Clark, Duncan (2001) "Shaping the Internet in China: evolution of political control over network infrastructure and content," *Asian Survey*, 41: 3 (May/June), pp. 378–498.

Ho, K.C., Kluver, Randolph and Yang, Kenneth C.C. (eds) (2003) *Asia.com: Asia encounters the Internet*, London and New York: RoutledgeCurzon.

Hong, Junhao (1998) *The Internationalization of Television in China*, Westport, CN: Prager Publishers.

Hughes, Christopher R. and Wacker, Gudrun (eds) (2003) *China and the Internet: Politics of the Digital Leap Forward*, London and New York: RoutledgeCurzon.

International Institute for Democracy and Electoral Assistance (International IDEA) (2001) "Democracy and the information revolution: values, opportunities and threats, democracy forum 2001 report." Online. Available HTTP: http://www. idea.int/2001_forum/Democracy_Forum_2001_Report.pdf (accessed January 5, 2003).

Kalathil, Shanthi and Boas, Taylor C. (2003) *Open Networks, Closed Regimes: The Impact of the Internet on Authoritarian Regimes*, Washington, DC: Carnegie Endowment for International Peace.

Lagerkvist, Johan (2003) "China's Internet problem: a threat to indigenous culture, youth and political thought?" paper presented at "A Global Interdisciplinary Conference, China and the Internet: Technology, Economy, & Society in Transition," Los Angeles, May 2003.

Lee, Paul Siu-nam (1994) "Mass communication and national development in China: media roles reconsidered," *Journal of Communication (JOC)*, 44:3, pp. 22–37.

Lessig, Lawrence (1999) *Code and Other Laws of Cyberspace*, New York: Basic Books.

Li, Gabriel and Wong, Edmond (2001) *The Rise of Digital China: Investing in China's New Economy*, San Francisco, CA: China Books and Periodicals.

Loader, Brian (ed.) (1997) *The Governance of Cyberspace: Politics, Technology and Global Restructuring*, London: Routledge.

Lynch, Daniel C. (1999) *After the Propaganda State: Media, Politics & "Thought Work" in Reformed China*, Stanford, CA: Stanford University Press.

Mueller, Milton and Tan, Zixiang (1997) *China in the Information Age*, Westport, CN: Prager Publishers.

Nagy, Hanna, Ken, Guy and Arnold, Erik (eds) (1995) *The Diffusion of Information Technology. Experience of Industrial Countries and Lessons for Developing Countries*, Washington, DC: World Bank (Discussion Papers, 281).

Nie, Norman and Erbring, Lutz (2000) *Internet and Society: A Preliminary Report*, Stanford, CA: Stanford Institute for the Quantitative Study of Society.

Nolan, Peter (2001) *China and the Global Economy*, London and New York: Palgrave.

Norris, Pippa (2001) *Digital Divide: Civic Engagement, Information Poverty, and the Internet World Wide*, Cambridge: Cambridge University Press.

Pavlik, John (2001) *Journalism and New Media*, New York: Columbia University Press.

Qiu, Jack Linchuan (2003) "The Internet in China: data and issues, working paper prepared for Annenberg Research Seminar on International Communication," October 1, 2003. Online. Available HTTP: http://annenberg.usc.edu/international_ communication/Papers/JQ_China_and_Internet.pdf (accessed March 3, 2004).

Reagle, Joseph (1999) "Why the Internet is good: community governance that works well," Berkman Center Working Draft, March 26, 1999. Online. Available HTTP: http://cyber.law.harvard.edu/people/reagle/regulation-19990326.html (accessed February 11, 2005).

Rheingold, Howard (1993) *The Virtual Community, Homesteading on the Electronic Frontier*, Reading, MA: Addison-Wesley.

Sunstein, Cass R. (2001) *Republic.com*, Princeton, NJ: Princeton University Press.

Tsui, Lokman (2003) "The panopticon as the antithesis of a space of freedom: control and regulation of the Internet in China," *China Information: A Journal on Contemporary China Studies*, 17: 2, pp. 65–82.

UNCTAD (2003) *E-commerce and Development Report, 2002.* Online. Available HTTP: http://r0.unctad.org/ecommerce/ecommerce_en/edr02_en.htm (accessed February 25, 2003).

UNCTAD (2004) *E-commerce and Development Report 2004.* Online. Available HTTP: http://www.unctad.org/en/docs/ecdr2004_en.pdf (accessed February 11, 2005).

UNESCO (2002) *Joint UNESCO and COMNET-It Study of E-governance.* Online. Available HTTP: http://www.comnet.mt/Unesco/CountryProfiles/Project/joint_unesco_and_comnet.htm (accessed April 20, 2004).

UNESCO (2005) *E-governance Capacity Building.* Online. Available HTTP: http://www.unesco.org/webworld/e-governance (accessed March 3, 2005).

United Nations (2004) *Global E-government Readiness Report 2004: Towards Access for Opportunity,* New York: United Nations.

Wang, Changsheng (ed.) (2003) *Zhongguo zhengwu fazhan baogao No.1 (China E-Government Development Report No.1). Dianzi zhengwu lanpi shu (Blue Book of Electronic Government),* Beijing: Shehui kexue wenxian chubanshe.

Winter, Carsten (1998) "Internet/Online-Medien," in Faulstich, Werner (ed.) *Grundwissen Medien,* München: Fink, pp. 274–95.

Wong, John and Nah, Seok Ling (2001) *China's Emerging New Economy: The Internet and E-Commerce,* Singapore: Singapore University Press.

Wu, Jiapei, Xie, Kang and Wang, Mingming (eds) (2002) *Xinxi jingji xue* [Economics of information theory], Beijing: Gaodeng jiaoyu chubanshe.

Xie, Kang (2001) *Shijie xinxi jingji yu guojia zhishi youshi* [World information economy and national knowledge advantage], Guangzhou: Guangdong renmin chubanshe.

Zeng, Qiang (Edward Zeng) (2001) *Zhongguo dianzi shangwu lan pi shu: China Electronic Commerce Blue Paper,* Beijing: China Economic Publishing House.

Zhang, Junhua (2001) "China's government online and attempts to gain technical legitimacy," *Asien* (July), pp. 93–115.

Zhang, Junhua (2002) "Chinas Steiniger Weg zum E-Government," in Schucher, Günther (ed.) *Asien und das Internet,* Hamburg Institut für Asienkunde, pp. 97–110.

Zhang, Junhua and Woesler, Martin (eds) (2002) *China's Digital Dream – The Impact of the Internet on the Chinese Society,* Bochum: The University Press Bochum.

Zittrain, Jonathan and Edelman, Benjamin (2002) "Real-time testing of Internet filtering in China: documentation of Internet filtering worldwide." Online. Available HTTP: http://cyber.law.harvard.edu/filtering/china/test (accessed February 27, 2003).

2 Government policy and political control over China's Internet

Eric Harwit and Duncan Clark

Since the early 1990s, Internet use in the People's Republic of China (PRC) has grown at a tremendous pace. As of the middle of 2004, statistics show there were 87 million Chinese with online access. Over the past five years, the country's international data bandwidth has expanded by a factor of more than 200. To a great extent, the Chinese government deserves praise for rapidly building the data network and seeing that access is being granted to a quickly expanding number of the country's population. The struggle for control of cyberspace information, physical data pipelines, and network revenue, however, will have a significant effect on the network's growth into the coming decade. The evolving demographics of Internet users and ways information is transferred within Chinese society is also shaping government attitudes toward regulation of the data highway.

This chapter examines three key factors that shape how the network is controlled in the PRC based on interviews carried out with Chinese academic researchers and business people active in the field. First, it discusses physical network control, asking who built the actual data pipelines through which information flows, and who now regulates and profits from these systems. And how do different parts of the government as well as the private sector vie for control of the network infrastructure? Second, we examine network content control. Who is able to post and send information across the network, and what political limits are placed on this content? What government/private sector dynamics affect competition for web audiences, and how do revenue flows affect content-providing companies? How do user demographics determine content, and how does user reaction to content shape sociological patterns that, in turn, influence the degree of government control over what appears on computer screens? Finally, we also consider the element of foreign influence on the network. How does foreign web content affect Chinese viewers, and what are the prospects for change in the near future? Furthermore, what are the implications of foreign participation for the management of the physical network?[1]

Past studies of China's media and the Internet

Early studies of post-Mao Zedong China's media focused on the evolving roles of print and television. They examined both the patterns of government control and the ways content developed as the new Deng Xiaoping reformist regime liberalized means of distributing information. Leonard Chu (1994) found evidence that media content in the 1990s had changed significantly since Mao's death in 1976. He noted the appearance of letters of complaint in newspapers, radio programs with free discussion of family social problems, and even soft-core pornography in some magazines. However, he described the Chinese Communist Party as "the owner, manager, and the practitioner" in the media sector and pointed out that no private media organizations had yet appeared (Chu 1994: 8). Paul Lee (1994) chronicled the growing number of television entertainment programs in the early 1990s, proposing that small-group discussion of broadcast fare had the consequence of building social consensus and, in turn, social stability. Joseph Chan (1994) examined foreign influence on China's media organizations and found domestic broadcasters, particularly in the south, sometimes improved their content when faced with outside challenges.

Studies from the later 1990s show continued transformation in these media tools. Junhao Hong (1998) saw openings to Western television programming as dependent on both domestic supply and demand, as well as on the liberal–conservative conflicts at top levels of the central government propaganda organs. Overall, improved domestic content seemed to be creating a viable rival to imported programming. Finally, Daniel Lynch (1999a) discussed trends in censorship of books, film, and also early Internet information up to 1997. He found many avenues through which these various media could circumvent government restrictions on both domestic production and import of foreign content.

The first works focusing specifically on the expansion of the Internet in China mainly came from those in the communications field. Scholars such as Zixiang Tan (1995) and Wu Wei (1996) have written on the early growth and expansion of the data network. Their work gave a thorough technical discussion of the Internet's first years, serving as a useful guide to some of the intra-governmental rivalry as the network grew in the early 1990s. However, these writers generally avoided discussion of other sociopolitical factors such as censorship, use of the network for information distribution, and regional access discrepancies. Other earlier writers, such as Bryce McIntyre (1997), focused almost exclusively on the network's hardware.

Work by Geoffry Taubman (1998) tried to put Internet development in a context of social change and threats to government control. He asserted the communist government's hold over domestic affairs would eventually be diminished because of the new technology. Taubman's work, however, failed to consider the demographics of current network users, or of the ways network subscribers are actually using instruments such as chat groups for social activity. He also gave relatively little attention to contradictions within the Chinese government or between China and foreign investors seeking to shape and profit from the Internet's development.

Milton Mueller and Zixiang Tan (1997), and Daniel Lynch (1999a) all consider the ways the government controls the Internet, with the first two researchers' joint-authored text concentrating on the physical network and the latter's on content. The Mueller–Tan study chronicles telecommunications ministerial control up to mid-1996, but does not anticipate the later moves by the Ministry of Information Industry (MII) to assert dominant control over international data traffic. The authors are also writing before the proliferation of content-providing companies in China, when the whole nation had only some 20,000 users. They therefore offer little analysis of the social impact the technology would have on a larger population, and predict that "foreign sources of information will be heavily restricted" (Mueller and Tan 1997: 98). Lynch's study gives an overview of Internet control, focusing on ways users can bypass government restrictions on access to foreign content. However, he also pays little attention to viewer characteristics or actual information seen by the users, and omits to mention newer ways of avoiding government blocking of web sites.

William Foster and Seymour Goodman (2000) provide a good overview of developments and a fine case study of Guangdong Province. This work tends, however, to give greater weight to technical features of the network and is partly predicated on a set of international comparative standards, some of which seem peripheral to analyzing China's network development.

Many of the analytical works on the Internet published in Chinese for a domestic PRC audience tend to be relatively policy-neutral. A book on telecommunications by Xiangdong Wang (1998) includes some focused attention on the information network's technical growth, but omits most discussion of the political conflicts related to the Internet's development and has little on the social implications of the communications web's growth. Other writers praise the general knowledge benefits the Internet promises larger society, explore potential boosts the network will bring to economic planning, note the benefits for natural science research, and point out the advantages of electronic commerce (Jin Wulun 1996: 22–31; Song Shiping 1997: 28–9; Zhao Wenli/Zhi Lihong 1998: 42–7, 51; Rui Mingjie 1998: 10–12). Work by Li Luting (1998: 24–8), however, does touch on some social problems of the information age related to young women.

Although some of the Western and Chinese authors examine political and sociological issues related to the Internet's growth, none of the writers focus on the ways network access may affect the formation of organizations functioning autonomously of government control. Past works on the formation of such civil society groups by authors including Margaret Pearson (1994, 1997), B. Sun (1994), Jonathan Unger (1996), and Minxin

Pei (1998) were composed before the Chinese started to enjoy broad access to the Internet. This earlier research on the growth of a civic consciousness found nascent autonomous social groups had little actual freedom from central control, and lacked the financial resources to develop their influence. Our own work analyzes the potential for independent group formation in light of the new technological tools, such as chat groups and e-mail, that the Internet now offers.

For comparative analysis, we find some recent work on the ways the Internet can affect US society. Norman Nie and Lutz Erbring (2000) asserted that network users spend so much time in front of their computer screens that they actually have fewer opportunities to personally interact with other human beings. Their study implied that future US society could be "atomized" as more of the population spends greater amounts of time shopping, doing research, and finding entertainment online. Of course, the new communication tools such as e-mail bulletin boards and chat groups also provide opportunities for virtual communities. We can also assess Chinese Internet development in the context of these sociological assertions.

In focusing on the recent development of Internet control in China and considering past studies of Chinese media as well as theoretical work on social effects of the data network, our own work fills several gaps in the political and sociological literature. We begin with an overview of the control over the Internet's physical growth over the past decade.

Construction and control of the physical network, 1987–2003

The US data network was initially conceived as a defense-related communications system, but quickly became a tool of academia in its early public deployment. Similarly, China's first efforts at creating a data network were focused mainly on the scholarly exchange of information. The country's first computer networks, the "China Academic Network," or CANet, and the Institute of High Energy Physics (IHEP) network, in Beijing, were established in 1987.[2] By the following year, the CANet system had begun sending international electronic mail through a gateway in Germany. At the same time, the organization chose ".cn" as the PRC's national domain name.

In the early 1990s, other educational networks arose to complement the first systems. The China Research Network, or CRnet, was established in 1990 and began by hosting more than ten research institutes. The IHEP began using the international Transmission Control Protocol/Internet Protocol (TCP/IP) standard, with a link to Stanford University in 1994. In 1996, the CANet, CRnet, and IHEP were combined, under the auspices of the Chinese Academy of Sciences (CAS), to form the China Science and Technology Network (CSTNet).

The State Education Commission (SEC) began building its own China Education and Research Network (CERNET) in 1993. This network constituted a nationwide backbone with further international links. CERNET's goal was to connect all the country's universities and, later, secondary and even primary schools to one network. Early control of the data network, then, generally fell under the auspices of the educational and academic sectors of the central government. Funding for CERNET's expansion, however, came from the larger central government budget. Perhaps more importantly, the network depended on lines leased from the state telecommunications regulator, the Ministry of Posts and Tele-communications (MPT) which, in March 1998, was reorganized as the MII.[3]

In 1993, a major change in network control and development began, as the MPT started to build its own packet-data network, CHINAPAC. By the early 1990s, the commercial value of packet-data service provision had become apparent to government telecommunications officials and they moved to harness the burgeoning data-transmission industry with their own competing network. Newly appointed MPT minister Wu Jichuan, a life-long telecommunications bureaucrat, took the ministry's helm at this important juncture and became a leading advocate of the ministry's main-taining control in virtually all areas of voice and data communication.

Two years later, the MPT's renamed network, ChinaNET, was launched and charged with providing public commercial services. The company was licensed as one of the government's major interconnecting networks and acted both as a wholesale provider of Internet bandwidth as well as a brand name for the regional provincial telecommunications administrations (PTAs) to offer their own retail service provision. Early ChinaNET customers were to be state corporations, private companies, or wealthy individuals who could afford connection fees (Tan 1996: 624).

The MPT, however, had other ministerial rivals for control of China's data networks. The Ministry of Electronics Industry (MEI) began to compete with the MPT by creating a new corporation in late 1993. Called Jitong, it was meant to be a satellite-based telecommunications network that used the MPT's land-based telephone lines for customer local access. The new company's larger mission was to promote the so-called "Golden Projects," which were intended to link China's customs and financial networks and provide vital information for users across the nation. Jitong's ChinaGBN (short for "Golden Bridge Network") data web was established in 1996. The MEI project was also seen as a top-level State Council attempt to instill some competition in the telecommunications sector. The Electronics Ministry's telephone operating company, China Unicom, and Unicom's new network, UniNET, were similar ventures created to chal-lenge the monopoly of MPT and its telecommunications corporation, China Telecom.[4]

A new rival emerged in mid-2000, as China Netcom began operation of yet another data network. The company clearly began outside MII control, with its managing partners consisting of Shanghai's municipal Information

Technology Office; the Chinese Academy of Sciences; the State Administration of Radio, Films, and Television (SARFT); and the Ministry of Railways. The latter, which has its own fiber optic network, reportedly supplied 420 million RMB (US\$ 50.6 million) to the new corporation. Netcom's chances of success increased as a result of the active interest taken by US-educated Jiang Mianheng, President Jiang Zemin's son, vice-president of the CAS and concurrently head of the Shanghai technology office, since both of these organizations had a financial stake in the new company (Greenberg 1999).

In late 2000, three new networks appeared. These included the mobile phone operating company China Mobile's CMNet, military-controlled telecommunications company China Great Wall's CGWNet, and the Ministry of Foreign Trade and Economic Cooperation's CIETNet. The China Satellite Network (CSNet) began construction in 2001. Each of these new networks had specific target audiences: for China Mobile, wireless Internet users would be a future market, while the foreign trade network would focus on international trade electronic commerce and the military network would be used primarily for defense-related purposes. Of course, each could look for larger customer bases in the future, though an already crowded field, as well as special restrictions such as those limiting the role of the military in the civilian economy, would put limits on the new entrants.

As of mid-2003, then, China had no less than ten interconnecting networks (though the CGWNet and CSNet were still in the construction stage). Table 2.1 gives details of each network's expansion. It uses international bandwidth (the size of their connections to the international data network) as a measure of their ability to channel information. The CERNET (under the Ministry of Education) and CSTNet (run by the Chinese Academy of Sciences) remained academically oriented networks, but each had less than 2 percent of China's total international bandwidth of 18,599 Megabits per second (Mbps). China 169, the successor to Jitong's ChinaGBN, had a capacity of 3,465 Mbps (some 19 percent of the total) and UniNet (which began operations in 1999 under China Unicom) had 1,435 Mbps, about 8 percent (CNNIC 7/2003).

The major player in running China's network, however, was ChinaNET, under the leadership of China Telecom, itself nominally controlled by the MII. With 10,959 Mbps of bandwidth, the company had nearly 60 percent of the nation's total international connection capacity. This allowed it near-monopoly control over China's data "pipelines" for international communication. Furthermore, as of mid-2000, ChinaNET offered connectivity in some 230 cities, using E-1 (2,048 Mbps) data lines (Foster and Goodman 2000: 50).

In the 1998 reorganization of the telecommunications sector, the MEI was merged with the new information industry ministry, which was now headed by former MPT chief Wu Jichuan. Jitong and Unicom were

Table 2.1 Major networks and their leased international bandwidth (selected years 1998–2003)

Month/Year	Network	Bandwidth (Mbps)	Percentage of total bandwidth	Total bandwidth (Mbps)
June 1998	CSTNet	2.1	2.50	84.6
	ChinaNET	78.0	92.20	
	CERNET	2.3	2.70	
	ChinaGBN	2.3	2.70	
June 2000	CSTNet	10.0	0.80	1,234.0
	ChinaNET	711.0	57.60	
	CERNET	12.0	1.00	
	ChinaGBN	69.0	5.60	
	UniNet	55.0	4.50	
	China Netcom	377.0	30.60	
June 2003	CSTNet	55.0	0.30	18,599.0
	ChinaNET	10,959.0	58.90	
	CERNET	324.0	1.70	
	China 169	3,465.0	18.60	
	UniNet	1,435.0	7.70	
	China Netcom	2,112.0	11.40	
	CIETNET	2.0	0.01	
	CMNET	247.0	1.30	
	CGWNet	0.0	0.00	
	CSNet	0.0	0.00	

Source: Authors' compilation based on data from CNNIC 7/1998, CNNIC 7/2000, CNNIC 7/2003.

Note: Rounding numbers causes some distortion in totals. China 169 service, launched in 2003 by China Netcom, incorporates parts of the ChinaGBN network previously owned by Jitong. Jitong was merged with China Netcom in 2001.

absorbed along with the rest of the MEI into the MII, meaning that Jitong's ChinaGBN and UniNet also came under MII authority. With the incorporation of the former State Council Information Leading Group into the new ministry, the MII emerged uncontested as the data systems' main regulator and policy director. Minister Wu, known for his fierce desire to maintain control over the course of the telecom sector, thereby assumed a role as the PRC's information czar. He and the MII would use this control at lower levels, such as for direct provision of Internet service to business and private consumers. The growth of these service providers is discussed in a later section.

As Table 2.1 indicates, however, ChinaNET's share of bandwidth did fall in the late 1990s as such rivals as ChinaGBN and UniNet increased their bandwidth capacity. The entry of China Netcom, with 377 Mbps international bandwidth capacity (mainly via its Shanghai connection) and high-speed OC-48 data lines represented a fresh challenge to ChinaNET and revealed a new, potentially significant inter-ministerial rivalry. The 2002 split of China Telecom into a new China Telecom in China's southern provinces, and an enlarged China Netcom in the north, was meant to further dilute the dominance of ChinaNET's hold on the network backbone.

Still, the MII's early plans to capture control of the network had resulted in its holding the lion's share of international bandwidth control as well as a significant hand in domestic Internet traffic. More importantly, it used its bandwidth control and widely developed network to garner a major portion of network user revenue, as the following section indicates.

Growth and control of Internet Service Providers (ISPs), 1995–2003

Though ChinaNET and the other data networks controlled large-scale information backbones, most of the direct sales of Internet service were left to retailing service providers. As noted above, ChinaNET in particular worked mainly as a wholesale network manager and leased its lines to provincial and other regional providers in cities across the country.

The need for a growing number of Internet Service Providers (ISPs) began with the explosion of Internet user numbers in the late 1990s. As of 1994, there were only around 5,000 users in the entire PRC. By the end of 1996, however, there were 120,000 with access, and the Internet population passed 2.1 million in 1998 before reaching 8.9 million at the end of 1999, 22.5 million at the end of 2000, and some 87 million in mid-2004 (Tan 1999: 263; CNNIC 1/1999, 1/2000, 1/2001, 7/2003, 7/2004).[5]

China's first commercial deployment of Internet services occurred in May 1995, when the Beijing PTA, or Beijing Telecom, the capital's municipal telecommunications unit of the former MPT, introduced its own ChinaNET-branded service. Shanghai's municipal PTA launched a service in June 1995 and PTAs in Guangdong, Liaoning, and Zhejiang began commercial Internet service in the second half of 1995. The first commercial service providers, then, fell clearly under the influence of the MPT's regional telephone companies (Clark *et al.* 1999: 96).

Not all of the country's service providers were local telephone companies. Accessing the Internet via bandwidth provided by the various major networks charted in Figure 2.1, other individual ISP companies, both collectively and privately owned, began to emerge from late 1995. All were at first required to obtain a license from network administrators, and many effectively operated as agents of ChinaNET. However, some ISPs did manage to develop a certain degree of independence. For example, InfoHighway was founded by entrepreneur Zhang Shuxin as the first private ISP in China, and began service in September 1995. Zhang sought to model her company on nascent American integrated content and service providers such as CompuServe and targeted eight major cities for service provision.

By the end of the year, there were some 20 companies, including the PTA providers, offering network connections to PRC residents. MPT-rival Jitong, at the time backed by the MEI and other ministries, launched its own ISP in September 1996, under the GBNet label (Clark *et al.* 1999: 97).

Some of the ISPs, such as ChinaNET/163 and NetChina in Beijing, were operated by, or secured licenses from, the local PTA and provided mainly coverage within limited localities. Others, including InfoHighway and China Online, secured inter-provincial licenses from the MPT and attempted aggressive cross-regional or nationwide expansion. China Online, for example, sought to offer dial-up services in 80 cities across the country. Figure 2.1 charts the organizational hierarchy of Internet service provision and revenue flows.

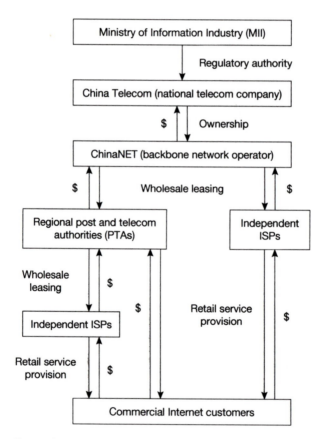

Figure 2.1 Control hierarchy and revenue flows of Internet service provision under the MII

Source: Authors' own compilation.
Note: The "$" sign indicates revenue flow. Similar wholesale arrangements with ISPs also exist for other backbone operators such as Netcom, though they fall outside of the MII purview. As of mid-2000, almost every commercial ISP used the ChinaNET backbone.

Many of the first ISPs, however, found themselves with excess capacity and thin profit margins. These early providers began by incurring immediate losses as they spent heavily on buying or renting dial-up lines, leased lines, Internet bandwidth, servers, and software. Furthermore, hefty online fees, averaging 400 to 600 RMB per month (about US$ 50–75) for 40 hours, limited customer numbers. These costs were quite high even for coastal citizens such as those in Beijing, where per capita GDP stood at only some 14,000 RMB (about US$ 1,700) (Clark *et al.* 1999: 155). Private companies, such as InfoHighway, were particularly hard hit, as they lacked the deep pockets of the government-backed telecommunications companies. Of these early providers, then, the ISPs owned by, or affiliated with, the local governments' PTAs emerged as dominant players. By late 1997, ChinaNET/163 in Beijing had nearly 10,000 subscribers, and NetChina about 4,000. High MPT leasing fees were also major hurdles for InfoHighway and other new ISPs. In late 1996, the ministry, via ChinaNET, charged as much as US$ 2 million for a 2 Mbps line; in the US, the equivalent rate would have been about US$ 500,000 (Triolo and Lovelock 1996: 26). Leased telephone lines from China Telecom, the MII's phone company, took up to 80 percent of the ISP costs in 1999, compared to about 6 percent for Internet providers in the US (Kuhn 1999: A2).

In essence, the MPT was using its near-monopoly on consumer Internet service leasing rights to draw disproportionate revenues from retailing service providers. Regional government-owned service providers could afford to wait until the number of consumers grew and profits would begin; private companies had a more difficult time. Consider the national subscriber numbers for some of China's major ISPs as of late 1999. ChinaNET-affiliated providers, such as ChinaNET/163 and MultiMedia/169, had the largest number of users, at approximately 700,000 and 500,000, respectively. The PTA-backed Capital Online also had managed to attract a large number of customers (200,000). GBNet (100,000), China Online (50,000), and InfoHighway (50,000) trailed the companies more closely associated with the MII.[6] InfoHighway's founder, Zhang Shuxin herself left the company in 1998, though internal management disagreements seem to have been the major reason for her departure. By 1999, however, the company seemed to be doing well, with some 50,000 customers. It claimed US$ 3 million in income for 1998, up from US$ 1.2 million in 1997 (*China Online*, July 15, 1999).

In early 1999, a popular campaign led by academics against the high cost of Internet access and other communications caught the attention of Premier Zhu Rongji. Zhu and other central leaders addressed several of the early problems for Internet access on March 1 of that year, as they ordered sweeping cuts in leased line fees, fixed line connections charges, and Internet access rates (*China Daily*, February 4, 1999; Wang 1999; Zhao 1999; Clark *et al.* 1999: 151; BDA [China] 2000: 35). These measures were meant both to help spread network access and to prevent the dominant MII and regional telephone company-controlled corporations from collecting excessive service fees. In the March moves, international leased line fees for ISPs were cut by some 25 percent, from US$ 52,000 per month to US$ 38,600 per month. At the consumer end, the price of a second line for residential users fell from US$ 130–300 to under US$ 30. Internet hourly rates were lowered to RMB 4 per hour (about 48 cents), bringing typical monthly bills for customers to a more affordable US$ 15–20 (Clark *et al.* 1999: 137, 151, 102). By mid-2003, dial-up rates in large cities such as Beijing and Shanghai cost some RMB 0.02 (about 0.25 cents) per minute. Broadband access cost as little as RMB 70 per month.[7]

Unfortunately for many independent ISPs, however, the cuts in the retail Internet rates they could charge Chinese consumers hit harder than any savings in lower leased-line fees paid to use ChinaNET's backbone network. As a result, a number of independent ISPs gave up their quest to manage their own service and announced they would simply re-sell the service of the regionally branded ChinaNET Internet connections. As of late 2000, some 85 to 90 percent of ISPs had such a re-selling arrangement (BDA [China] 2000: 35).

Independent ISPs have struggled for a controlling stake in the physical data network structure, but the MII and its operating companies have been reluctant to allow them to collect large revenues for providing Internet access. The central telecommunications authorities and their regional carriers were able to ride out the high early costs of investing in equipment and paying leasing fees, and have become the survivors while network costs fall and the number of users skyrockets. The only hope for independent ISPs may lie in cooperation with foreign corporations. If they can offer better service and learn to function more efficiently, they may stage a comeback in the face of central and regional governmental challenges to service provision. We discuss the potential role of foreign corporations in post-WTO China in a later section. In the meantime, however, we note that the central and local governments have effectively used their greater financial resources and pricing structure to maintain control over the service part of the Internet's physical network.

Overall, the main priority of the MII and its operating companies seems to have been to retain as much control as possible over the data network for two reasons. First, the information ministry sees great profits by selling access at both wholesale and retail level. Second, it sees itself as a kind of government guardian for ownership control of the communications network and its content, in the same way as physical and editorial control of television and newspaper companies remain in other state hands. On the first point, recent moves to create competition, in the form of rapidly growing Netcom, may eventually weaken the MII's position and create benefits for consumers. Furthermore, if independent service providers can give better quality network access than the government-linked companies, we may see a reduced role for government agents in control of the network systems. On the second point, although outright ownership of the network infrastructure will probably remain in government hands for the time being, we must also consider the government's attitude toward network content.

Internet content: regulation and control of domestic and foreign web sites

Content for Chinese users grew slowly in the early 1990s, but had greatly accelerated by the end of the decade. As Figure 2.2 shows, China has followed the pattern of other nations in corporate domain name registration, with nearly 75 percent of all registered names in early 2003 labeled ".com," while fewer than 1 percent belonged to the early academic domain, ".edu."

The number of registered domestic web sites derived from Internet Content Providers (ICPs) numbered about 626,600 in mid-2004 (CNNIC

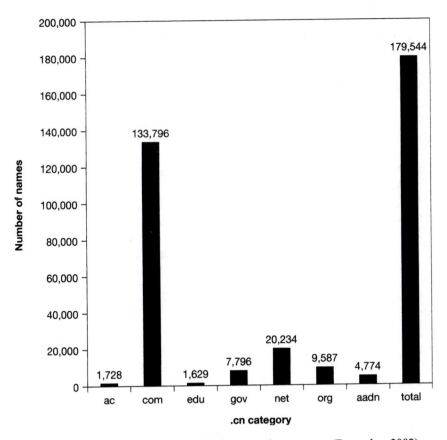

Figure 2.2 Numbers of registered domain names by category (December 2002)

Source: Authors' compilation based on data from: CNNIC 1/2003.

7/2004: 7), and, in contrast to most of the physical network ownership and management, many of the main content providers were private or cooperative companies. Popular sites currently include Netease (aka "163.com"), Sina.com, and Sohu.com. These sites provide mainly news, entertainment, and sports information, but often rely on officially sanctioned agencies for their own content. Some, such as Sohu.com and Sina.com, had provided links to foreign news about China and Chinese language sources published in various foreign countries, but have been adopting more links to the state-news organization Xinhua since 2003.

Control of Internet content, in contrast to the physical infrastructure, generally falls outside of the MII's purview. The ministry's mission statement of August 1998, for example, stresses its role in areas such as planning network construction and expansion, developing standards and coordinating production, and promoting "informatization" (*xinxihua*) of the economy (Foster and Goodman 2000: 124–6). Minister Wu Jichuan's own statements at public venues also tend to focus purely on matters related to telecommunications business regulation and strategies for developing the industry and maintaining competitiveness in a more open international environment.[8] We should not, however, take Wu's emphasis on economic issues as a sign of indifference to political content control. Wu more than likely agrees with political regulations on Internet content (discussed below), but as long as the activities of his own ministry remain relatively unaffected, he tends to avoid crossing into the realm of other parts of the government that focus on these issues.

It is the central State Council and top Communist Party propaganda organs that establish guidelines on what material is deemed sensitive. Although most rules were unpublished as of early 2000, draft laws included provisions that anyone seeking to operate "Internet and multimedia network services" had to apply for a license from the authorities under the State Council (*Business Wire*, September 28, 2000). In early October, 2000, State Council decree 292 required ICPs to provide the authorities upon demand with all content that appeared on their sites as well as records of users who had visited their sites for up to 60 days prior to the request. ICPs were responsible for policing their own sites for "subversive materials" (*Agence France Press*, October 3, 2000).

In contrast to Minister Wu's focus on mainly economic regulatory aspects of the Internet, former Publicity Department chairman and Communist Party politburo member, Ding Guan'gen, had been the government's point man for keeping Internet content focused within allowable political boundaries. In early 2001, for example, he made several statements promoting the importance of official government information web sites such as Xinhuanet.com, and pledged that the government would "tighten control and delete 'harmful' material from Internet news reporting" (*South China Morning Post*, February 9, 2001).

Of course, the national government has long had restrictions on such activities as the spread of pornography, gambling, and publication of "counterrevolutionary" materials. In late 2000, Anhui became the first of China's provinces to set up an "Internet police force," but 20 other provinces and cities were also reportedly preparing such organizations (*Xinhua News Agency*, August 4, 2000).[9] Over the past few years, we have seen some examples of sanctions for those violating government content rules. For example, a relatively new ICP, Netbig, was attacked for providing an independent ranking of some Chinese universities (Einhorn and Roberts 1999). Activist Lin Hai was arrested in March 1998 for sending some 30,000 e-mail addresses to an online, pro-democracy newsletter in the US. He was released in September 1999, but not before news of his crime and punishment spread rapidly through domestic chat groups and bulletin boards, to serve as a warning for those who would commit similar acts (Platt 2000: 7).

In mid-2000, in one of the first high-profile cases of prosecution for Internet activities, an activist in Sichuan province named Huang Qi was arrested for posting information on his web site, http://www.6-4tian wang.com, about victims of the 1989 Tiananmen demonstrations. In early March 2001, Huang went on trial for "subverting state power," a crime that carried a penalty of up to ten years in prison. Huang's web site, however, was based outside China, so, as of mid-2001, the site continued to report on his trial as well as post information alleging police violence and abuse of Chinese citizens, and more general information on missing persons (*Asiaweek*, March 2, 2001: 14). In May, 2003, Huang was sentenced to five years in prison, and, as of September 2003, his web site became a forum for sales of Viagra and other pharmaceuticals (Yu 2003: 4).

The goal of these measures seems to be to intimidate users into censoring their own web content. As it is technically impossible for the Chinese government to screen all domestic web sites at all times, the tactic of "killing the chicken to scare the monkeys" (publicizing punishment to intimidate the masses) is one of the few tools the authorities can use to prevent ICPs from crossing politically acceptable boundaries. Some ICPs have admitted they actively check the content put on web pages. For example, InfoHighway's Zhang Shuxin stated in a 1996 interview that if the topics her audience addressed in discussion groups turned out to be too political, "I cut them off" (Richburg 1996: A01). As noted above, new rules place the burden for policing their web content on ICPs themselves.

Many of the most popular domestic web sites are private, but some regional government organizations try to attract viewers with useful material. Capital Online in Beijing is popular for its free e-mail service, while the Shanghai city government recently launched Eastday.com to provide local news about the municipality. According to Shanghai city government officials, this site, launched in the summer of 2000, had become the city's most popular site within two months.[10] At Eastday.com, Shanghai audiences can view news from several of the city's main newspapers and television stations.

It is unclear how well these state-owned enterprises will fare in competition with the private, mainly Beijing-based, corporations. However, private content companies face problems similar to those of American and other foreign content providers: how can they generate profits without directly charging viewing customers? One of the main revenue generators, online advertising, brought only US$ 3 million to all Chinese ICPs in 1998 and some US$ 10 million in 1999 (*Asiaweek*, March 2, 2001: 33). One 1999 survey in Beijing found only three out of 67 Internet companies were profitable (*China Online*, July 19, 2000). Many of the private ICPs faced looming debts in late 2000 and sought new infusions of foreign venture capital. In contrast, municipally owned web sites could feel secure with the financial backing of the city government to support them over the longer term. However, as an IAMASIA corporate survey from February 2001 indicates, none of the state-backed web sites ranked in the top ten most popular web pages. The most popular web pages were (users in millions): sina.com.cn (4.6), sohu.com (4.5), 163.com (Netease) (4.0), chinaren.com (3.0), yahoo.com (2.3), microsoft.com (2.1), etang.com (2.0), 163.net (1.9), 263.net (1.6), china.com (1.3) (IAMASIA 2001).

In the same way that domestic government-backed ISPs weathered early financial squeezes in the late 1990s, the domestic ICPs with government backing could also emerge as survivors in the competition for viewing audiences. Furthermore, the government web sites will generally be resistant to posting material that violates the country's content rules and will therefore be viewed more favorably by policing organs. Of course, if state-backed content-providers fail to include information that meets viewers' needs, the private content-providers can still win by satisfying broader consumer demands.

Although the number of domestic ICPs has grown quickly over the past few years, a large portion of the web content for Chinese readers comes from overseas sources. Some of the first foreign web sites to target Chinese audiences came in the wake of Beijing's Tiananmen Square demonstrations of 1989. Overseas Chinese scholars founded China News Digest to spread news of the PRC derived from mainly Western news wire services. Readers could subscribe through e-mail accounts and receive daily briefings that could be displayed in the Chinese language if they had the proper software.

As ICPs saw a great expansion in the US in the mid-1990s, Chinese also turned to foreign content for information and entertainment. Yahoo!'s English-language page became the most popular site in China for a time, as it provided a useful portal to the main American web pages. In May 1998, Yahoo! itself launched a Chinese-language site. Domestic web sites, however, dominate lists of the most popular web sites in China, as mentioned above. Only three foreign web sites – those of Yahoo!, Microsoft, and the Hong Kong-based China.com – made the list. Still, the table indicates that users do have broad access to the kind of information useful for understanding a broad range of economic, scientific, and cultural topics from a wide variety of sources.

Central government control of access to foreign web pages remains schizophrenic, as the goal of exploiting the international network's educational and commercial advantages conflicts with the desire for information monitoring. Since the mid-1990s, the Chinese government has made several attempts to regulate access to some sites by targeting specific web site Internet protocol numerical addresses. In particular, officials have tried to block Western news sources sometimes critical of China, such as the *New York Times*, the *Washington Post*, and *Time* magazine. Following rules similar to those for controlling domestic ICPs, other targets for control attempts have been pornographic sites, web pages printing, or even broadcasting, anti-government propaganda, and gambling sites.

In a 1996 move to intimidate users, the government required ISP customers to register with the police when they opened an account. Recently, more sophisticated efforts have been made to selectively block access to foreign sites through dynamic blocking enforced at the level of the interconnecting network, rather than at the service provider. This method is a response to criticism over the earlier slow access speeds resulting in part from the heavy-handed attempt to block permanently a large number of foreign web sites.[11]

Many of the attempts to control access to foreign sites have failed. The survey by IAMASIA on the ten most popular web pages in China clearly indicates that many millions of viewers have access to sites such as Yahoo! and Microsoft, in spite of the fact that these have what the government would probably consider useful though policy-neutral content. Government regulations are also unevenly enforced. For example, while *Time/CNN* web sites are sometimes blocked, *Newsweek* and *ABC News* sites are usually open. Rules announced in January 2000 that would have required web companies – domestic and foreign – that used encryption software to register each individual user, were quickly withdrawn after American companies argued they were too restrictive (Shanker 2000: 4). Furthermore, the 1996 requirement to register with the police is, in fact, a passive regulatory tool and has a more psychological than practical effect on user habits.

As for skirting blocked foreign web pages, several companies outside China, such as Rewebber, http://rewebber.de, have offered free "anonymous" web surfing services.[12] The user accesses the free site, then enters a new address on the site's internal window, and connects to the new, perhaps controversial, page. The Chinese server, therefore, does not have a chance to block access, as it believes the user is still accessing the free anonymous web page. As of late 2000, the government had not yet blocked all the anonymous server sites, which would effectively stop this practice. Furthermore, as Lynch pointed out, "objectionable" foreign web sites, such as those supplying pornography or anti-government materials, can change web addresses or proliferate to such a degree that the government cannot keep track of them (Lynch 1999a: 196–7). Evidence of such use comes from one European survey firm, which found that some 60 percent of web hits by users monitored in Beijing in 1999 were adult-oriented sites.[13] In sum, the high degree of government control over foreign web access foreseen by Mueller and Tan has yet to materialize and, according to one foreign technician who has close ties with the MII, there is actually no intention of developing or deploying omniscient monitoring tools.[14]

Of course, the Internet is not the only tool Chinese citizens have for receiving uncensored foreign information. According to Chan (1994: 73) it is expected that China will have up to 30 million illegal satellite dishes. By mid-2003, China had more than 400 million telephones and millions of fax machines. These communication tools are available to a broad segment of Chinese society and, in the short term, are probably more likely to be used for communicating with disaffected members of Chinese society than the Internet. Be that as it may, we do see some tangible evidence of foreign web sites affecting domestic Chinese social behavior. In early 1999, for example, members of the Falun Gong spiritual exercise group, led by a Chinese individual in exile in the US, staged demonstrations in China that were reportedly coordinated via an American-based Chinese language web page. Such activity shows the potential power of sites located outside Chinese government jurisdiction, and indicates that the regulation of domestic portals is something of a moot point.

Although the domestic ICPs practice some self-censorship in their content, they have so far been allowed some financial cooperation with foreign sources. Sina.com, for example, is backed by Goldman Sachs, Softbank, Pacific Century Cyberworks, and Dell, among others, while Zhaodaole.com was supported by a Malaysian conglomerate. However, Sina.com's US$ 80 million initial public offering in April 2000 on Nasdaq, the US stock exchange, shows some limits to foreign financial access to China's ICPs. The stock offering was allowed to proceed only on condition that actual ownership of the domestic Chinese company was taken out of the listed enterprise. The domestic enterprise was created to operate the ICP, and this company entered into a service contract with a wholly owned subsidiary of the foreign entity (a Cayman Islands company) that was listed on the Nasdaq (Netease.com, Inc. 2000: 21).

Part of the MII strategy in allowing limited foreign investment in ICPs may reflect earlier trends in similar media content. As Joseph Chan documented, the government was keen to allow restricted joint ventures in television program production so that domestic producers could both absorb needed capital and learn foreign techniques. He described a significant audience shift in southern China away from Hong Kong radio content and toward local production after stations actively emulated Hong Kong presentation styles using regional content (Chan 1994: 79, 76).

To sum up, the MII may be allowing foreign capital in during the nascent growth of ICPs, but it still maintains some restrictions on how foreign investors can influence content provider management. The Chinese government could possibly even try to force out foreign corporations when the domestic companies achieve greater economic viability. China's accession to the WTO, discussed later in this chapter, speculates on future foreign investment opportunities. Unlike the builders and managers of the physical Internet infrastructure, the early pioneers of Chinese web content are mainly private, non-governmental organizations. Foreign companies have greater access to providing content through their foreign web sites and even have some limited ability to invest in domestic web companies. The government continues to maintain some control over the most sensitive of network content through a combination of rules and public examples to inspire self-censorship among Chinese domestic ICPs. It also employs limited blocking techniques to try to prevent the most controversial foreign materials from reaching Chinese audiences. The phenomenon of municipal government web pages attracting large audiences and, perhaps, stealing viewers from struggling private corporations could, however, mark a movement toward greater government control over network content.

Before examining factors that will shape the control of China's Internet use in the future, we are going to focus on the ways current demographics of Internet users affect web page content as well as the possible social implications of network viewing. The profile of current Internet audiences in China helps us understand not only what material viewers will demand, but also allows us to apply broader sociological and political theories about how network users' world views will develop in the coming decade. As we will see, these world views, in turn, represent a feedback mechanism, one that determines the degree of social and political control that the Chinese government organs will seek to exercise.

Internet user profiles and social implications

Striking features of Chinese user profiles include the predominance of young and male users of the data network system. Figures 2.3 and 2.4 and Table 2.2 indicate demographic patterns as of late 2002 and mid-2003. As a whole, users tend to be young men of college age. Older citizens represent a significantly smaller percentage of the network community than their proportion of the population would indicate. These characteristics reflect similar patterns to those seen in early use of the Internet in the US as well as Europe. As the figures indicate, however, women's Internet usage has begun to grow over the past five years and will likely soon begin to reflect patterns now seen in Western countries, where age and gender features on the Internet now more closely mirror those of the wider population.

Table 2.2 compares the percentage of respondents to a nation-wide survey with their respective percentages of the country's population. Geographically, we see wealthy coastal areas with a higher proportion of users than their overall populations would warrant. Cities such as Beijing and Shanghai had user survey response several times that of the proportional populations, while poorer provinces such as Yunnan, Guizhou, and Tibet were underrepresented in the survey. However, such regional deviation may be ameliorated as government measures and the Internet itself contribute to broader economic growth in China's inland regions.

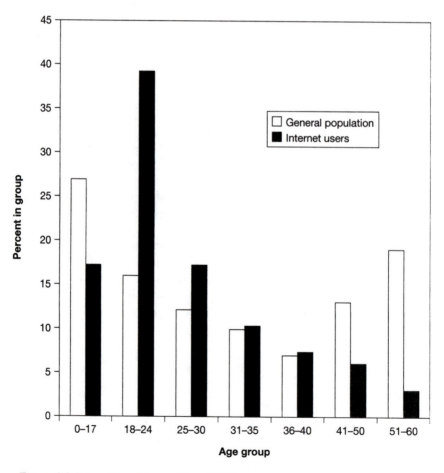

Figure 2.3 Internet use by age (June 2003)

Sources: Authors' compilation based on data from: CNNIC 7/2003: 7. For general population (figure is for year 1997) see Clark *et al.* 1999: 167.

Overall, according to the data, the typical Internet user in China is currently a 20–30-year-old male living in either an urban area or a relatively wealthy province such as Guangdong. Noting that, in the 1980s, young college-age students were among the leaders of several democracy campaigns that culminated in the 1989 Tiananmen Square movement, we wonder, could or will this age cohort use new network tools for social activism purposes? When answering this question, we shall consider ways that Chinese use the Internet and compare them to the findings of Nie and Erbring. Table 2.3 compares American and Chinese activities when using web accounts.

We see that Chinese patterns of use are similar to those in the US and indicate utilization of the network for informational, educational, as well

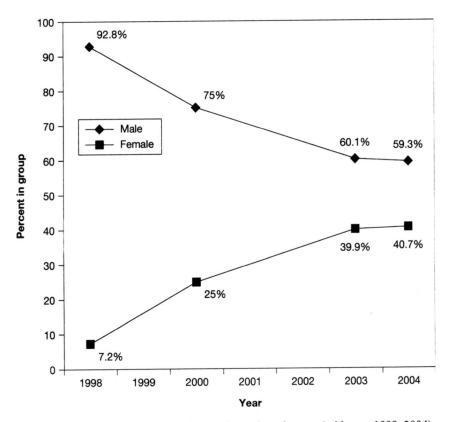

Figure 2.4 Changing Internet use by gender, selected years (mid-year 1998–2004)

Sources: Authors' compilation based on data from: CNNIC 7/1998, CNNIC 7/2000, CNNIC 7/2003, CNNIC 7/2004.

Table 2.2 Internet use by selected geographic location (2002)

Province or municipality	Percentage of users by region	Region's population as percentage of national total	Ratio of users to population percentage
Beijing	6.6	1.10	6.00
Shanghai	7.1	1.30	5.50
Tianjin	2.3	0.79	2.90
Guangdong	9.5	6.90	1.40
Liaoning	4.8	3.40	1.40
Heilongjiang	3.8	2.90	1.30
Hubei	5.4	4.80	1.10
Qinghai	0.3	0.39	0.80
Sichuan	5.2	6.60	0.79
Hunan	2.9	5.10	0.57
Hebei	3.7	5.40	0.69
Yunnan	1.7	3.40	0.50
Tibet	0.1	0.21	0.50
Anhui	1.9	4.80	0.40
Guizhou	0.8	2.80	0.29

Sources: Authors' compilation based on data from CNNIC 1/2003, *China Statistical Yearbook 2002*, CD-ROM version, section 4–8.

Note: Selection of regions reflects areas of greater, medium, and lesser Internet penetration in the base year of 2000.

as entertainment purposes. There are some exceptions such as travel information and online purchase that reflect different levels of disposable income in each society. Furthermore, Nie and Erbring's study found social isolation increasing when Internet use was greater than 10 hours per week – in their study some 15 percent of American users spent that long per week. In mid-2000, however, some 53 percent of Chinese users reported spending more than 10 hours per week using the network, and in mid-2003 the average accessing time was 12.3 hours per week (CNNIC 7/2000, CNNIC 7/2003: 13). Surveys of Chinese users do not exactly replicate Nie and Erbring's queries on whether they spend less time with family and friends, but the long hours spent in front of screens indicate some similarity to American user patterns.

Should China follow the American trend outlined by Nie and Erbring, then the likelihood of greater "civil society" autonomous group formation in the PRC might actually diminish. Rather than organizing movements that might fall outside political control, Chinese citizens could end up more isolated, and less likely to challenge the rule of the established authorities. Of course, the communication outlets for Internet users also can work against this isolation trend. Chat groups in China (as well as the US and other countries of the world) allow virtually unrestricted opportunity for

Table 2.3 Comparison of selected activities of American and Chinese Internet use patterns

Activity	Percentage of American users	Percentage of Chinese users
E-mail	90	91.8
General information	77	n.a.
Search engine	n.a.	70.0
Downloading/uploading software	n.a.	43.0
Entertainment	36	44.9
Travel information	54	6.7
Buying/online purchase	36	11.7
Job search	26	20.3
Chat rooms	24	45.4
Trading stocks	7	5.4
Matchmaking	n.a.	2.6

Sources: Authors' compilation based on data from Nie and Erbring 2000: 9, CNNIC 7/2003: 11–12.

Note: Not all categories were solicited in each survey.

communication among like-minded individuals. For the Chinese, such an outlet for discussion offers a potentially powerful medium for anonymous expression of a wide variety of opinion and thought.

In practice, however, many current chat groups seem to contain rather bland discussions. Online browsing conducted by the authors found, for example, that one of the most popular sites in China, Sina.com, mirrors many other content providers by including such chat rooms as "sports," "living," "travel," "games," "food," as well as match-making areas and others, and has attracted up to 13,000 users at a time. However, repeated random visits to the chat rooms in 2000 and 2001 found that visitors seldom adhered to the category guidelines. In fact, the "chat" tended to be quite repetitious, with many users simply extending greetings to others in the room, making some references to their social lives, or complaining about how slow their connections or computers were. There was little discussion of politics or current events. None of the more widely known web sites in Chinese, including Sina, had a chat room labeled "politics," though China.com had an area for discussing general "news."

There are exceptions to these observations. In the wake of the October 2000 rules on ISP monitoring, some chat room visitors posted critical comments. "Totally nuts!" said one posting on Sina.com on October 3 adding: "Could anybody pass my question to the people who made the new regulations on the Internet? Do these people know how the Internet works? If China requires a licence, shall we move overseas?" Another on October 9 said: "The domestic ICPs are doomed" (Clark 2000).[15] Part of the problem for users of these chat rooms has been the slow speed of modem connection. Replies made with slow-response computers are delayed so long that the train of thought is difficult to maintain. Even as connection speeds improve, the types of police monitoring noted above are probably also inspiring a kind of self-censorship among many chat room users.

These and less widely used chat rooms do, however, occasionally contain bursts of frustration with China's political system, and sometimes heated discussion of contentious issues. The bombing of the Chinese embassy in Yugoslavia in 1999, for example, unleashed various political debates on several web sites. However, attempts by Western scholars to quantify such content and categorize it as "political dialogue," or "anti-government senti-ment," is complicated by the virtual impossibility of knowing whether the chat room participant actually lives in China and is thereby subject to secu-rity bureau retaliation, or whether the person is based in the US, Taiwan, or some other country.

Chinese chat groups do, on occasion, have some influence on Chinese government officials and policy. For example, former Premier Zhu Rongji apparently took a more conservative stance toward improving ties with Japan during an October 2000 visit to Tokyo when chat groups expressed some hostility toward his seemingly conciliatory views.[16] In March 2001, Zhu made a televised apology to the nation after a school explosion; his action followed fierce chat room criticism of the government investigation of the incident (Browne 2001).

The more controversial communications to and within China on the Internet are probably carried out through conventional e-mail. These forms of dialogue are more difficult for police to monitor. Currently, we have no data on how many e-mail messages are of a socially disruptive nature. However, to protect against police infiltration of e-mail groups, sensitive communication is likely limited to a few users at a time. In this way, e-mail loses some of its ability to affect large numbers of citizens and may then be relegated to the same kind of one-to-one communication now available through telephone, fax, or even postal letter contact.

The demography of Internet users also has implications for the types of potential political challenge we might expect in the near term. For example, many of the members of the Falun Gong are reportedly older citizens, who may turn to the group's exercises for health reasons. We would expect, then, that relatively few members of the Falun Gong are active Internet users. Reports that the Falun Gong communicates with its members through the Internet may, in fact, reflect network use mainly among the group's leaders. Directives to the group's members would more likely be spread through more traditional methods of communication, such as the telephone or word of mouth.

For many of the young, mainly urban, male users, there may be little incentive to endanger their future careers by discussing politics. As social scientists such as Andrew Walder (1986) and Margaret Pearson (1997) have found, those members of Chinese society who see a secure career path within the existing political system may be reluctant to disrupt it.[17] The potential danger of random government checks of these chat groups may suffice to institute self-censorship among current Internet users. Futhermore, if Internet content creates the same kind of consensus building that Chan saw with television content, stability may be further reinforced.

In sum, the avenues for greater political dialogue are expanding, and as the numbers and demographics of users change in the coming years, the kinds of discussion will undoubtedly evolve. At the moment, however, there is little indication that Internet forums are contributing to a greater degree of Chinese civil society. The kind of future challenge seen by Taubman (1998: 255–72) and others who forecast net-based autonomous group formation, and perhaps eventually democracy, has yet to materialize.

The lack of an immediate political challenge, then, influences the methods the government will employ to control both the Internet's physical infrastructure and its network content. If user demographics indicate a challenge to the ruling authority may be muted, the need for control will also be softened. As access to data network tools spreads to less-privileged members of society in coming years, however, we may expect new voices to change at least some of the current tone of network content.

The future role of foreign corporations

As seen above, foreign web content is already widely available to Chinese audiences, and foreign companies have even been able to take limited financial stakes in Chinese ICPs. According to the conditions for the PRC's accession to the world trade body, the WTO, the country opens up to 49 percent ownership in China's Internet service providing companies, and as much as 50 percent in other services such as e-mail and online information over the coming years. These steps could allow some significant foreign influence on how Chinese consumers gain access to the network, as foreign companies could aid nascent private ISPs in their drive to take a market share from regional network companies. The influence of municipal and provincial companies in controlling revenue flows could effectively be curtailed. Private ICPs could benefit, in a similar way, from foreign capital and expertise and ensure that state-backed content companies faced continued competition.

Increased economic strength could embolden Chinese service and content providers to exercise greater creativity and perhaps reduce their willingness to follow Chinese government rules and restrictions. Of course, being punished by the police for violation of government rules would still deter even the strongest companies from challenging political edicts, but the government would lose some of the control now held in its economic levers. Increases in wholesale leasing fees, for example, might have less effect on foreign-backed ISPs, and cash-burning ICPs could last longer against deep-pocketed municipal and regional government web sites. Furthermore, if foreign companies themselves chose to partner with the state corporations, the private companies would face an even greater challenge for control of service and content.

Conclusion

In conclusion, we see that government control of the physical network does not necessarily imply control over content. The MII may have both direct and indirect dominance over the data pipelines, but the ministry's main goal seems to be collecting revenue from those who use the system. As long as the MII can accomplish this goal, it tends to shy away from conflict with the party organs and publicity offices more fully charged with regulating Internet content. Conservative members of the government leadership probably also believe that the actual tools of communication should remain in state hands for the same reasons that there are no private newspaper printing presses or television transmitting stations.

On the other hand, much of China's Internet content is in private hands. Self-censorship is probably a big factor in controlling the political nature of this content, but the composition of the audience also shapes what is put on Chinese screens. We see, however, that, if detected, those few who violate unspoken government limits of expression face severe sanctions.

Nascent government-backed web sites, such as Eastday.com in Shanghai, and others, also stand as a potential challenge to the free market forces working among the private dot.com content companies and service providers. The utilization of superior financial resources by the government sites also contradicts the government's goal of taking state enterprise out of the economy's forefront, and encouraging the growth of private business. In the wake of the (perhaps temporary) global weakness among Internet content providers, national and local government moves in China to develop state-owned web enterprises could retard free market forces, at least in the short term.

Finally, with the possible exception of the Falun Gong demonstrations, access to foreign information via the Internet has had little socially disruptive impact. Internet demographics indicate that user profiles, in fact, work toward social stability, at least in the coming few years. Younger users may avoid controversy, and use the network more for education and entertainment purposes.

A key turning point may come if foreign companies are allowed full ownership of web content providers or service providers, although even here police restrictions could thwart a free flow of information. Furthermore, as today's elite Internet users age and perhaps encounter financial or political difficulties in their lives, and as more disaffected members of society find access to the network, we may see it emerge as a tool to be utilized more frequently to channel discontent.

In short, the government seems intent on tapping the most lucrative parts of the Internet – here is where we see the greatest desire for control. As for content, political controls will remain schizophrenic because the value of an open network conflicts with conservative political philosophies and because the nature of the Internet's audience means that the Internet will remain an unlikely tool for precipitating socially disruptive forces.

Notes

1 An earlier version of this essay appeared as "Shaping the Internet in China: evolution of political control over network infrastructure and content." It has been revised and reprinted: © 2001 by The Regents of the University of California, Asian Survey, Vol. 41, No. 3, pp. 377–408 by permission of the Regents.
2 Some of the following history is derived from Mueller and Tan 1997: 81–91.
3 Interview with Chinese Academy of Social Sciences researcher, by Harwit, Beijing, May 19, 1999.
4 For detail on the conflict between the MPT and China Unicom in the mid-1990s, see Harwit 1998, Lynch 1999b: 165–75.
5 Interactive Audience Measurement Asia (IAMASIA), a Hong Kong-based survey organization, reported a lower figure of some 12 million users (defined as someone who has used the Internet within the past four weeks) in mid-2000, when the CNNIC found nearly 18 million users (with an unclear definition of "user," although the January 2001 survey defines users as "Chinese citizens who use the Internet at least one hour per week." We note that the official statistics are in the same order of magnitude. See the IAMASIA home page at http://www. iamasia.com/ and CNNIC 7/2000.
6 Author's own telephone interview survey with companies in Beijing 1999.
7 From September 2003 discussion between Harwit and Chinese government official in New York State.
8 For a lengthy speech by Wu on the growth of the information industry, see *Renmin youdian* 1998: 1. See also *New York Times* (December 6, 2000).
9 In February 2001, the Ministry of Public Security released details of its own equivalent of "NetNanny" filtering software, named "110" after China's equivalent of "911." From April 2001 interview with a foreign telecommunications consultant in Beijing.
10 Interview with Shanghai academic researcher, by Harwit, Shanghai, July 19, 2000.
11 Telephone interview with foreign business consultant operating in Beijing, by Harwit, October 2000.
12 See also the chapter by Chase, Hachigian and Mulvenon in this volume.
13 Interview with researcher at foreign survey firm, by Harwit, Beijing, June 2000. The company placed software on Internet users' computers, and provided them with a small stipend and a guarantee of anonymity in return for their cooperation in the survey project.
14 Interview with foreign consultant, by Harwit, Beijing, June 12, 2000.
15 However, we do not know whether those who posted these comments actually reside in China.
16 Informal discussion between Harwit and Chinese central government official, April 2001, Beijing. This official commented that others in the official's ministry use chat sentiment as a kind of unofficial public opinion poll. Of course, as noted above, such official attention to chat groups leaves them open to manipulation by overseas Chinese seeking to distort chat discussion content.

17 Pearson came to these conclusions after examining private business people and joint venture employees in the early 1990s.

References

Agence France Presse (October 3, 2000) "China issues long-awaited Internet rules." *Asiaweek* (March 2, 2001) "Web renegade on trial," pp. 14, 33.

BDA (China) Ltd (2000) *Broadband Access in China: Focus Report*, Beijing: BDA (China) Ltd.

Browne, Andrew (2001) "China's Zhu apologizes over deadly school blast," *Reuters World Report*, (March 15).

Business Wire, Inc. (September 28, 2000) "2dobiz.com inside track to mainland China."

Chan, Joseph Man (1994) "Media internationalization in China: processes and tensions," *Journal of Communication (JOC)*, 44: 3, pp. 70–88.

China Daily (February 4,1999) "China's Internet fees expected to decrease." Online. Available HTTP: http://www.chinadaily.com.cn/cndydb/1999/02/d5-4net.b04. html/ (accessed February 8, 1999).

China Online (July 15,1999) "China infohighway in no rush for overseas investment." Online. Available HTTP: http://www.chinaonline.com/ (accessed July 18, 1999).

China Online LLC online news service (July 19, 2000) "For most China Internet companies, profitability means improbability." Online. Available HTTP: http://www.chinaonline.com/ (accessed July 25, 2000).

Chu, Leonard L. (1994) "Continuity and change in China's media reform," *Journal of Communication (JOC)*, 44: 3, pp. 4–21.

Clark, Duncan (2000) "Decree clearly adds to confusion," *"Beijing Byte" e-mail information service*, posted October 16, 2000. Online. Available HTTP: http://www.bdaconnect.com (accessed October 25, 2000).

Clark, Duncan, Rehak, Alexandra and Dean, Ted (1999) *The Internet in China*, Beijing: BDA China Ltd.

CNNIC (1/1999) *Statistical Report of the Development of China Internet (1999.1)*. Online. Available HTTP: http://www.cnnic.net.cn (accessed February 15, 2003).

CNNIC (1/2000) *SemiAnnual Survey Report on Internet Development in China (2000.1)*. Online. Available HTTP: http://www.cnnic.net.cn (accessed February 15, 2003).

CNNIC (7/2000) *Semiannual Survey Report on the Development of China's Internet (2000.7)*. Online. Available HTTP: http://www.cnnic.net.cn (accessed February 15, 2003).

CNNIC (1/2001) *Semiannual Survey Report on the Development of China's Internet (2001.1)*. Online. Available HTTP: http://www.cnnic.net.cn (accessed February 15, 2003).

CNNIC (7/2003) *12th Statistical Survey on the Internet Development in China (2003.7)*. Online. Available HTTP: http://www.cnnic.net.cn (accessed August 17, 2003).

CNNIC (1/2004) *13th Statistical Survey on the Internet Development in China (2004.1)*. Online. Available HTTP: http://www.cnnic.net.cn (accessed March 23, 2004).

CNNIC (7/2004) *14th Statistical Survey Report on the Development on Internet in China*. Online. Available HTTP: http://www.cnnic.net.cn (accessed August 21, 2004).

Einhorn, Bruce and Roberts, Dexter (August 2,1999) "China's web masters," *Business Week (International edition)*. Online. Available HTTP: http://www.businessweek.com/datedtoc/1999/9931.htm/ (accessed October 25, 1999).

Foster, William and Goodman, Seymour E. (2000) *The Diffusion of the Internet in China*, A Report of the Center for International Security and Cooperation, Stanford University.

Greenberg, Jonah (December 7,1999) "China Netcom," *Virtual* China. Online. Available HTTP: http://virtualchina.com/infotech/news/stories/120799-netcom. html (accessed December 7, 1999).

Harwit, Eric (1998) "China's telecommunications industry: development patterns and policies," *Pacific Affairs* (Summer), pp. 175–94.

Hong, Junhao (1998) *The Internationalization of Television in China*, Westport, CN: Prager Publishers.

IAMASIA (2001) "Top ten web domain sites for all users," corporate survey from February 2001. Online. Available HTTP: http://www.iamasia.com/ (accessed June 7, 2001).

Jin Wulun (1996) "Kexue shehuixue yu keji zhengce" [Scientific sociology and technology policy], *Ziran bianzhengfa tongxun* [Natural dialectic communication] 5/1996, pp. 22–31.

Kuhn, Anthony (February 13,1999) "State phone monopoly makes using the Internet difficult," *Los Angeles Times*, p. A2.

Lee, Paul Siu-nam (1994) "Mass communication and national development in China: media roles reconsidered," *Journal of Communication (JOC)*, 44: 3, pp. 22–37.

Li, Luting (1998) "Xinxi shehui yu qingnian nuxing wenti" [The problems of the information society and female youth], *Zhongguo qingnian zhengzhi xueyuan xuebao* [The Chinese youth policy institute journal], (January), pp. 24–8.

Lynch, Daniel C. (1999a) "Dilemmas of 'thought work' in *Fin-de-Siecle* China," *China Quarterly*, 157 (March), pp. 173–201.

Lynch, Daniel C. (1999b) *After the Propaganda State: Media, Politics, and "Thought Work" in Reformed China*, Stanford, CA: Stanford University Press.

McIntyre, Bryce T. (1997) "China's use of the Internet: a revolution on hold," in: Lee, Paul S. N. 1997 (ed.) *Telecommunications and Development in China*, Cresskill, NJ: Hampton Press, pp. 149–69.

Mueller, Milton and Tan, Zixiang (1997) *China in the Information Age*, Westport, CN: Prager Publishers.

Netease.com, Inc. (June 29, 2000) *Prospectus for Issue of American Depository Shares of Netease.com, Inc.*

New York Times (December 6, 2000) "Last word in China's phone industry."

Nie, Norman and Erbring, Lutz (2000) *Internet and Society: A Preliminary Report*, Stanford, CA: Stanford Institute for the Quantitative Study of Society, (February 17).

Pearson, Margaret (1994) "The Janus face of business associations in China," *Australian Journal of Chinese Affairs* (January), pp. 25–46.

Pearson, Margaret (1997) *China's New Business Elite*, Berkeley, CA: University of California Press.

Pei, Minxin (1998) "The growth of civil society in China," in James Dorn (ed.) *China in the New Millennium*, Washington, DC: Cato Institute, pp. 245–66.

Platt, Kevin (March 21, 2000) "After prison, dreams of China's democracy," *Christian Science Monitor*, p. 7.

Renmin youdian [People's posts and telecommunications] (September 6, 1998) "Wu Jichuan buzhang zai kexue huitang fabiao zhuanti baogao" [Minister Wu Jichuan delivers a special report at the scientific auditorium], p. 1.

Richburg, Keith B. (April 8, 1996) "A Great Wall of China slowly gives way; entrepreneur creates online network despite official controls," *Washington Post*, p. A01.

Rui, Mingjie (1998) "Hulianwang lingshouye fazhan tansuo" [Exploration of Internet retail industry development], *Shangchang xiandaihua* [Market modernization], (April), pp. 10–12.

Shanker, M. K. (March 21, 2000) "Security software creators find openings as curbs ease," *South China Morning Post*, Technology Post section, p. 4.

Song, Shiping (1997) "Internet yu tongji xinxi tongxin wanglu jianshe" [The Internet and construction of the statistical information network], *Tongji yu xinxi* [Statistics and information], (January), pp. 28–9.

South China Morning Post (February 9, 2001) "Ding calls for more 'influential' Internet development." Online. Available HTTP: http://china.scmp.com/technology/ZZZV5PKVPGC.html/ (accessed February 9, 2001).

Sun, B. (1994) "Xiangzhen shetuan yu Zhongguo jiceng shehui" [Township associations and the Chinese society at the grassroots], *Chinese Social Sciences Quarterly* (H.K.) (autumn), cited in Pei 1998.

Sydney Morning Herald (July 25, 2000) "Content licensing ducks China's media blockade," p. 33.

Tan, Zixiang (1995) "China's information superhighway," *Telecommunications Policy*, 19: 9, pp. 721–31.

Tan, Zixiang (1996) "Internet in China," *Pacific Telecommunications Conference Proceedings* (January), p. 624.

Tan, Zixiang (1999) "Regulating China's Internet," *Telecommunications Policy*, 23: 3–4, pp. 261–76.

Taubman, Geoffry (1998) "A not-so World Wide Web: the Internet, China, and the challenges to nondemocratic rule," *Political Communication*, 15 (March), pp. 255–72.

Triolo, Paul and Lovelock, Peter (1996) "Up, up, and away – with strings attached," *China Business Review* (November/December), p. 29.

Unger, Jonathan (1996) " 'Bridges': private business, the Chinese government and the rise of new associations," *China Quarterly* (September), pp. 795–819.

Walder, Andrew (1986) *Communist Neo-Traditionalism*, Berkeley, CA: University of California Press.

Wang, Chuangdong (March 1, 1999) "Ministry unveils fee adjustments," *China Daily*. Online. Available HTTP: http://www.chinadaily.com.cn/cndydb/1999/03/d1-1post.c01.html (accessed May 5, 1999).

Wang, Xiangdong (1998) *Xinxihua: Zhongguo 21 shiji de xuanze* [Informatization: China's choices in the 21st century], Beijing: Shehuikexue wenzhai chubanshe.

Wei, Wu (1996) "Great leap or long march: some policy issues of the development of the Internet in China," *Telecommunications Policy*, 20: 9, pp. 699–711.

Xinhua News Agency (August 4, 2000) "Chinese Internet Police."

Yu,Verna (2003) "Webmaster given five years for publishing essays," *South China Morning Post* (May 19), p. 4.

Zhao, Huanxin (March 2, 1999) "Internet hook-up cost reduction to enhance extension access." Online. Available HTTP: http://www.chinadaily.com.cn/cndydb/1999/03/d2-5inte.c02.html (accessed March 3, 1999).

Zhao, Wenli and Zhi, Lihong (1998) "Dianzi wanglu yu kexue gongzuo de shehui jiegou" [The electronic network and social construction of scientific work], *Ziran bianzhengfa tongxun* (July), pp. 42–7, 51.

3 In the crossfire of demands

Chinese news portals between propaganda and the public

Johan Lagerkvist

The evidence from China's online news industry presented in this chapter shows that the delicate relationship between news making and news control is undergoing interesting changes. While self-censorship is practiced in Chinese cyberspace, and the Chinese government is firmly determined to keep news reporting within limits set by the Communist Party, economic logic and changed value orientations among China's Internet surfers equip editors of online news organizations with arguments they can use to negotiate online spatial freedom with government officials. This analysis of the "soft" negotiation processes for China's online news networks, most notably the administration of municipal online news portals, is primarily based on in-depth interviews with editors and journalists of Beijing's *Qianlong Wang* and Shanghai's *Dongfang Wang* in 2003 and 2004. Issues raised in the analysis concern the role the online news genre may play in the development of more independent news making in China. Optimistic assumptions that online news media in a globalizing China will offer less controlled news coverage and follow-up commentaries than offline news outlets such as print media and television are not altogether wrong. But such forecasts must be qualified against continued government censorship, and self-censoring among online journalists and news consumers. Constraining contextual factors such as Communist Party propaganda and the authoritarian tradition also need to be factored into the equation.

I shall, in this chapter, describe and analyze one particular difficulty in managing Chinese news portals on the Internet, namely the constant concern about government reaction to news production. One may wonder how new communications technology, effects of globalization and commercialization, and public demand for alternative sources of news are affecting the ideological and political framework of China's hitherto tightly controlled media system. I argue that the commercial logic of online news media is impacting on, and changing, the negotiation process involving editors of online news portals and government officials, with implications for both online and offline municipal and state news media. The analysis of news production in Chinese cyberspace in this chapter is primarily based on interviews with managers and operators of bulletin board services (BBS) of Beijing's *Qianlong Wang* in 2003 and 2004. To contrast the case of *Qianlong*, an analysis of interviews conducted at Shanghai's *Dongfang Wang* is also used. In all these interviews, the changing dynamics between the administration of municipal online news portals and Communist Party control through the local propaganda department is accounted for in detail. Readings of general Chinese policy documents on relevant Internet regulations and official speeches are also incorporated into the analysis. The perceptions of the daily work routine and the negotiations with officials from the propaganda department regarding online news content and online news commentary are outlined in block citations, since news editors' views on what they call "an on-going" learning process between professional news workers and the propaganda cadres offer a rare glimpse into the changes this important relationship is going through today.

According to Chinese law, only officially approved news units are allowed to publish online news (Baker and McKenzie 2001: 362). But technological developments are making these regulations increasingly yeasty and blurred. For instance, news dissemination among individual surfers in the Chinese blogosphere and on various electronic bulletin boards is becoming more prevalent.

In a strict legal sense, new online media such as blogs and BBSs cannot be defined as news media outlets, although they have already come to play an important role in distributing alternative news information. Legal necessity makes for the use of commercial agreements whereby important domestic or international news items are bought from official national-level news organizations such as *Xinhua News Agency* and then pasted onto the website of the municipal news portal. An individual online editor or reporter may publish local political news on a municipal web portal. This activity is something editors at a local private web portal such as *Sina*'s East China branch are not allowed to do.

Establishing municipal online news organizations

The municipal online news networks occupy an important position in China's media system since they are part of the Chinese state's large-scale effort not to lose the initiative in making news online. At the end of the 1990s, the Internet was not as regulated as it is today. At that time, web portals such as *Sina, Sohu, Netease, tom.com*, and other private or semi-private mainland media organizations, were able, if not directly allowed, to copy news items from abroad and also publish political news. If the Chinese state had not begun to limit political news publishing by these web portals, and if national and municipal party-controlled mass media had not started to enter cyberspace, the setting of the online news agenda would have been a freer enterprise than it is today. Interestingly though, these municipal news portals are now themselves, under the pressure of media commercialization, forced to negotiate the boundaries of online space with those in the Communist Party supervising and defining what is tolerable and harmful content in Chinese media types.

Chinese mainland mass media started to become involved with advanced communications technology, including the Internet, at the beginning of the 1990s. Since, however, the number of Chinese Internet users at that time was limited to only a few high-tech businesses, the research community, and the higher levels of the bureaucracy, there was no mass base to read online news. All that changed after the grand opening of the national news portal *People's Net* (*Renmin Wang*, hosted by the *People's Daily*), *Xinhua News Agency*'s online version *Xinhua Wang* in 1997 and several other important nation-wide media organizations. By 2001, however, only four years later, there were more than 700 online news media competing in Chinese cyberspace (Min 2003: 57).

The municipal online news networks *Dongfang Wang* and *Qianlong Xinwen Wang* (hereafter called *Dongfang* and *Qianlong*) are located in Shanghai and Beijing respectively. Moreover, as *Qianlong* is based in the political capital, Beijing, and *Dongfang* is located in the finance and banking capital, Shanghai, they stand out as models for other news networks around the country to study and emulate.[1] Thus, an analysis of how these two online news networks interact with news censors within the government and municipal bureaucracies may offer an insight into the actual level of control exercised over online state-sanctioned media initiatives.

From the start, it seemed that the government had the upper hand and was in control of the development of the national online news genre. The Ministry of Education's monthly magazine, *China Scholar* (*Shenzhou Xueren*), marked the beginning of the mainland news media going online in 1995. Shortly afterwards, however, privately owned commercial web companies began to invest heavily, and to push ahead with the rapid dissemination of news on the Internet. When these start-ups, mostly run by IT-savvy young men, opened the doors to interesting news stories online, both regulators and state-owned media organizations were alerted to the need to scramble for public opinion (ibid.).

Qianlong, a consortium consisting of nine media organizations altogether, was formally inaugurated in Beijing on March 7, 2000, notably in the presence of Xu Guangchun, vice-minister and director of the State Administration of Film, Radio and Television.[2] When its news service was launched on May 25, 2000, Long Xinmin, head of the Publicity Department of Beijing Municipality was present to witness the inauguration. The attention that *Qianlong* and other municipal online news networks received and continue to receive from leading propaganda officials is testimony to the importance that the Chinese Communist Party and the central government attach to creating an ideologically and politically correct Internet environment. The State Council Information Office specifically set up an Internet Propaganda Administrative Bureau, which was assigned the tasks of coordinating web news content, and ordering major state media organs to utilize the Internet fully to accomplish the political objectives of the party (Kalathil 2003: 494). On July 30, 2000, *Qianlong's* BBS was opened to the surfing public. At the time, it was primarily targeting the web audience of the capital, Beijing. According to the wishes of both the Central and Municipal Departments of Propaganda, the name of this flagship BBS was later changed from Discussion Forum for All and Everything under Heaven (*Tianxia luntan*) to Discussion Forum of Beijing (*Jinghua luntan*) (*Qianlong* 2001). Thus it can be seen that, in the interests of political correctness, seemingly peripheral details are also designed and changed at will by officials in charge of supervising propaganda and news work in China. On its website, *Qianlong* simply presents itself as "the biggest and most influential portal in the Beijing area," and is the web media alternative that most comprehensively and directly contributes to the motto "Beijing understands the world, the world understands Beijing" (ibid.). One news editor outlined his company's vision as follows:

> I believe our company's goals and objectives are embodied in our emphasis on the economy and welfare of the nation, that we exhort a healthy life-style, that we offer healthy information. It should be said that everybody here thinks this position is very important.
>
> (Interview with *Qianlong* news editor
> in Beijing, January 6, 2003)

The battle of the online news market

All Chinese online media companies, whether state-owned, owned by municipalities, private, or owned by cooperatives, are nowadays subject to the logic of the market. But the political logic of an authoritarian regime continues to inform how, by whom, and what kind of political news should be presented to the public. In an increasingly profit-driven media landscape but still Communist Party-controlled media system, it seems safer to break social taboos than publish non-sanctioned views on politics.

Two news stories, one from 2003 concerning public morals, and one from 2004 concerning the sensitive Taiwan issue, aptly illustrate the Chinese government's unease about cyber culture and the evolving online news genre in the People's Republic: on March 19, 2004, in the southern city of Tainan, during the last days of the Taiwanese presidential elections, an alleged attempt was made on the life of Chen Shui-bian, President of Taiwan. In the immediate aftermath, it would have been reasonable to expect that a piece of news of this importance would have appeared in some corner of China's state-controlled media space, or at least in part of the monitored, albeit less controlled cyberspace.[3] Even if BBSs and chat rooms were not flooded by comments on the assassination attempt, at least some postings on the incident should have been made by China's surfing citizens, so called netizens. None of this happened however. Apart from a few sparse comments on the *People's Daily*'s Strong Country Forum (*Qiangguo luntan*),[4] and a few lines found on the official website of the *Xinhua News Agency*, Chinese cyberspace remained mute on this serious event of great interest to Chinese people the world over, because it concerned sensitive "Taiwan Straits politics."

In sharp contrast, when burgeoning interest in the sex-dominated columns of blogger,[5] Mu Zimei, began to appear on China's Internet in 2003, the private web portal *Sina* decided to make the strategic move of publishing her online diary on their national website. For *Sina*, the profit motive justified taking the risk of affronting the Communist Party's Central Propaganda Department in going public with the sex stories of a new celebrity. Nevertheless, the *Sina* news staff has certainly not been over-quick in putting sensitive political news items on Taiwan online. In the case of the alleged assassination attempt on Chen Shui-bian's life, this was partly due to the lack of an official news organization from which a story could be purchased, but the most overwhelming reason was probably the fear that violating the laws on news-making in China would incur a heavy cost in this particular case.[6]

Many would argue that the World Wide Web, online news, blogs, and BBSs in China at least allow more space for open-minded discussions and postings of critical articles than the traditional news media does, even if they are not safe havens for dissidents.[7] The inherent logic is that external forces of globalization are important. This is the main theme of communications scholars, Curran and Park, who, in the introduction to their anthology, *De-Westernizing Media Studies*, argue that "globalizing influences are viewed as progressive in their effects in China and Taiwan," and that the market there is viewed as "being on balance an important agency contributing to the emergence of a more independent and critical media system" (Curran and Park 2000: 13–14). Nonetheless, what may ultimately contribute to liberalization and reform in the Chinese media sector are internal factors of an economical, organizational, and educational nature. Nowadays there is much more pressure on newsroom staff to be efficient, well educated, and, not least, to have a profit-oriented instinct. It is important to recognize that the pressures associated with media globalization are, in fact, originating from market liberalization of the domestic media system.

While the programming and format of multi-national media giants such as *Star-TV* and Google are exposing Chinese audiences to different value orientations, it must be noted that their desire to get a foothold within the Chinese media system have made these companies as anxious as domestic media not to offend the Chinese Communist Party. The pressures felt by the conservative elements of the Chinese government and Communist Party are of a commercial kind, whose origin is national. As a consequence, the officials in charge of propaganda and news control in the

State Administration of Film, Radio and Television, and the General Administration of Press and Publication have had to lower their guard and play a more subtle game than before. Most notable is the need to shift the focus from enforcing a "correct political discourse" in the media towards a stance where foreign influence over and cooperation with the largely unreformed media industry is acceptable to the government. Needless to say, much of the incipient foreign impact on the domestic media industry is only a natural consequence of China becoming a member of the WTO.[8]

The attention paid to the so-called "Great Chinese Firewall," has increased, as has the quantity of tracts written about censors and censorship in Chinese cyberspace in the last few years (see Qiu 1999, Kalathil and Boas 2003).[9] This kind of research mostly focuses on the blocking of certain websites whose content Chinese authorities consider harmful to China.[10] Less attention has been paid to the management of online news organizations, BBSs, and chat forums such as the Strong Country Forum hosted by *Renmin Wang*, or the *People's Net*, and how these work. It is a fact that self-censorship is practiced online in the PRC. But to what extent are news editors and journalists able to negotiate online space with the officials in charge of propaganda work in the Chinese bureaucracy? There is little research literature available on this extremely important aspect of the Chinese media system.

In order to be able to "win the war on public opinion" in the information age, state and municipal media actors such as *Qianlong* and *Dongfang* need to muster and energize their forces if they are to compete with Nasdaq-listed web portal giants such as *Sina* and *Sohu*.[11] Needless to say, the international, or Taiwan branches of these web portals have much more journalistic freedom than their mainland counterparts. And when the interviewees in this chapter mention *Sina*, they always refer to the headquarters in Beijing or the regional East China branch with its head office located in Shanghai. A project director of *Qianlong* Academy, leading the unit's mission to produce new knowledge about Internet businesses in general, and online news-making in particular, stated in an interview that:

> the difference between *Qianlong*'s news service and those of *Sina*'s and *Sohu*'s concern political limits. Yes, they do their own reporting on big sporting events and stories related to entertainment, but they are very wary about stepping on somebody else's toes.
>
> (Interview, January 5, 2003)

This may seem counter to conventional wisdom, but other evidence is also available to support this finding (Kalathil 2003: 495). As municipal news portals are administered, financed, and supervised under the auspices of the municipal government in Beijing and Shanghai, state officials may in fact entertain a false notion of security. That may account for the municipal online news organizations, in some cases, appearing to have more room for maneuver than their sensationalist private competitors. When asked to elaborate in some detail on the competition between the news items of *Qianlong* and *Sina*'s copied or purchased online news items, the *Qianlong* project director responded:

> Credit must go to them for fast news production, which to some extent originates from their having it much easier to acquire the latest computer equipment than their state-owned competitors. [...] The central government well understood it had to establish a strong presence and capacity online in order to be able to "guide the opinion" (*yulun daoxiang*) effectively also in the Internet age.
>
> (Interview, January 5, 2003)

A news worker at Shanghai's *Dongfang* website also discussed in detail the difference between the municipal and private portals: "Sure the conditions are different between privately owned web portals such as *Sina* and *Sohu* and us, the municipal ones. Just take a look at the rooms and interior design here at our place." With a lot of pride, however, he also added: "On the other hand, these private enterprises do not assume any social responsibility either." The obvious counter-argument to that statement would, of course, be that private and semi-private web portals are not permitted by the government to shoulder such a task either. Nevertheless, this editor did not rule out such a role for them in the future: "In a few years time, say ten to twenty years, private media companies like them will probably play the same role as such companies do today in the West."[12]

Thus, it is evident that the fast moving private web portals alerted the Central Propaganda Department of the Communist Party to the fact that they had to catch up – and catch up fast. A new strategy for catching-up was clearly illustrated in a speech delivered to the 16th Central Party Committee in September 2004 by China's vice-president and member of the politburo standing committee, Zeng Qinghong. In his speech, he stated that:

> the Party must take very seriously the influence the Internet and other new types of media have on public opinion, and thus strengthen the system for managing the Internet and the buildup of a corps of online propaganda personnel, and form up strong momentum in straightforward propaganda.
>
> (Zeng 2004: 2)

One *Qianlong* manager described the Communist Party's dilemma regarding the Internet in this way:

> That is actually the major reason behind the establishment of the huge news networks *Qianlong* in Beijing and *Dongfang* in Shanghai [...]

there is also great encouragement from the central government's side to establish news networks at regional and local levels [...] sometimes *Qianlong* confronts the problem of accommodating and satisfying the demands from propaganda workers and censors within the Communist Party and the municipal Beijing government. These people have strong views about how many of our stories should carry elements of Party ideology and current "correct opinion" on some outstanding policy issues, and this is something that ordinary surfers do not wish to see.

Obviously, to accommodate market demand and, at the same time, to assume the traditional role of mouthpiece in the global information age poses a dilemma. And online journalists have to adjust to this situation of being caught in the crossfire of demands from both Chinese government propaganda officials and the Chinese public. This particular informant actually admitted that there are, indeed, clashes of viewpoints between the Party's ideologues and news reporters. Today, reporters show less readiness than before to satisfy the commands of the propaganda apparatus, since these orders increasingly conflict with the interests of reporters and the reading public, which is tired of viewing, reading, and listening to old-fashioned propaganda.

The credibility of online news

Media researchers Deuze and Yeshua (2000) have discussed how online journalism by some actors is viewed as lacking institutional credibility, professional standards, and not making a clear distinction between commercial and editorial content. When it comes to news-making, popularity is apparently not the twin of credibility. And in China, people's trust in online news media has been on a roller coaster ride ever since this new media type saw the light of day in the mid-1990s. In the late 1990s, several surveys showed that online news scored low in trustworthiness among respondents. But recent Chinese reports measuring the credibility of the online news genre indicate that young people, in particular, have gone from a negative attitude regarding the trustworthiness of online news to a more positive attitude.[13]

In all likelihood, this newer attitude was reinforced when the Chinese people were informed of the seriousness of the SARS virus, not by the state-controlled media, which remained silent, but by online news media, both foreign and Chinese-language news sources, outside the PRC. The cover-up by government and state-controlled media outlets, and the lack of serious investigative reporting drove many Chinese citizens online in their search for more truthful news. During the SARS crisis of spring 2003, the number of SMS-messages, e-mails, and Internet accounts made a quantum leap in the PRC (Clark 2003). Now, in the aftermath of the crisis, news-hungry Chinese people are flocking to the web in increasing numbers, in their search for news stories. In fact, in a comparison of online behavior between China, Germany, and the US, it was shown that China's netizens use the web the most for searching news (Hu 2004: 176).

What must be noted, however, is the way in which state-controlled media organizations are trying to score points on the question of reliability, and they are succeeding quite well in portraying themselves as reliable. It is certainly something of a paradox that as an increasing number of China's Internet users rush to get online in order to access first-hand and less censored political news, the traditional mass media continue to score high on trustworthiness (Hu 2004: 184). Chinese citizens, so long accustomed to the language and style of official news propaganda, might be expected to think more critically of these official media outlets, especially after the SARS crisis. In essence, official media organizations are persuading people to believe that they are not as sensationalist as privately owned web media businesses and, furthermore, that they are fulfilling a social responsibility by not randomly distributing unchecked facts in the blind pursuit of profit. This was precisely the view given by several interviewees at both *Qianlong* and *Dongfang*. It shows that a new self-image is developing among media professionals in state-owned online media units. While they want to lessen their role as mouthpieces of government propaganda, they may be forced, or in some cases may even be willing, to adopt some of the reservations held by the government and Communist Party regarding privately owned media companies – not for the sake of ideology or political stability, but for the sake of profit. Apparently, trustworthiness may sell just as well as sensationalism, at least in some quarters. Despite the fact that ordinary people began to seek independent news sources and that more trustworthy, less sensational online journalism started well before the outbreak of the SARS virus, the people's need for alternative sources of news with a less politicized agenda than the state-controlled media was clearly intensified by the crisis that followed. In that sense, the response of the Chinese people to the medical curfew and media silence in Beijing of Spring 2003 was a landmark in the media history of the PRC.

Propaganda in the online news genre

Is there any difference between news content and political propaganda material in contemporary China? The intensity and scope of propaganda, *xuanchan*, in the mass media has changed a lot since the 1949 communist revolution. As a consequence of the economic reforms initiated by Deng Xiaoping in 1978, the Communist Party and the state no longer dominate the daily life of ordinary Chinese people. In the post-Mao period, party propaganda shifted its focus from class struggle to emphasizing party-led economic modernization. Nowadays, propaganda has become increasingly sophisticated (Lagerkvist 2003). It is more often presented as rational information with the goal of persuading people to realize the importance of the continued dominance of the Communist Party in Chinese society. And, more specifically, how do the journalists and editors working in online news media organizations perceive their role vis-à-vis the powerful propaganda officials in the Chinese media system?

The interviews conducted in Beijing and Shanghai confirmed the continued relevance, albeit changing in nature, of a special relationship between reporters and censors. This relationship is not very much influenced by the ongoing globalization of China, which has led to more openness than ever before with the rest of the world and its government representatives going abroad to study models and ideas from other countries.

Issues of freedom of speech and media liberalization have been recurring themes ever since Deng Xiaoping initiated economic liberalization in 1978. The censorship institutions in China came under repeated attack from dissidents, academics, and professional journalists during the period of Deng's program of economic reform and opening up to the world (*gaige kaifang*). The most outspoken and dramatic criticism of mass media censorship revealed itself among the many journalists, editors, and dissidents who were roused to action during the student demonstrations of spring 1989. In 2004, mainland media scholars again attacked the system of news control maintained by the party-state's propaganda apparatus. The vitriolic attack on the Communist Party's Central Propaganda Department by Beijing University media professor, Jiao Guobiao, in February 2004, received much attention in the international press. Jiao's paper argued that this department was the only unit in the Chinese bureaucracy unable to reform, and that by maintaining news control and continuing to stifle the press, it was blocking necessary political reform.[14]

In an interview, a journalist with *China Central Television*, CCTV, expressed confidence that the authorities and "the ruling Party" would be successful in both regulating the Internet *and* turning it into a tool for propaganda: "For them it is difficult and time-consuming, but it's happening. A few years ago it was all a mess online. Nowadays it's more orderly, and there's clarity about what may be published."[15] One *Qianlong* news editor outlined the mission of his media organization and the special circumstances involved when one is routinely scrutinized by the officials of various propaganda units and the State Administration of Film, Radio and Television in these terms:

Online media organizations run by the government have a primary responsibility, and that is to spread the voice of the Party and the Government. At the same time, we must offer netizens news information of a fresh kind, including information about entertainment. There are some contradictions in all this, but that doesn't mean you have only one thing and not another, or that there is a sharp dichotomy between them. While spreading the message of the Party and the

Government we can also make good on offering netizens the things they like. It's not as incompatible as fire and water. On the issue of handling reporting, we are learning from each other: we [the journalists] say that reporting is an art form where you must avoid mechanical copying and the simple and crude "I-decide-what's-right" ways of reporting.

This statement is very interesting: it shows that as the relationship between news content and propaganda changes, the relationship between newsmakers and the propagandists of the Communist Party is also affected. This is also reflected in an article written on October 8, 2004 by China's vice-president, Zeng Qinghong, on strengthening the party's ability to govern the country. In the article, published in the *People's Daily*, he outlined the decision of the Fourth Plenum of the 16th Party Committee "to uphold the principle of the Party controlling the media, guide the media in combining the embodiment of what the Party advocates and the reflection of public sentiment" (Zeng 2004: 2). Zeng's exhortation illustrates well the perceived need for continued Communist Party control of the mass media and a confirmation that the learning and negotiation process mentioned by one *Qianlong* news manager is really going on.[16] Without taking into account what the public wants to read, or reflecting their sentiments, the online public will vote with a click on the mouse. This ongoing learning process involving news managers and officials from the propaganda corps is, at least to some extent, not only one-way. To the *Qianlong* news editor, the fundamentals to be learned by the propaganda apparatus are very straightforward:

You know that the comparative cost of the Internet is very low. To go from one website to another, you only need to make a small movement with your mouse, and you've made another choice. That means to get out is very simple, so you can't rely on a simple way of telling others you have to watch this story and not that. [. . .] Because the most terrifying thing is what I have just mentioned – the cost of online networks is low. Newspapers are different, if I subscribe to a newspaper for a year, it will arrive regularly. Or, if I only want to read the sports pages in this newspaper, the comparative cost is rather high, isn't it? Whereas the cost of online news is extremely low. If somebody, after having arrived at your website twice, thinks there's no interesting stuff worth reading, then perhaps he won't return to your website for half a year. This is a very real problem. So you really must attract him with something if you want him to stay. [. . .] And online news in contrast to those printed newspapers has more means of reporting and thus a larger output of information. If we take the 16th Party Congress as an example, the *People's Daily* will tell you, "The 16th Party Congress has successfully closed and Hu Jintao made an important speech." So, how will we in our news organization report on it? We will pick out the most important resolutions at this 16th Party Congress, the ones taken that are most cared for by common people [. . .] so there's no contradiction, only that you have to deal with this relationship.

The propagandists defending the monopoly on power held by the Communist Party are becoming increasingly aware that, as explained by the *Qianlong* news editor, there is a need to deliver the most interesting content in a very enticing way. Otherwise, in an extremely competitive environment such as the online world, no one will ever surf near to home and thus be persuaded of the Communist Party's perspective and view of an evolving news story. The negligible cost of producing online has been a contributing factor to the enormous increase in participatory journalism and blogging in the world, and this phenomenon of the democratization of journalism is also impacting on the very strict gate-keeping and leading role of China's state-owned media. Nowadays, almost anyone hooked up to the World Wide Web can produce and distribute news content (Pavlik 2001: 201).

This kind of website competition and commercialization was clearly illustrated in *Sina*'s decision to go public with the story on the Mu Zimei sex blog. The suppressed resentment among *Qianlong*'s editors and management vis-à-vis their giant private competitor was evident in all interviews:

> In this, official news websites are carrying out an important task. While having a character of their own, there is also the ambition to ensure the high reliability of the news. And since all news in Chinese cyberspace originates from official channels, netizens often go to e-government websites or official news websites to verify something they have seen at commercial websites. This is where the reliable side of official news websites shows itself.

In response to a concrete question on how their web-age propaganda may reveal itself, one editor confirmed that *Qianlong* is a website influenced by the propaganda officials of Beijing municipality, and that *Qianlong* was currently helping out in propagating the benefit of Beijing's third ring road. From this rather innocent form of non-ideological propaganda, he went on to discuss the much more far-reaching Maoist propaganda concepts of "thought work" and the phrase, often reiterated in official speeches, of "ideologically guiding opinion":

> Now, we do not emphasize this. We often have a rather narrow understanding of the meaning "thought work." Like telling you that thinking this way is incorrect, you have to change and agree with the thinking

of the Party. This concept has thinned out. Now, the goal of news production is no longer about changing people. Today's news making no longer carries with it the "smell of heavy gunpowder." So, when speaking of the role of acting as the Party's mouthpiece, there are a few tasks involving political propaganda, such as when the 16th Party Congress opened. This was perhaps one of our most important propaganda tasks. Now, how did we do it? We tried to find perspectives and alternative issues. For example, the Party Congress raised the issue of how many years it would take to achieve full welfare provision for everybody. Of course, this welfare society issue gets much attention from, and is closely related to the interest of, ordinary people. Well, how to realize this notion of *xiao kang* then.[17] What kind of guarantees are there for it? There are questions like these that the masses of netizens are intensely interested in reading. This is not only simply shouting out empty slogans, there is also real and original content to be found, not of the empty sort.

(Interview with *Qianlong* news editor,
Beijing, January 6, 2003)

This shows that if thought work in online propaganda itself contains elements of political analysis, it sometimes brings forth modest attempts to examine critically the concrete meaning of the theoretical concepts and objectives of the Chinese Communist Party. This online editor, on the subject of the sensitive relationship with the propaganda units and the heated feelings the discussions with officials occasionally evoke, described a recent case involving another of *Qianlong*'s online editors who had gone too far in the eyes of the local propaganda officials:

Last year, for example, we published a piece on the Korean war ("helping the North, resisting the United States"), as you know, people's views have changed a lot since the period of reform and opening up started. Now, there are a few things that can be debated in academic circles. [. . .] Our country has a certain view of this issue, and our editor who has knowledge of this topic published some of these different academic perspectives. Afterwards he received a lot of criticism [. . .] of a very severe and serious kind (ibid.).

Propaganda and entertainment in online news

The Chinese Communist Party needs its propaganda apparatus to positively reflect on the leading role of the party and its goals for China's future. That is especially evident in the medium of television. How is party propaganda showing itself to the online world? The channels of information available to Chinese citizens, the Internet and Internet news media, are increasing. China's Internet users are motivated to go online for three primary reasons: to obtain information (46.2 percent); to find enjoyable entertainment (32.2 percent), and to exploit the Internet for educational purposes (7.9 percent). And according to these CNNIC statistics of July 2004, what comes first is searching for news and information. The use and checking of e-mail accounts score second place. For the managers of Chinese online news organizations, these numbers are of great interest as they form the basis for any informed guess about the changing face of China's growing web audience, which, according to the CNNIC report of January 2005, amounts to 94 million users. Statistics of this kind lay the foundation for corporate strategic planning, and also facilitate the arguments needed in negotiations with officials in charge of news control. How do you attract traffic to your particular website? The managing editor of *Qianlong* elaborated extensively on this in the interview:

> Right, you cannot find a lot of people and lead them by the nose telling them you must view only this network and not that. So, if you genuinely want to attract netizens, while at the same time disseminating the voice of Party and government, you must also provide an artistic touch to the content of news and information. [. . .] The other part concerns information of a less political and economic nature, i.e. information on entertainment, etc. News websites can also with full force offer this kind of information, this is not the sole prerogative or exclusive right of commercial websites. Official and government websites can do this just as well. [. . .] Speaking generally about news websites, when it comes to political news reportage the superiority is quite obvious. But online news networks are not only carrying political news, entertainment news will also become an important part of their work. All online news networks are investing ever more manpower and other resources in this segment. After having guaranteed the accuracy, timeliness and authority of political news, more and better work will be put into entertainment news, including life-style issues, private housing, cars et cetera.
>
> (Interview with *Qianlong* news editor, Beijing, January 6, 2003)

It is evident that this editor is envisioning and emphasizing a broader role, not only in catering to online political news but also in online entertainment news. One explanation is, of course, purely related to economic concerns, but there may also be a propaganda strategy underlying this logic:

> After the new Hu Jintao leadership ascended to power they started to emphasize the importance of news work, and wanted to reduce the reports on high-level political meetings, giving, instead, more priority to the news that was closer to the lives of ordinary people.

Transparency has also increased somewhat. As we want to further improve our news work and to offer netizens more of the contents they like to read, this is really a very good signal [. . .]. It is also a very positive phenomenon that the space for reporting has expanded. [. . .] so, I think that while disseminating the voice of government we also provide entertainment news and information about entertainment products and this does not produce any contradictions.

(ibid.)

Shanghai's municipal online news network, *Dongfang*, has a different visual appearance and a leaner organizational structure than its Beijing counterpart *Qianlong*. According to news workers at Shanghai's *Dongfang* news network, only a very small part of their online content is in any way related to propaganda (Interview, October 28, 2003).[18] Moreover, only a small section of the *Dongfang* website is dedicated to political news. This particular editor elaborated on the conventional wisdom that the Shanghainese, in contrast to Beijingers, do not take an interest in political affairs. If they do show any interest, this is then restricted to matters concerning neighborhood politics. This is also reflected in a comparison of the two online news networks, *Dongfang* and *Qianlong*:

There are regional differences between the municipal news networks. In Shanghai, it's more of everyday practical matters like traffic, housing or school issues that concern or upset people. In Beijing there are more often issues of national importance that draw people's attention.

If this is correct, especially with regard to propaganda playing a minor role in the daily work routine, this is in marked contrast to *Qianlong* in Beijing. Moreover, if one only looks at print media in the Chinese media system there is more scope for investigative reporting in the capital than in Shanghai, where reporters usually keep a very low profile on issues deemed to be sensitive to the government. But in the online world, there is apparently less pressure on news workers to conduct propaganda tasks on behalf of the local propaganda department. Unlike their off-line colleagues in the traditional print media organizations, online editors in Shanghai are not as constrained as their Beijing colleagues by propaganda directives. Rather counter to expectation, then, it would seem that online editors in Shanghai have more space for maneuver than either their local print media colleagues or the Beijing online editors.

Globalization and online public opinion

In general, it can be argued that Internet opinion is gaining a certain influence over how Chinese leaders dare to act in the international arena. Popular nationalism online is setting a standard of what may be called "true patriotism" in contrast to state nationalism, and, in a way, it is thereby deterring more nuanced foreign policy and state-media reporting on sensitive international relations concerning Japan, the US, or Taiwan. It is also interesting in China nowadays that since government censorship and regulatory practices effectively control traditional media, the Internet at times functions as an alternative arena for agenda setting. This may be a surprise for the occasional China observer, perhaps accustomed to thinking of authoritarian countries as being extremely effective also in repressing deviating voices in cyberspace (see for example Kurlantzick 2004). In fact, critical, sensitive, or political news items, are, in many controversial issues, first reported in Internet chat forums devoted to news commentary. With a significantly large critical mass of chat room postings, a minor issue may quickly be transformed into a major one requiring the attention of Chinese political leaders. Only then does it become easier for traditional media to conduct follow-up reports and seriously probe into the issue at hand. This contrasts strongly with the way the agenda-setting function works in a Western media system and in a democratic polity, where journalists in the traditional media engage in questioning and seeking out the truth behind a social or political problem.[19] After this process, what has been disclosed by mass media becomes the object of lively discussions in web chat rooms. To be able to gauge and monitor public opinion online, both swiftly and cost-effectively, is of course a great boon for China's authoritarian leaders. In that process, though, we are also witnessing today how pockets of politically interested citizens on the Chinese Internet are becoming important drivers of change in the way public opinion is formed in the PRC.

Even now, in a relatively calm period in which Chinese citizens are experiencing record economic growth and increasing prosperity, we are witnessing how these new electronic meeting-places on the Internet have shown themselves able to influence Chinese courts and party officials and how agenda is set in the traditional mass media (Lagerkvist 2005: 128). One may assume that if a very turbulent phase were to occur in the future, perhaps as a result of widening income gaps, public frustration and discontent might swell to find expression on the web. While it is possible to sketch out the rise of online public opinion as a result of electronic news production and online political commentary in contemporary China, this knowledge must be balanced against the continued relevance of the authoritarian tradition. Here the argument of Loa Aldisardottir (2000: 249) that globalization theorists ignore cultural communities is important. She contends that the Western focus on economic interests has edged aspects of culture into the shade, dismissing them as unimportant in modern high-tech societies. It has been discussed by various media scholars such as Curran and Park that nation-states still continue to be important, if not the most important, shapers of media systems in the age of globalization. Not only do they issue the laws and regulations that frame the activities of media organizations, they also have many informal ways of influencing the media. As Curran and Park (2000: 34) rightly point out: "Different nations have different languages, political systems, power structures, cultural traditions, economies, international links, and histories." Naturally, if too much national history or too many contexts are left out when analyzing changes in the specific media systems of this world, a perception of newness may obscure what is really taking place. It can be argued that the globalization of the world's media industries and the universal market logic according to which most of them operate are bringing challenges to the Chinese media system. A clear example is the view above of one *Qianlong* news editor on the on-going learning process in the Chinese media sector that involves also the officials in charge of propaganda. With the advent of new communications technology, it is dawning on the Chinese Communist Party and its officials who are responsible for news control and propaganda that the Internet is facilitating alternative channels of news and information. The understanding that is taking root is that new information and communications technology will inevitably help to pluralize the Chinese media system. Now the task is to steer it in directions favorable to the objectives, policies, and continued power ambitions of the Communist Party state.

Still, one may well argue along the lines of Curran and Park (2004: 13) that there is "a familiar pattern in which commercial media controllers keep their heads down, and avoid political retribution, by mixing tame journalism with profitable entertainment." This logic still holds true if we take a broader view of online journalism among China's state-controlled news websites. Fully commercialized and Nasdaq-listed web portal companies such as *Sina* and *Sohu* have to bow to government demands in order to conduct business in mainland China. The leaders of these privately or semi-privately owned successful enterprises regularly demonstrate a willingness to kow-tow to leaders of the propaganda units of the Communist Party and state bureaucracy in public (Interfax 2004). And the fear of being criticized by the government or perhaps ostracized by the Chinese media market also haunts non-Chinese online media companies such as Yahoo! and Google.

Therefore, it is reasonable to argue that the challenges to China's state-controlled media system and the changes it is undergoing have more of a national than an international dynamic. The pressures on Chinese media organizations are coming more from inside the PRC than from the outside world. It is likely that the state's all-encompassing monopoly on what may constitute "the truth," and the influence of the Communist Party on public opinion is diminishing with the arrival of new Internet services and online news providers. Nevertheless, in this era of a rapidly globalizing China, the power of the propaganda units involved with controlling the online news flow continue to be felt by newsmakers.

Conclusion

Private or semi-private web portals such as *Sina* are more inclined to test moral conventions in Chinese cyberspace than their state-owned or municipally owned competitors. This became evident in 2004 with *Sina*'s daring photojournalism and readiness to publish the "immoral" sex stories of Mu Zimei online. Her provoking online diary caught the attention of both ordinary people and the Chinese authorities. While the managers of municipal online news networks such as *Qianlong* and *Dongfang* constantly argue that they are more motivated by credibility, accuracy, and honesty in their news production than *Sina*, these organizations controlled by the municipalities of Beijing and Shanghai are, however, not prepared to engage their reporters in any kind of investigative journalism. In China, that role is still played by a handful of print media products such as the Guangdong-based newspaper *Southern Weekly* (*Nanfang Zhoumo*). Nevertheless, the evidence from Beijing Municipality's *Qianlong* news network presented in this chapter show that people involved in the management of online news media organizations are informed by a new logic. The ways online editors and journalists think about their professional norms, notions of format, form, audience, and news values are being affected by the tough competition among all types of domestic news media today. Consequently, more resources are going into programming, research, and fashionable online layouts.

The most important finding presented in this chapter is that as market demand pushes the amount and intensity of propaganda in the news into the background, the relationship between newsmakers and the propagandists of the Communist Party is also affected. By using their new logic in discussions with state officials in charge of monitoring media organizations, the administrators and managers of online news networks are, to some extent, brokering new space for public opinion by trying to publish diverse news stories and allowing alternative voices to circulate in the online world their website is hosting: especially the news comments posted by ordinary Chinese surfers on their organizations' electronic bulletin boards. Without the guidance of the logic of the growing media market in China, online news organizations will lose page views and advertising revenue, and consequently these media outlets controlled by local government and local branches of the Communist Party will be less able to promote the party's views on current affairs. And clearly the Chinese Communist Party is slowly beginning to realize how the growing dependency of news organizations on a steady consumer base is also affecting the media industries in the PRC. The ongoing learning process in the Chinese online media sector outlined in this chapter is testimony to that realization. Moreover, the extent to which online news, news commentary, and, increasingly, blogging, are already changing the media landscape of today's China is evident from the way that agenda setting in the Chinese news industry is beginning to be altered. Since government censorship and regulatory practices effectively control traditional media, the Internet at times functions as an alternative arena for agenda setting. This situation is seldom mirrored in Western observations of the role of online news content in China. Interestingly enough, and rather counter to expectations, although an increasing number of China's Internet users are going online to gain access to less censored news stories, the traditional media still scores very highly on trustworthiness. One would assume that Chinese citizens long accustomed to official propaganda in news programming would be more critically inclined towards the official mass media. One reason for this could be that state propaganda is increasingly fine-tuned nowadays. Television or computer screens are no longer showing high percentages of Party propaganda. This gradual turnaround shows how the learning process involving both journalists and propaganda officials is having some tangible results. Therefore, while it is possible to sketch out the slow emergence of alternative news channels and online public opinion as a result of electronic news production in Chinese cyberspace, this knowledge must still be balanced against the political culture of contemporary China. Occasionally, optimistic forecasts from foreign observers about a globalizing China contend that online news media, the rise of the blogging phenomenon, and chat room culture will offer less controlled news and news commentary than offline news outlets such as print media, radio, and television. While potentially attractive, *and* containing elements of truth, such musings must be qualified by other constraining contextual factors such as the authoritarian tradition, the effectiveness of government propaganda, and the remarkable persistence among the Chinese public of continuing to trust government news sources.

Notes

1 Researchers at *Qianlong*'s Academy routinely send their young scholars on missions throughout the country to help establish and consult on issues related to online news. They also send out regular comprehensive newsletters on what is happening in the new media industry, especially with regard to Internet media. (Interview with project director, *Qianlong* Academy, Beijing, January 5, 2003.)
2 These are: *Beijing Daily* (*Beijing ribao*), *Beijing Evening News* (*Beijing wanbao*), The People's Radio Station in Beijing (*Beijing renmin guangbo diantai*), Beijing TV (*Beijing dianshi tai*), Beijing Cable TV (*Beijing youxian guangbo dianshi tai*), *Beijing Youth Daily* (*Beijing qingnian bao*), *Beijing Morning News* (*Beijing zaochen bao*), *Beijing Economic Daily* (*Beijing jingji bao*), *Beijing TV Daily* (*Beijing guangbo dianshi bao*).
3 While the commercialization of the Chinese media, a product of China's economic reforms, has added a new dimension to China's state-controlled media space, two centerpieces of Leninist control of the media remain strong. The first principle is the continued administrative monopoly of production of political news; the second concerns the control and weeding-out of content deemed to go against the policies of the communist party, social stability, and economic development.

4 The Strong Country Forum is part of the state-run *People's Net* (*Renmin Wang*), owned by the *People's Daily*. It can be accessed at HTTP: http://bbs.people.com.cn/bbs/mlbrd?to=47.

5 A blogger is a person (or a collective) writing a web-log, or simply a blog, which is a web application containing periodic posts on a common webpage that often discuss social phenomena or news. As blogs may contain comments from, and links to, other bloggers, they constitute a virtual global space called the blogosphere. In China, it was the Mu Zimei blog that made blogging popular among the urban young.

6 According to the "Provisional regulations for the administration of Internet sites engaging in the business of news publication," effective from November 6, 2000, Internet companies that are wholly, or partly, privately owned are only permitted to publish news that has already been published by approved news organizations in China (see Baker and McKenzie 2001: 362–6). These companies do, however, employ journalists, and allow them to publish their own reports on soft news such as entertainment and sports.

7 Since China lacks a transparent and concise media law, there is a large grey zone for what may be considered illegal web content. Chinese legal scholars petitioned the National People's Congress in February 2004 on this issue. The problem is that online journalists or Chinese citizens may discover they have become cyber dissidents in the eyes of the government, when, in their own view, they have merely written about social ills or debated democratic elections in the countryside.

8 China became a member of the WTO on December 11, 2001. In the accession documents, China agreed to open up and liberalize the Chinese media market step by step, and also allow for more foreign investment in Chinese media industries.

9 For a recent analysis of surveillance practices in China, see also Tsui 2003.

10 The websites of some foreign news organizations such as *CNN*, Chinese political and religious groups in exile, such as Falun Gong, and websites containing pornographic material, are regularly but quite randomly blocked for Chinese Internet users (see Edelman and Zittrain 2005).

11 For a recent analysis of liberal journalism and public opinion formation in the PRC, see Chan 2002.

12 Interview conducted with a BBS operator of *Dongfang* news network, October 28, 2003.

13 Research conducted by the Horizon Group in Beijing and statistics from China Network Information Center (CNNIC) all point in this direction; see *China Daily*, August 13, 2003.

14 For an interview with Jiao Guobiao, see Kan 2004.

15 Interview with a *Central China Television* (CCTV) reporter in Beijing January 5, 2004.

16 Negotiations for online space amount to the very concrete cases of physical meetings between persons, telephone calls, or the joint conferences where portal management discuss with propaganda officials what content should not be published. On the other hand, negotiations also involve the incremental push on, and mutual learning process of, the current limits enforced in chat rooms, on BBSs and mailing lists. This is the individual surfers' trial-and-error method of negotiation of online space.

17 The concept of *xiao kang* has a history stretching far back into Chinese history. Its contemporary meaning is "a reasonable level of welfare and livelihood for all people."

18 The interview was carried out with one of *Dongfang*'s bulletin board masters.

19 It should be mentioned that with the rising importance of blogging, the way the news agenda is set is also changing in the West.

References

Aldisardottir, Loa (2000) "Research note: global medium – local tool? How readers and media companies use the web," *European Journal of Communication*, 15: 2, pp. 241–52.

Baker & McKenzie (eds) (2001) *China and the Internet: Essential Legislation*, Hong Kong: Asia Information Associates Ltd.

Chan, Alex (2002) "From Propaganda to hegemony: *Jiaodian fangtan* and China's media policy," *Journal of Contemporary China*, 11: 30, pp. 35–52.

China Daily (August 13, 2003) "Survey says Net is major news source." Online. Available HTTP: http://www.chinadaily.com.cn/en/doc/2003-08/13/content_254 275.htm (accessed January 26, 2005).

Clark, Duncan (2003) "From the web to wireless," paper presented at "A global interdisciplinary conference, China and the Internet: technology, economy, & society in transition," Los Angeles, May 2003.

Curran, James and Park, Myung-Jin (eds) (2000) *De-Westernizing Media Studies*, London and New York: Routledge.

Deuze, Mark and Yeshua, D. (2000) "Online journalists face new ethical dilemmas," research paper. Online. Available HTTP: http://home.pscw.uva.nl/deuze/publ15. htm (accessed October 10, 2004).

Edelman, Benjamin and Zittrain, Jonathan (2005) *Empirical Analysis of Internet Filtering in China*, Berkman Center for Internet & Society, Harvard Law School. Online. Available HTTP: http://cyber.law.harvard.edu/filtering/china/China-highlights.html (accessed February 3, 2005).

Hu, Xianhong (2004) "Zhong, Mei, De, san guo wangmin he fei wangming yanjiu bijiao" [A comparative study of netizens of the three countries China, USA, and Germany]," in: Cheng Manli (ed.) *Beida xinwen yu chuanbo pinglun* [Beijing University's Journalism and Communication Review], Beijing: Beijing daxue chubanshe [Beijing University press], p. 176.

Interfax (2004) "Chinese government organizes trip for China's Internet elite to improve their political quality," *Interfax*, Online. Available HTTP: http://www. interfax.com/com?item=Chin&pg=0&id=5769699&req (accessed November 12, 2004).

Kalathil, Shanthi (2003) "China's new media sector: keeping the state in," *The Pacific Review*, 16: 4, pp. 489–501.

Kalathil, Shanthi and Boas, Taylor C. (2003) *Open Networks, Closed Regimes: The Impact of the Internet on Authoritarian Regimes*, Carnegie Endowment for International Peace.

Kan, Joseph (2004) "Let freedom ring? Not so fast. China's still China," *The New York Times*, May 3.

Kurlantzick, Joshua (2004) "The web won't topple tyranny. Dictatorship.com", *The New Republic*, March 25.

Lagerkvist, Johan (2003), "China's Internet problem: a threat to indigenous culture, youth and political thought?" paper presented at "A global interdisciplinary conference, China and the Internet: technology, economy, & society in transition," Los Angeles, May 2003.

Lagerkvist, Johan (2005) "The rise of online public opinion in the PRC," *China: an International Journal*, 3: 1, March, pp. 119–30.

Min, Dahong (2003) "The value of the Chinese network in the era of globalization," *Contemporary Chinese Thought*, 35: 2, Winter 2003–4, pp. 51–67.

NewScientist.com news service (2004) "Google omits controversial news stories in China," Online. Available HTTP: http://www.newscientist.com/article.ns?id=dn 6426 (accessed September 4, 2004).

Pavlik, John (2001) *Journalism and New Media*, New York: Columbia University Press.

Qianlong (2001) "Qianlong wang 2000 nian da shiji" [Major events of Qianlong net in 2000]. Online. Available HTTP: http://www.qianlong.com (accessed September 15, 2004).

Qiu, Jack Liu (1999/2000) "Virtual censorship in China: keeping the gate between the cyberspaces," *International Journal of Communications Law and Policy*, 4, pp. 1–25.

Reporters Without Borders (2004) "Reporters without borders calls on US officials to impose code of conduct on Internet firms," July 26, 2004. Online. Available HTTP: http://www.rsf.org (accessed October 17, 2004).

Tsui, Lokman (2003) "The panopticon as the antithesis of a space of freedom: control and regulation of the Internet in China," *China Information: A Journal on Contemporary China Studies*, 17: 2, pp. 65–82.

Zeng, Qinghong (2004) "Jiaqiang dang de zhizheng nengli jianshe de ganglingxing wenjian (xuexi guanqie shiliu jie si zhong quan hui jingshen, jiaqiang dang de zhizheng nengli jianshe)" [A programmatic document strengthening the construction of the Party's governing ability (Study and implement the spirit of the Fourth Plenum of the 16th Central Party Committee, strengthening the construction of the Party's governing ability)], *Renmin Ribao*, October 8, 2004, p. 2. Online. Available HTTP: http://www.people.com.cn/GB/paper464/13101/1175378.html (accessed February 2, 2005).

4 Comrade to comrade networks

The social and political implications of peer-to-peer networks in China

Michael Chase, James Mulvenon, and Nina Hachigian

Chapter 4 adds another perspective to the debates on political and technological influences and the CCP's attempts to exert efficient control. Predictions about the impact of peer-to-peer (P2P) technology on both commercial computing and the free flow of political information have been breathtaking. Because it allows users to exchange information without a centralized point of contact, P2P technology makes such sharing difficult for authorities to control, be they corporations or governments. While the political stakes of this battle in the affluent democracies of Europe and North America are significant, the consequences are potentially even greater in countries where governments restrict information flow for political reasons. What impact will the P2P phenomenon have on the balance of power between these governments and their citizens? P2P is sure to play a role in the ongoing cat and mouse dynamic between the Chinese government and citizens interested in "subversive" activities. This chapter examines how P2P technology may affect the balance of information control in China. It analyzes how P2P is being used, the methods the Chinese government might use to counter the growing phenomena, and the potential impact of P2P. P2P is a hot topic among tech-savvy Internet users in China. As for average Chinese web users, most of those who are familiar with P2P are undoubtedly more interested in the use of the technology for entertainment than politics. But P2P is also beginning to attract the attention of some netizens whose agendas are considered subversive by Beijing. Some Chinese Internet users are already exchanging documents and accessing blocked websites through P2P networks. If the Chinese authorities were to make a concerted effort to restrict the use of P2P technology, they would probably employ a mixture of high-tech and low-tech countermeasures, as they have against Internet use for subversive purposes generally. In the short term, neither the Internet nor P2P technology will lead to profound shifts in political power. But in the long term, such effects are not difficult to imagine.[1]

Predictions about the impact of peer-to-peer (P2P) technology on both commercial computing and on the free flow of political information have been breathtaking. Advocates of P2P ardently insist that it is a "revolutionary" (see, for example, Minar and Hedlund 2002: 4) technology that will "reshape the Internet" (Kan 2002: 94) and "permanently shift the Net's balance of power" (Borland 2001),[2] because it allows users to exchange information without a centralized point of contact. As a result, it is predicted that P2P technology will undermine the ability of authorities, be they corporations or governments, to control content or its distribution.[3] While the political and commercial stakes of this battle in the affluent democracies of Europe and North America are significant, the stakes are potentially even higher in countries where governments restrict information flow for political reasons. A country where P2P technology could have a significant impact is China, which is unique in its simultaneous encouragement of technological progress and its desire to control online information. This combination makes China a natural locus of activity for tech-savvy users who are working to defeat the government's various attempts at censorship of politically sensitive information.

There has been a great deal of speculation about the potential political impact of general Internet usage in China. Some argue that the Internet will dramatically shift power to the Chinese people by allowing them to organize and by channeling information, particularly about democracy and better standards of living, from outside the country. Others claim that because the Chinese government can control aspects of Internet use and content, because few mainland citizens have Internet access, and because even fewer are interested in subversive information, the Internet is unlikely to have any significant effect. Yet others argue that the Internet's most important impact will be its delivery of information to the Chinese people about events within China, especially during crises.

Whichever theory turns out to be the most accurate, P2P is sure to play a role in the ongoing cat and mouse dynamic between the Chinese government and citizens interested in "subversive" activities. As broadband access and user sophistication increase, encouraged by Chinese officials, the number of people able to use P2P technologies in China will also likely rise. The key questions, of course, are who might use it, for what purposes, and with what results? Some activists believe P2P technology will enable Chinese Internet users and overseas dissidents to circumvent the Chinese government's cyberspace controls. As one Chinese dissident remarked, "The peer-to-peer networking model has great potential for sharing politically sensitive information" (McLaughlin 2000). For some observers, however, optimism about P2P's political potential is tempered by the failure of other communications technologies to live up to the expectations of their most enthusiastic promoters. "In the long run, P2P may break down barriers to free speech," said Bobson Wong, executive director of the

Digital Freedom Network, "but then again, a few years ago, people thought the Web would do that, and that hasn't played out" (Interview, April 2002). This chapter will examine how P2P technology may affect the balance of information control in China. We will analyze how P2P is being used and to what degree, the methods the Chinese government might use to counter the growing phenomenon, and the possible impact of P2P on communication and politics in China.

The politics of the Internet in China

The Internet has been at the forefront of the information revolution in China. While penetration of the Internet is still quite limited when measured in either relative or absolute terms, growth in the number of users since 1995 has been virtually exponential and is expected to increase at a tremendous rate in the near future. The number of Internet users in China had reached 45.8 million by July 2002, up from only 2.1 million in January 1999, according to the CNNIC.[4] China's international connectivity and the number of computers with Internet access are also increasing rapidly. International data bandwidth grew dramatically during the research period, increasing almost tenfold between January 2000 and July 2001, and more than doubling between July 2001 and January 2002, while the number of computers connected to the Internet, which only stood at around 750,000 in January 1999, had exceeded 16 million by July 2002.[5]

As a result of the rapid growth of the Internet in China, the leadership of the Chinese Communist Party faces a series of challenges that are testing its ability to balance the competing imperatives of modernization and control (for more on this topic, see Chase and Mulvenon 2002). On the one hand, the regime believes that information technology is the driving force behind economic development, despite the bursting of the Internet bubble and the dashed hopes of numerous Chinese "dotcom" companies, and that future economic growth in China will depend in large measure on the extent to which the country is integrated within the global information infrastructure. This is of particular importance because economic growth is directly linked to social stability for the Beijing leadership, and, in the absence of communism or any other unifying ideology, maintenance of prosperity has become the linchpin of regime legitimacy and survival. Since economic growth has required the modernization of China's relatively poor communications infrastructure, China has quickly become one of the world's largest consumers of information-related technologies. Moreover, Chinese leaders view the development of information technology, particularly the Internet, in China as an indispensable element of their quest for recognition as a great power.[6]

At the same time, however, China is still an authoritarian, single-party state, whose continued rule relies on the suppression of anti-regime activities. The installation of an advanced telecommunications infrastructure to facilitate economic reform greatly complicates the state's internal security goals (for a comprehensive rendition of this argument, see Kennedy 1999). Faced with these contradictory forces of openness and control, China has sought to strike a balance between the information-related needs of economic modernization and the security requirements of internal stability. In doing so, the authorities are actively promoting the growth of the Internet even as they place significant restrictions on online content and the political use of information technology (Hachigian 2002: 51–8; see also Harwit and Clark 2001: 378–498). The challenge for the regime is to "prevent this commercial goldmine from becoming political quicksand" (Hachigian 2001: 118–33).

Peer-to-peer technology: some background

What effects will the introduction of P2P technologies have on the tensions within China over information control? A review of the concept and state of P2P technologies is generally helpful in addressing this ultimate question.[7]

The concept of peer-to-peer networking dates back to the 1960s and the original ARPANET, the Internet's predecessor, which directly linked its participating computers together. However, as personal computers (PCs) proliferated in the 1980s and the Internet and World Wide Web exploded in the 1990s, "client-server" became the prevailing network architecture. In the client-server model, depicted in Figure 4.1 and discussed further below, client computers (mostly PCs) connect to a (usually larger) central server in a hub and spoke fashion. The PCs send messages to, and request data or information from, the server, and the server, in turn, delivers data or information and relays messages to its clients. For example, if Jane user points her browser to the site of CNN.com, the large CNN server, or perhaps the server of her ISP which has cached the information, sends the CNN homepage to her PC.

While there is no precise, common definition in use today,[8] we use peer-to-peer (P2P) in this article to mean network architectures that do not strictly conform to the client-server model. P2P technologies offer a variety of advantages to network designers, including:

- reduction of bottlenecks;
- scalability;
- anonymity for producers and consumers of information;
- resistance to third-party attempts to deny access to information;
- support of massively parallel computation and storage;
- decentralization of network functions.

These attributes enable a number of attractive applications. On the commercial side, some examples of popular uses are file sharing that circumvents intellectual property laws; collaborative workspaces among colleagues located in different physical locations;[9] "instant messaging;" and distributed computing that spreads a computing burden over many

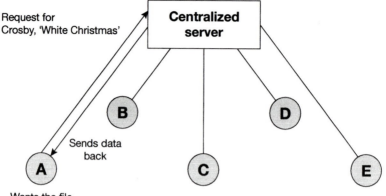

Figure 4.1 Schematic of client-server architecture

client computers.[10] For politics, the key P2P applications are the increased ability to share files among peers without government interference, to visit blocked websites, and to preserve the anonymity of Web users.

Client-server architecture

Networks can range from completely centralized (client-server with no links between clients) to completely decentralized ("pure" or "un-brokered" P2P). Client-server is the most heavily used architecture in today's Web infrastructure. The model allows for two classes of computers: clients that consume information, and servers that distribute it. As illustrated in Figure 4.1, Client A knows that the centralized server has a large library of music files available. Thus client A simply directs a formatted query to the server, asking for a copy of a particular file.

The server will compare that request with its own internal database, and if a match is found, it will send the file back to client A. Once client A has the file, the user that controls client A is free to view the file, store it, or simply delete it. In other words, the server has no control over the status of the file once it has been sent.

Brokered P2P architecture

Brokered P2P architecture, while having elements of a peer-to-peer system, employs a centralized index.

Napster

First introduced on the Web in June 1999, Napster is the highest profile example of brokered P2P technology used to share a particular type of content: MP3 music files. Napster users first download a proprietary application that can act as both a server and a client.[11] Users who wish to share music files they already have can put these files into a directory on their hard drive. Users who wish to search for a particular music file send a request to a centralized index server that keeps track of all the files available from other users (peers) on the network. These requests are fairly easy for the centralized index server to process, because they are exclusively for a particular type of content and have already been formatted and structured by the user.

As shown in Figure 4.2, when peer A sends a request to the centralized index server, the server sends back a list of peers that have the requested file stored, along with the speed of each of these peers' connections to the Internet (illustrated by the thickness of lines between peers). In this sense, the centralized Napster index server acts as a search engine that indexes content for participating peers on the network. User A can choose which peer to ask for the file itself. A will generally choose the fastest connection that can be found (E in this case), consistent with his or her own connection to the Internet (e.g., if A has a DSL connection, he or she will likely select another peer with a DSL or faster connection). A will then establish another connection directly with E to obtain the file.

The brokered P2P model scales relatively well. At its peak in late 2000–early 2001, Napster reportedly had some 38 million users sharing 98 million music files, and the system could handle more than 1 million simultaneous users (Luman and Cook 2001, Truelove and Chasin 2001, Black 2001). However, a centralized index makes brokered P2P networks

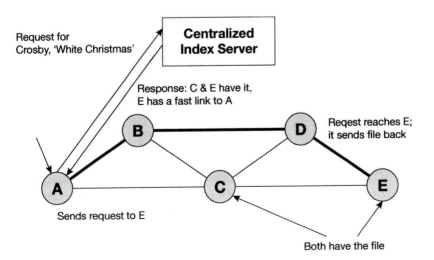

Figure 4.2 Schematic of brokered P2P architecture (Napster)

inherently more vulnerable to attack, whether from lawsuits as in the case of Napster, from hackers who seek to corrupt or bring down the system, or from governments who seek to arrest file-sharing.[12]

SafeWeb and Triangle Boy

The company SafeWeb began by providing a form of "anonymizing, privacy-enhancing, application-layer web proxy" in October 2000. The service did not require software download or local installation.[13] A network diagram of SafeWeb's server model is provided in Figure 4.3.[14]

As with a typical anonymizing server, users could go to the Safe-Web home page, http://www.safeweb.com, and type the URL (Uniform Resource Locator) of the website they wished to visit into the address window. The SafeWeb service then set up a connection between the user's computer and the website through an SSL (Secure Socket Layer) connection. All data (including URLs and domain names) transmitted to and from the user's computer passed encrypted through SafeWeb servers, so that no one could pry into that user's online activity. The user's identity and personal information was hidden from everyone en route, including advertisers, websites, government agencies, employers, ill-willed hackers, ISPs, and even SafeWeb itself. At its peak, the proxy handled 120 million users per month, with hundreds of thousands of users worldwide, according to company materials. In 2001, the proxy servers reportedly delivered over 1.5 billion encrypted pages. Over time, however, SafeWeb's website was blocked by retail censorware programs (SurfWatch, Cyber Patrol, Net Nanny, CYBERSitter, X-Stop, PureSight, CyberSnoop, etc.), corporate firewalls, and repressive governments, forcing commercial service to be shut down in late 2001.

After other governments, such as China, began to block access to the company website and install anti-proxy auto-blocking software, SafeWeb, in April 2001, released its "second phase" technology, a variant brokered peer-to-peer network dubbed "Triangle Boy." Funded in part by the Voice of America (VOA), TB is designed to allow Chinese Internet users unfettered access to blocked sites. SafeWeb's white paper on Triangle Boy describes the specific purpose of the application: "Triangle Boy is our answer to Internet censorship. Triangle Boy defeats all attempts to prevent users from accessing sites on the Internet."

According to Stephen Hsu, SafeWeb's CEO, "SafeWeb's Triangle Boy software exploits the encryption capability of browsers and creates a distributed network which allows individual users in China to access the entire Web through an unbreakable encrypted channel" (SafeWeb 2002). The company's press release asserted that "volunteers can turn their PCs into 'packet reflectors,' or proxies, for SafeWeb by installing the Triangle Boy application" (SafeWeb press release 2001). A network diagram displaying TB's model can be found in Figure 4.4.[15]

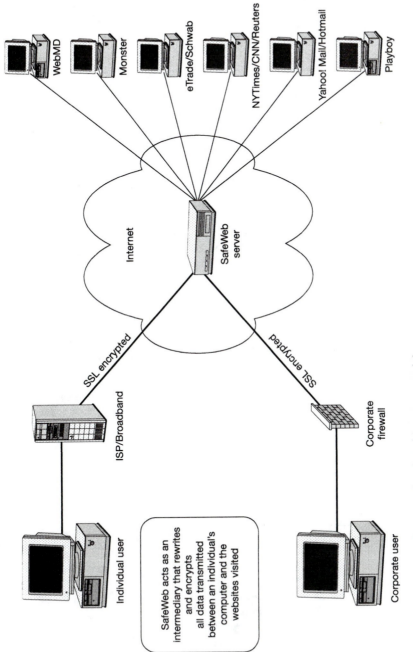

WebMD

Monster

eTrade/Schwab

NYTimes/CNN/Reuters

Yahoo! Mail/Hotmail

Playboy

Internet

SafeWeb server

SSL encrypted

SSL encrypted

ISP/Broadband

Corporate firewall

Individual user

SafeWeb acts as an intermediary that rewrites and encrypts all data transmitted between an individual's computer and the websites visited

Corporate user

Figure 4.3 Network diagram of SafeWeb's server model

Note: Figure printed with permission by Stephen Hsu.

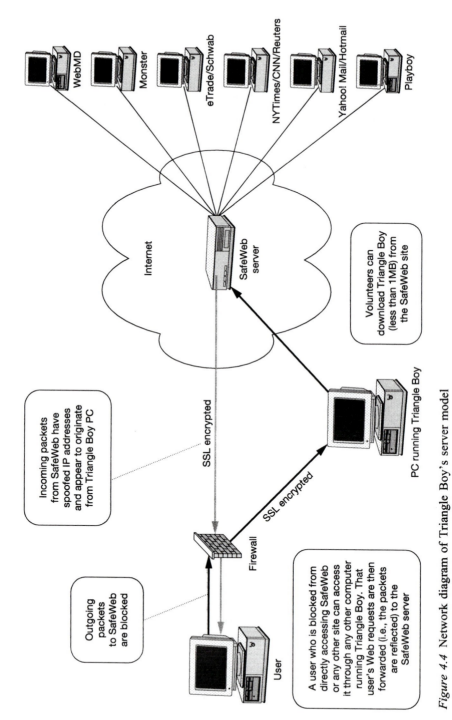

Figure 4.4 Network diagram of Triangle Boy's server model

Note: Figure printed with permission by Stephen Hsu.

Based on the twin assumptions that "a large number of volunteers will be willing to deploy Triangle Boy to support freedom of information on the Web" and that the Chinese government would be "unlikely to block access to the volunteer PCs," the TB nodes would "act as encrypted gateways to the Internet and allow Chinese citizens full access to an uncensored Web (ibid.)." Packet routing and IP spoofing would theoretically reduce the load on volunteer PCs, none of whom would be able to see the content of the encrypted packets. SafeWeb asserted that it would become more and more difficult over time for the Chinese security services to block access to its network as the number of Triangle Boy machines increased. Furthermore, the use of dynamic IP addresses by some Triangle Boy machines, according to SafeWeb, would "make the censor's task even more daunting and the likelihood of success even slimmer" by making it more difficult for censors in Beijing to harvest IP addresses for blocking.

According to some reports, however, the Chinese authorities have been relatively successful in their attempts to block the system. Pro-democracy activists initially touted Triangle Boy as "the most effective method to date for breaking through the CCP's Internet blockade," but they say it was not long before the Chinese authorities began to block access to the system thoroughly enough to make it difficult for mainland Internet users to obtain usable IP addresses (Shi *et al.* 2001). Computer-savvy Internet users have reported that they are often unable to access SafeWeb's Triangle Boy servers in the PRC (Interview, April 2002). One major problem with the current system is communicating the IP addresses of Triangle Boy servers to people in China without the authorities also finding out and quickly blocking access to the sites. Currently, SafeWeb sends out an email containing the information in response to user requests. Personnel from the Ministry of Public Security's Computer Monitoring and Supervision Bureau simply request the information through email as often as necessary and block the IP address on the routing table (Interviews, Western computer technicians, Beijing, January 2002). In addition, SafeWeb was never able to rally enough "volunteers" to fully frustrate the efforts of the Beijing government to block the IP addresses.

At its peak, it is estimated that Triangle Boy was used to view about 300,000 web pages per day. After only a few months, however, Beijing's blocking of the addresses caused an 80 percent decline in the use of Triangle Boy by Chinese web surfers, according to a Western media report (Yatsko 2001). However, the Chinese authorities have not been able to eliminate Triangle Boy's use entirely, and this report may be exaggerated. According to Hsu, "currently, [Triangle Boy] is used approximately 100,000 times per day despite vigorous efforts on the part of Chinese security forces to hunt down and block access to the network" (Hsu 2002). SafeWeb stopped supporting the network in late 2001.

Unbrokered P2P architecture

The second, more robust form of P2P architecture, which we call here "unbrokered," does not employ a centralized index server. Compared to the Napster-like brokered technologies, these networks are even more difficult to monitor and control because there is no central point at which information is gathered.

Gnutella

In March 2000, only nine months after Napster hit the Web, a programmer working for an AOL Time Warner subsidiary released software for a different P2P technology using no centralized index servers.[16] This technology, named Gnutella, is depicted in Figure 4.5.

How does a user, after downloading the Gnutella software, locate a particular file without a centralized index? In the example illustrated in Figure 4.5, Gnutella user A broadcasts a data request to all neighboring peers with which it maintains a network connection (only B in this example). Once B receives the request and determines that it does not have the data, it re-transmits the request to all its neighbors (C, D, and E in this case). In this example, C will simply bounce the request back to B as a failure (because C is not connected to anyone else), E will attempt to forward the request to D, and at the same time D will forward the request

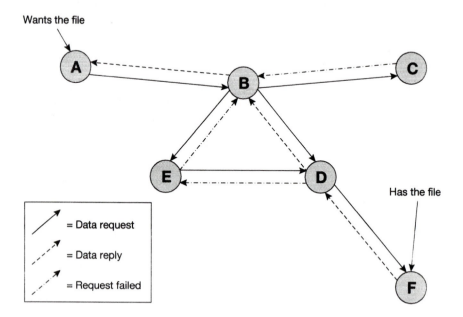

Figure 4.5 Schematic of unbrokered P2P architecture (Gnutella)

(initially received from B) to F. During the next time step, F will have received the request from D, recognize it has the data requested, and return the data in a message back to D. The other failed requests will propagate back in the form of messages, while the requested data moves backward through the chain of peers to A.

Eliminating the central index supports anonymity for both requesters and sharers, but at a price of lower efficiency and less scalability. Gnutella's essentially random search protocol is relatively inefficient and increases network traffic exponentially as more peers participate. Some current versions deal with these problems by limiting the number of simultaneous connections to other peers and/or the number of search "hops" before timing out (Ripeanu 2001). A sample of Gnutella usage over a 24-hour period in August 2000 also identified a "free rider" problem, in that almost 70 percent of Gnutella users shared no files, and nearly 50 percent of all responses were returned by the top 1 percent of users (Adar and Huberman 2000). Nevertheless, a dedicated group of software developers continues to support and improve Gnutella technology, and the Gnutella architecture has been embraced by several commercial start-ups.

Moreover, pure, unbrokered P2P models do not scale as well as brokered ones, so the current Gnutella-like networks encounter difficulties when serving more than about 50,000 simultaneous users. As a consequence, hybrid networks such as Morpheus[17] and KaZaA[18] have emerged for music and media sharing on a larger scale. Both Morpheus and KaZaA use P2P technology developed by FastTrack,[19] a Netherlands-based company. FastTrack networks recognize computers with more processing power and faster connections, and automatically designate these machines as "Super-Nodes" to act as search hubs for requests from other computers. Super-Nodes emerge dynamically from the network as the number of requests increases and disappears when the demand subsides. Using this dynamic hybrid approach, Morpheus and KaZaA have proved workable with some 300,000 simultaneous users (Truelove and Chasin 2001); and the company believes it can serve up to one million users today and many more in the future as computing and communications technologies continue to improve.

Some P2P applications have been designed specifically for use in countering government censorship attempts. The primary goals of the developers of programs such as Freenet, Publius, SafeWeb, and others, are to allow users to either share banned material anonymously, visit blocked websites, or have anonymous discussions without fear of government monitoring.

Freenet

Two relatively early P2P developments, Freenet and Publius, are non-commercial projects designed to keep online content readily available despite attempts at censorship or malicious attack. Ian Clarke came up with the Freenet design concept in July 1999 for his fourth-year project in computer science at the University of Edinburgh (Clarke 1999). As described above, Freenet is a pure unbrokered architecture without a centralized index.

"Freenet uses a decentralized P2P architecture to create an uncensorable and secure global information storage system," according to the project's developers.[20] Like several other P2P applications, Freenet was designed explicitly to "address information privacy and survivability concerns" (Clarke *et al.* 2002: 40–9).

Each user's computer stores the content files it has handled most recently – both its own requests and files it has received and passed on to others. Consequently, the more demand for a specific content file, the more copies will be distributed throughout the network. All files and messages are encrypted, providing anonymity to both those who store content and those who request it. Thus, Freenet aims to make content available freely and anonymously, and to distribute it widely in such a way that efforts to censor or destroy particular content would result in the distribution of even more copies of it. The technology is continuously evolving, and the Freenet community regularly makes new releases publicly available.[21]

Freenet differs from Gnutella in two principal respects: first, it indexes content to provide a "best guess" on where a particular file might be found on the network; and, second, it forces users to store a small cache of files that have passed through them most recently (Langley 2002: 123–32).[22] Both content indexing and forced caching are intended to give a more efficient system performance.

Freenet's features of indexing and forced caching increase its search efficiency relative to Gnutella. Caching makes it easy to retrieve popular content and also supports localized storage of specialized content (e.g., Japanese fiction – "docs/books/japanese/fiction/. . ." – within Japan). However, Freenet encrypts all files and requests, which enhances security and anonymity but may reduce efficiency. Freenet's approach to indexing also raises the problem of sensitivity to small variations in filenames,[23] as well as the semantic issue of what constitutes "closeness" for different types of content. Freenet, along with all other P2P approaches, is susceptible to denial of service attacks, including interruption of network connections. Finally, with its emphasis on anonymity for requesters and content providers, Freenet may be more vulnerable to spoofing (e.g., publishing pornographic material under the false filenames) than are other P2P technologies.

Publius

Billed by its creators at AT&T labs and New York University as a "censorship resistant publishing system," Publius is named for the collective pseudonym under which James Madison, Alexander Hamilton, and John

Jay published the series of articles known as the Federalist Papers in 1787–88, advocating the ratification of the US Constitution. The Publius system allows users to publish and access several types of files, including pdf documents, images, and web pages.[24] The developers of Publius promote it as the perfect vehicle for dissidents to access and distribute politically sensitive materials in defiance of controls imposed by the governments of authoritarian countries:

> A file published with Publius is replicated across many servers, making it very hard for any individual or organized group to destroy the document. Distributing the document also provides resistance to so-called distributed denial of service (DDoS) attacks, which have been used in highly publicized incidents to make a resource unavailable. Another key feature of Publius is that it allows an individual to publish a document without providing information that links the document to any particular computer. Therefore, the publisher of a document can remain anonymous.
>
> (Waldman *et al.* 2002: 145)

The content, posted anonymously, is encrypted and split into fragments, which are then distributed randomly among participating web servers. There is no central index. A request for the document goes from peer to peer among the participating servers, and only a few fragments are needed to reconstruct and decrypt it. The principal developer, Avi Rubin, says "Publius is ideal for corporate whistleblowers and dissidents in authoritarian countries who are barred from accessing or posting political material because the government controls Internet domains" (Abreu 2000). Waldman, Cranor, and Rubin (2002: 158) highlight six key features of the Publius system:

- It allows users to publish documents in a "censorship-resistant manner" by placing it on numerous servers.
- Documents retrieved through the system can be checked for tampering and unauthorized changes.
- A document's publisher can easily update it and users searching for it are redirected to the new document.
- Publishers can use a password to delete a document if they so choose.
- Documents can be published anonymously, though users are still advised to take additional precautions to protect their identities from being ascertained indirectly.
- Stored documents can be retrieved even if many servers are unavailable, making the system highly resistant to DDoS attacks.

Aware, perhaps, that the popularity of some other P2P applications is limited because they are difficult or inconvenient to use, the developers of Publius say that the system "has been designed with ease of access for end users in mind" (Waldman *et al.* 2002: 145). The Publius website presents clear, easy to follow, step-by-step instructions on how to use the system. The instructions cover a wide range of topics, including connecting to a Publius proxy server, installing a Publius proxy (an option available only to Unix users), viewing sample documents, and performing operations such as publishing, updating, or deleting documents using Publius.[25] Dedicated users will undoubtedly be willing to devote the necessary time to this, but like many other P2P systems, Publius demands enough effort to deter some casual surfers.

As with other P2P applications that seek to give users in authoritarian countries the option of publishing anonymously (as well as widely available encryption and steganography programs that allow users to communicate securely over the Internet) there is always the risk that criminals or terrorists could use Publius for purposes never envisioned by its creators.[26]

Peekabooty

Another emerging P2P technology is Peekabooty, a software product which, according to its developers, will enable Internet users to circumvent the firewalls and censorship measures that China and more than 20 other countries use to restrict access to websites. To thwart government censors, Peekabooty uses the encryption standard for e-commerce to make P2P exchanges look like regular e-business transactions (see Salkever 2002). The Peekabooty project has been an all-volunteer effort since its inception and several groups have been involved in its development. Originated by the hacker group, Cult of the Dead Cow, and subsequently developed by Hacktivismo, a hacker group dedicated to social activism, the Peekabooty project is now led by Internet freedom activist Paul Baranowski. A posting on the Peekabooty website estimates that if the development of Peekabooty had been undertaken as a commercial effort it would have cost more than US$ 450,000 (Baranowski 2002).

The Peekabooty system is designed to enable Internet users in countries where the Internet is censored to exchange files and to gain access to officially banned web pages (see, for example, McDonald 2001). According to the developers, "the goal of the Peekabooty Project is to create a product that can bypass the nation-wide censorship of the World Wide Web practiced by many countries. [. . .] The theory behind it is simple: bypass the firewalls by providing an alternate intermediary to the World Wide Web" (Peekabooty n.d.).

The Peekabooty website explains how the system works:

> Peekabooty is software run by "global-thinking, local-acting" people in countries that do not censor the Internet. A user in a country that censors the Internet connects to the ad hoc network of computers running Peekabooty. A small number of randomly selected computers

in the network retrieves the Web pages and relays them back to the user. As far as the censoring firewall is concerned, the user is simply accessing some computer not on its "banned" list. The retrieved Web pages are encrypted using the de facto standard for secure transactions in order to prevent the firewall from examining the Web pages' contents. Since the encryption used is a secure transaction standard, it will look like an ordinary e-business transaction to the firewall.

Users in countries where the Internet is censored do not necessarily need to install any software. They merely need to make a simple change to their Internet settings so that their access to the World Wide Web is mediated by the Peekabooty network. Installing the software makes the process of connecting to the Internet simpler and allows users to take fuller advantage of the Peekabooty network.

"Global-thinking, local-acting" people in countries that do not censor the Internet install Peekabooty, which can run "in the background" while they use their computer for their day-to-day work. It doubles as a screen saver that displays its status as well as information about human rights and censorship.

(http://www.peek-a-booty.org)

The developers of Peekabooty also assert that because of its "distributed nature" it would be difficult for a hostile government or organization to successfully attack and disable the Peekabooty system: given enough users, it would be almost impossible to block access to or otherwise disable all the computers in the Peekabooty network. Each computer in the Peekabooty network "knows" of only a few other computers in the network. This makes it more difficult for a hostile government to discover the Internet addresses of Peekabooty machines and add them to their "banned" lists or target them for "cracking."

Peekabooty's release was delayed by problems that could have presented security risks for its users, but an open source release was announced on the Peekabooty website on July 11, 2002 (Anonymous, July 11, 2002). Peekabooty has already generated a great deal of media attention and it is possible that Chinese Internet users and exiled pro-democracy activists will soon begin to experiment with it.

Specific Chinese P2P applications

A number of P2P applications have been developed specifically for the Chinese dissident or commercial market.

Freenet China

The Freenet China project was founded in early 2001 by several Chinese engineers now living in the US. The first version of the program was released last fall. The project is managed by a small, dedicated group of computer specialists, including one full-time volunteer and a few individuals who work on it in their spare time. The philosophical motivation of the group that manages the Freenet China project is support for freedom of information on the Internet; the group promises users, "when you use Freenet, you will have the rights to freedom that you ought to have" (http://freenet-china.org/freenet/4all.htm). These ideals are embodied in a posting, entitled "Free Speech as the Highest Principle," which can be found on the Freenet China website:

> Freenet is built on the conviction that every person in the world has the inalienable right to express his or her opinions without fear of oppression. For instance, people in totalitarian regimes, or employees of powerful corrupt organizations, may want to blow the whistle on mass abuses of human rights. In such situations, the traditional Internet protocols – web, email, ftp, chat etc. – offer no protection for privacy. People using these protocols can easily find their lives in grave danger. Therefore, Freenet is built from the ground up to completely disguise the identity of anyone who posts material. The Freenet community strongly believes that the right to free (and optionally anonymous) expression is the highest truth. Due to its unique architecture, Freenet usage cannot be policed. Compare Freenet to a hammer. A hammer can be used to provide shelter for starving children. A hammer can also be used to bludgeon people to death. No one calls for hammers to be banned or modified because of a few violent or careless individuals.

Members of the group say that apart from opposing censorship and promoting Internet freedom, the project does not have a specific political agenda (Interview, May 2002).

The Freenet China program can be downloaded from the group's website, http://www.freenet-china.org. The Chinese authorities have already blocked the site on the mainland, but the program can also be obtained via email. In addition, it is rumored that the Chinese version of Freenet is being distributed on floppy disks to make it available to users in China who cannot access the Freenet China website from the mainland (Interview, March 2002), and that activists in China are installing the software on computers in Internet cafés (Interview, May 2002).

While their numbers are still relatively small, some Chinese Internet users are using Freenet China to download politically sensitive documents and to view websites blocked by the Chinese authorities (the use of P2P applications by Chinese Internet users is the focus of the second section of this essay). As of May 2002, Freenet China had a "core, dedicated group" of a few thousand users (Interview, May 2002). The popularity of Freenet China may be limited in part because some Internet users, particularly those who lack experience with computers,[27] have found it "rather difficult to use," according to one source (Interview, March 2002). Aware of this limitation, members of the Freenet China team have identified, as one of their most important goals, expanding the popularity of the program by making it more accessible to the broader population of casual Internet surfers in China (Interview, May 2002).

For now, even though use of the Chinese variant of Freenet is not yet widespread among the general population of PRC netizens, the application has already become a potentially useful tool for some relatively computer-savvy Chinese Internet users. Indeed, it purports to offer several advantages over systems such as Napster and Gnutella. With those systems, "anyone can find out who posted or downloaded a document," but Freenet is different, according to the introductory guide to using the Chinese version of Freenet. "If you publish a document on Freenet," the guide asserts, "the system will not allow anyone else to know that you posted it, and if you search for or read a document, it is almost impossible for other people to discover that it was you who was trying to find a certain document."[28]

Dynaweb

Launched in March 2002 by US-based Chinese activists and computer technicians from Dynamic Internet Technology and dajiyuan.com, Dynaweb is one of the newest anti-censorship software applications. It can be used to view blocked websites and download banned documents. According to technicians associated with the project, Dynaweb already has more than 10,000 subscribers (Interviews, May–June 2002). They say that, on an average day, several thousand Chinese web surfers use Dynaweb; log files indicate daily traffic ranges from 100,000 to 300,000 hits.

In contrast to Freenet, Publius, Peekabooty, and SafeWeb's Triangle Boy network, which were all designed to undermine censorship, other P2P applications were developed with commercial considerations in mind. Like their counterparts in many other countries, Chinese software developers are trying to create P2P applications and commercially viable business plans in their pursuit of profit. Two of the most widely used P2P applications created by Chinese technology companies are Openext and Workslink.

Openext

Openext is a Chinese P2P software based on Gnutella.[29] Designed by Openext in cooperation with the Chinese Academy of Sciences (Jiang Mianheng, son of Jiang Zemin, the Chinese leader, is a Vice President of this Academy), it is "a fully-distributed information-sharing technology."[30] The Openext website hosts numerous discussion forums on topics related to P2P. These include several forums on the Openext system, as well as discussion boards that focus on P2P software, the development of P2P technology in China and throughout the world, and news about P2P from Chinese and foreign sources.[31] One recent posting warned about vulnerabilities in the Morpheus P2P program that can result in the exposure of the personal data of users exchanging files through the system (Anonymous, 2002).

Workslink

Shenzhen All Talent Digital Technology, the company that produces Workslink, was founded in January 2001 and has a staff of eight. The company claims on its web page that Workslink is the "Chinese language peer-to-peer software with the most users in China today."[32] It is described by a US-based Chinese software engineer as "the number one Napster-like service in China" (Interview, March 2002). The software allows users to exchange music, videos, pictures, games, software, and documents. Workslink can also be used for P2P chat. Its producers advertise it as an application that enables users to "swap their data and files directly, safely, freely, quickly, and conveniently." Their goal is "to be the best provider of P2P service and software and to form Chinese P2P standard."[33] The version currently available for download is free, but the company founders believe they eventually will be able to charge membership fees. As they acknowledge implicitly on the Workslink website, however, widespread availability of broadband connections in China is a precondition for the popularization of P2P in China.[34]

The use of P2P technology in China

This section examines the use of P2P technology in China. It addresses the following questions: How popular is P2P in China? How are groups or individuals using P2P in China? What technologies are being used in China? Are applications for sharing music files popular? What other types of information are people sharing with P2P? How many people have used P2P to circulate *The Tiananmen Papers* or other politically sensitive documents or to view banned websites?

P2P is a hot topic among tech-savvy Internet users in China. Chinese computer magazines and technology websites have been abuzz with discussion of P2P for the past several years. Many articles are devoted to explaining the technical aspects of P2P computing, as well as its potential commercial applications (see, for example, *Weidiannao shijie* 2002a). One story published in the popular Chinese computing magazine *PC World China* in 2001, for example, outlines the basics of P2P computing, contrasts it with the client-server model, and provides a brief history of P2P, which the authors describe as "new wine in an old bottle," or, in other words, a network design that is being used in new ways, but is not really so novel as is sometimes assumed (*Weidiannao shijie* 2001a). The article also discusses various uses of P2P, such as online collaboration, instant messaging, file exchange, and distributed computing, and briefly describes several well-known P2P applications such as Napster, Groove, and SETI@home (ibid.). The articles provide factual coverage of developments in the P2P field, but some, like their Western counterparts, are almost breathtaking in their predictions about the potential effects of P2P. For instance, a recent article from *PC World China* proclaims, "P2P is bringing back the essence of the Internet," and predicts that in the next few years "P2P will enter into a new period of extremely rapid development" (*Weidiannao shijie* 2001b). Perhaps even more common are Chinese translations of Western articles on P2P, interviews with well-known American computer entrepreneurs, and news reports from international computing magazines and overseas websites. There are also scores of bulletin board sites (BBS) dedicated to discussion of P2P and related issues.[35] Through these numerous magazines and websites, Chinese computer technicians and other interested readers can keep abreast of everything from the latest trends in P2P technology to the most recent developments in the legal battle over the downloading of free music files. The Napster legal saga is a particularly popular subject. For example, in its annual awards issue in 2000, a popular Chinese computer magazine awarded Napster a tongue-in-cheek prize as the "computer technology most likely to be declared illegal."[36]

Music sharing

Discussions with Chinese Internet users and recent coverage of P2P in Chinese computing magazines suggest the most popular uses of P2P are not inherently political in nature. Indeed, Chinese IT industry executives are eager to explore P2P's commercial possibilities, as is demonstrated by the establishing of the China P2P Alliance earlier this year by Shenzhen All-Talent Digital Science and Technology, the producer of Workslink, one of China's most popular P2P applications (Workslink is discussed in greater detail on p. 82). Among the alliance's goals are "speeding up the process of the commercialization (*shangyehua*) of P2P technology in China" and "promoting the development of China's software industry" (*Weidiannao shijie* 2002b). The China P2P Alliance's other founding members include Openext, Ezpeer, and Kuro. Its website, http://www. cnp2p.org, provides links to the latest P2P news, software downloads, technical documents on P2P, a P2P discussion board, and an invitation to apply for membership of the organization.

As for average Chinese web users, most of those who are familiar with P2P are undoubtedly more interested in the use of the technology for entertainment than politics. This is a valid claim on at least two counts: first, because only a handful of Chinese citizens are political activists and second, because downloading and exchanging music files is one of the most popular applications of P2P technology for Internet users in countries throughout the world. Similarly, in China, limited survey data and anecdotal evidence indicate that many mainland Internet users are downloading MP3s, and that while the most popular sources of music files are simple websites, some Internet users are taking advantage of P2P applications to download and exchange their favorite songs.[37] In a survey on Internet usage in China conducted by researchers from the Chinese Academy of Social Sciences (CASS), more than 54 percent of respondents said they had downloaded entertainment files, and over 45 percent said they had downloaded music files or enjoyed them online (see Guo and Bu 2001: 14).[38] In a similar CASS survey of teenage Internet users in China, about 35 percent of users said that they sometimes listen to MP3s or watch videos online, some 33 percent said that they did so regularly, and just over 10 percent said that they did so on a daily basis. Only about 22 percent of respondents said that they had never downloaded an MP3 or video file (ibid.). Indeed, the general consensus of several Chinese students and expatriates in Beijing and Shanghai interviewed for this report is that MP3s already enjoy widespread popularity in China. This is especially so among Internet users who can download music files with ease through fast connections at work, and among students who enjoy access to broadband Internet connections at their universities. While websites are almost certainly the main source of free online music at present, P2P is also used frequently. It seems likely that exchanging music files over the Internet by various methods, including the use of P2P applications, will become even more popular in China when broadband connections become more widely available.

In China, as elsewhere, the popularity of free online music has raised concerns about copyright violations. For its part, the Chinese government has stated publicly that websites offering free music downloads must comply with copyright laws and has warned that proprietors of websites that flout the regulations, may face lawsuits (see FT Asia Intelligence Wire Business Daily Update, July 4, 2001). Chinese Internet companies are already adapting. In response to Chinese government pressure to curtail free online music trading on its websites, Netease.com, a Chinese Internet company, has formed a partnership with the Taiwan-based Internet music and entertainment company Kuro to create a membership-based P2P music community.

Dissent

P2P is also beginning to attract the attention of some netizens whose agendas Beijing considers subversive. Discussions with pro-democracy activists, Chinese computer engineers, and proponents of free speech on the Internet confirm that the use of P2P technology for transmission of politically sensitive materials, coordination among activists, and other such purposes is not yet widespread in China. One Chinese activist with a background in computer technology even said he does not know anyone in the dissident community or exile democracy movement who is using P2P to exchange documents (Interview, April 2002).

However, interviews with other activists suggest that some Chinese Internet users are already exchanging documents and accessing blocked websites through P2P networks. While the numbers appear to be small at present, dissidents, Falungong practitioners, and other activists in the PRC and abroad are turning to emerging P2P technology in their protracted online struggle with the Chinese authorities. For two primary reasons, which are alluded to above, many P2P technologies are ideally suited, even designed, for such purposes. The first reason is that several of these information-sharing technologies allow users to exchange files without using a central repository that can be easily shut down. The second is that some of these technologies have the potential to provide dissidents with a relatively high degree of anonymity.

Postings on Chinese language websites dedicated to promoting freedom of speech on the Chinese Internet suggest that a growing number of users have turned to one such application, Freenet China (discussed in greater detail on p. 79), since the Chinese authorities intensified their efforts to block access to SafeWeb and Triangle Boy in late 2001. When SafeWeb first introduced the Triangle Boy application, according to an article posted on the Chinese language website, http://www.Internetfreedom.org, mainland Internet users could effectively use a server address for a relatively long period of time, but recently the amount of time a server can be used before it is blocked has become shorter and shorter (Freenet, December 11, 2001). "Now it is basically impossible to use it," the posting laments (ibid.).

Instead, it suggests that Freenet can be used as an alternative means of accessing politically sensitive information on the web. The posting predicts that the number of people using Freenet on the mainland will increase. It also provides instructions for mainland users, including those who log on at Internet cafés, on downloading, installing, and using Freenet, and urges users to install Freenet on computers at work and in public places so as to allow more computers to be used to "break the information blockade." In addition, the posting promises that users of Freenet can count on a high degree of privacy and security: "Because of its characteristics, Freenet cannot be blocked, the data is completely encrypted, and even if someone accesses your computer the most they can know is that you may have used Freenet – they won't be able to find out what you have been reading" (ibid.).

For their part, exile dissidents are looking to P2P technology as a potential tool for reaching Internet users in China. Richard Long and Lian Shengde, the Washington-based editors of *VIP Reference*, a daily compilation of uncensored Chinese language news reports that is emailed to perhaps as many as a million mainland Internet users, are reportedly developing their own P2P program. "I don't think the government will be able to shut it down," Long told a reporter. The technology has not been widely adapted within China yet, but as Long points out, "The peer-to-peer networking model has great potential for sharing politically sensitive information" (McLaughlin 2000).

File sharing

Some Chinese Internet users have been taking advantage of technology to read electronic versions of politically sensitive books and documents, including some that have been banned by the Chinese authorities. To date, P2P technology has played a secondary role in the distribution of such books and documents online.

The dissemination of *The Tiananmen Papers* online provides an illuminating case study of how Chinese web users are utilizing the Internet – including websites, email, and P2P – to circumvent the barriers of official censorship. Although *The Tiananmen Papers* was officially banned by Beijing, this book, which contains what are purportedly excerpts from highly classified Chinese Communist Party and government documents on the suppression of the 1989 Tiananmen democracy protests, is widely available on the Internet in both English and Chinese. When highlights of *The Tiananmen Papers* were first released on the web in English, university students and intellectuals fluent in the language rushed to read excerpts on the website of *Foreign Affairs*. The authorities hurriedly attempted to block sites that carried the text of *The Tiananmen Papers*, but their efforts met with only partial success and some sites that provided links to excerpts from the book, such as that of the Council on Foreign Relations, which publishes *Foreign Affairs*, remained easily accessible. At the same time, students and intellectuals were reading excerpts of the Chinese version of *The Tiananmen Papers* on the Internet even before the book was published, as rough Chinese translations of the English version (which had been translated from the original Chinese) quickly began to appear on BBSs and other web pages. These excerpts were also transmitted by email.[39] Some users turned to P2P, and the complete text of the Chinese version of *The Tiananmen Papers* was made available on the Chinese version of Freenet. In May 2001, *VIP Reference* published an article containing instructions for using Freenet to download copies of *The Tiananmen Papers* in Chinese.[40] Freenet China was used to view *The Tiananmen Papers* several thousand times, according to one estimate (Interview, May 2002. This figure cannot be independently verified). In addition, a zip file containing *The Tiananmen Papers* is the document most frequently downloaded by users of Dynaweb, an anti-censorship service established earlier this year by US-based Chinese activists. They estimate that tens of thousands of copies have been downloaded through Dynaweb (Interview, June 2002. This figure cannot be independently verified).

In addition to *The Tiananmen Papers*, many other documents can be downloaded using P2P applications. One that is available in English and

Chinese on Freenet, for example, is China's Golden Shield, a report by freelance researcher Greg Walton on the contributions foreign corporations have reportedly made to the development of electronic surveillance technology in China.[41] There are also somewhat dated news articles about China's princelings, the children of high-ranking Party and government officials. For users of Dynaweb, apart from *The Tiananmen Papers*, the most frequently downloaded files include a collection of Tiananmen-related pictures, reports on the Yuanhua corruption scandal, and a collection of Falun Gong books (Interview, June 2002). Interestingly, some files containing information on sensitive political topics are available even through P2P networks that are operated by Chinese companies. For instance, a video entitled *Xue Lu* (The bloody path to Tiananmen square) is available through one such application, but the video is more than 45 minutes long and the file is very large, so it is unlikely that Internet users with dial-up connections could download it. However, most of the material exchanged by users of these applications is not political; much of it falls into the entertainment category, and some of it is pornography, as pointed out by several interviewees.

Facilitating access to blocked websites

The emergence of P2P will also have implications in other areas related to censorship on the Internet. Like other P2P technologies, Freenet can be used not only to search for and exchange documents, but also to access websites that are blocked by the Chinese authorities. For example, the main websites of the banned Falungong group, websites containing back issues of *VIP Reference*, and a variety of Chinese language news sites hosted by Chinese exiles can be visited using Freenet China. According to postings on a Chinese language website that carries the latest information on technologies that allow Internet users on the mainland to circumvent barriers imposed by Beijing, some users have complained that it is too slow. But as one posting puts it, hopefully, "If everyone uses Freenet more, it will become even faster" (Freenet, December 11, 2001). Some of the other blocked websites that Chinese surfers are using Freenet China to visit include those of the Chinese language e-magazine *VIP Reference*, the Chinese-language news services of the BBC and VOA, and several websites hosted by US-based activists that provide uncensored Chinese-language news updates.[42]

Despite Chinese attempts to block SafeWeb's Triangle Boy system, Chinese Internet surfers are reportedly still using it to visit a variety of websites. On January 4, 2002, for instance, VOA's server logs show that Triangle Boy was used to access 110,013 web pages (Communication with Stephen Hsu, June 2002). Among the most popular destinations for Triangle Boy users are news web sites, such as http://www.chinese newsnet.com, which provides Chinese-language news on a wide variety of topics including Chinese, US, and international politics, sports, and health,[43] and http://www.wenxuecity.com, a site with a broad range of content that aims to "let China enter into the world, and let the world enter into China."[44] The websites most frequently visited by users of DynaWeb include Chinese language news sites such as http://www.dajiyuan.com, http://www.kanzhongguo.com, http://www.renminbao.com, http://www.bignews.org (the website of *VIP Reference*), and the Falun Gong website http://www.minghui.ca (Interviews, May 2002). Dynaweb's log files indicate that visiting forbidden websites is far more popular than downloading banned documents. In addition, there have been a number of reports that Tibetan activists are also using Freenet and other similar programs (Interviews, April 2002).

Structural constraints

While the popularity of P2P is apparently increasing, there are a variety of constraints that have implications not only for casual Internet users who want to download their favorite songs, but also for those in China who would use P2P to promote reformist political agendas. Regulations on copyright violations notwithstanding, surveys conducted by CASS indicate that the most significant problems related to Internet access in China are slow access speeds, connection difficulties, and high costs, and suggest that these shortcomings are also the strongest constraints on the appetite for online music, including the use of P2P applications to download music files. Of the more than 1,000 users surveyed by CASS, over 68 percent said connections were too slow, nearly 40 percent reported problems with connecting, and about 55 percent complained that access was too expensive (Guo and Bu 2001). Regarding connection speed, it is worth noting that over 60 percent of Chinese Internet users connect to the Internet with a 56k modem connection and nearly 5 percent are still reliant on even slower modem connections (ibid.).

For now, slow connections and the high cost of Internet access, along with the ready availability of inexpensive pirated CDs of a reasonably good quality,[45] make it uneconomical for many users to download MP3s. The comments of a Chinese graduate student at Beijing University illustrate this point. "I usually don't download music from the Internet," he said. "It's too slow and resource-consuming, and the Internet and telephone fees are so expensive that downloading a dozen songs will leave you broke" (Interview, February 2002). The result is that while some Internet users in China are using P2P applications to share MP3 files and other multimedia files, P2P technology is not as widely used in China as it is in the US, according to well-informed observers.

Many of the same constraints that have apparently slowed the growth of P2P technology for exchanging music files in China are also likely to pose some obstacles to the use of P2P applications for political purposes, though it could be argued, of course, that the problem of connection speed is not a particularly serious impediment to the use of P2P applications for exchanging documents, since these files are typically much smaller than music or video files. In addition, technological constraints are frequently cited as among the main reasons that P2P applications are not widely popular among the few citizens dedicated to political change in China. Pro-democracy activists with extensive information technology experience point to several factors that limit the usage of P2P technology in China. These include difficulty in searching keywords in Chinese because of the various encoding systems, inadequate bandwidth, and the relative scarcity of dedicated lines or "always-on" broadband connections among Internet users in China (Interview, March 2002).[46]

Another constraint they cite is that many of the P2P programs are not particularly user-friendly. "At this point," one knowledgeable source points out, "most of the available software is too difficult for the average Chinese user to learn how to use" (Interview, April 2002). This, in particular, has reportedly limited the popularity of some P2P applications, such as Freenet China, that were designed to help Chinese Internet users undermine official censorship.

Chinese government responses to P2P networks

This section focuses on the Chinese government's possible countermeasures to any use of P2P technology for purposes it sees as subversive or threatening. We attempt to answer the following questions: what efforts has the PRC government made to control or restrict use of P2P? What are the technical barriers to control of P2P? What is the regulatory environment? Can Beijing promote self-censorship to prevent "subversive" use of P2P technology?

The ease with which mainland Internet users can read *The Tiananmen Papers* and other politically sensitive materials online is a striking illustration of the way in which the Internet has contributed to the decline in Beijing's ability to control the flow of information into and within China.[47] This trend toward the erosion of information control has alarmed the Chinese authorities and Beijing has been able to respond effectively in a number of ways, ranging from regulations that promote self-deterrence and self-censorship to the physical arrests[48] of individuals.[49]

If the Chinese authorities make a concerted effort to restrict the use of P2P technology specifically, they will probably employ a similar mixture of high-tech and low-tech countermeasures as they have against suspected Internet use for subversive purposes generally. The low-tech response would rely heavily on tried and true techniques of issuing broad regulations, making selective arrests, spreading propaganda, and encouraging self-policing. The last of these tactics has proven a particularly effective component of Beijing's Internet control strategy. The Chinese authorities use administrative punishments and the threat of economic penalties to encourage Internet providers to police their own websites, contributing to a climate of self-censorship. In the most recent example of this tactic, the Beijing Public Security Bureau in early June punished several Chinese Internet companies, including the popular portals Tom.com and Sina.com, for allowing "unsuitable content" to appear on their websites. In an apparent effort to discourage other Internet companies from permitting politically sensitive material to appear on their sites, the punishments were publicized in the *Beijing Youth Daily*, an official newspaper. It was also reported that checks of content provided by portals would be conducted regularly for the next several months (*South China Morning Post*, June 6, 2002).

High-tech responses to P2P networks

From a security and intelligence perspective, the big question from the outset is to decide whether you want to block this traffic or keep it under surveillance. Blocking traffic may solve the latest iteration of the network penetration, but surveillance could potentially allow the authorities to identify and arrest the members of a P2P network or poison the online "health" of the network by injecting disinformation.

Countermeasure one: IP blocking

Certain classes of brokered P2P nets, such as Triangle Boy, require the use of a set of known IP addresses for access to the network. If these addresses are static, then Beijing can block the IP addresses on the national-level routing tables or at the ISP level using software such as the Ministry of Public Security's Internet Police 110. Changing the IP addresses on a regular basis to foil any authority attempting to block them creates a significant coordination problem: how do you provide the IP addresses for the users in China without also tipping off the authorities? In the case of Triangle Boy, users were required to send an email to SafeWeb to receive the new addresses, but there was nothing to prevent the PRC authorities from simply requesting the IPs of the current node list for themselves and then adding those to the blocked list on the routing table. Later, the Chinese government went so far as to prevent users from requesting Triangle Boy IP addresses via email by blocking the IP address of SafeWeb's email auto-responder, so that it could not connect to email servers in China. This led SafeWeb to encourage users to sign up for web-based services hosted outside China, such as Hotmail and Yahoo! (Lee 2001). Finally, SafeWeb tried to assign IP addresses dynamically, by publishing one IP address at a time via volunteer web pages running CGI scripts that grabbed a "live" IP address from the SafeWeb database each time the page loaded. To prevent mass "harvesting" of addresses, SafeWeb did not allow more than a certain number of IPs to go to a particular web page per day. Beijing responded by systematically blocking the addresses of the volunteer web pages, whose number never grew large enough to overwhelm the censors.

Countermeasure two: port-blocking

P2P nets can be divided into two categories, based on their use of port connections. The first set are those that use unique port numbers, such as Napster (port 6699), Gnutella (port 6346), and KaZaA (port 1214). These are easily blocked by system administrators at every level, denying traffic to specific ports at the server level. Most of the more sophisticated P2P nets try to hide their traffic on common-use ports that do not handle encrypted traffic (e.g., port 21 FTP, port 23 Telnet, port 25 SMTP, port 80 HTTP://WWW., port 110 POP3, etc.), reasoning that system administrators would not want to sacrifice the functionality of their server to the user in order to block potential use of P2P nets. For example, Triangle Boy uses port 443 (HTTPS/SSL), Peekabooty uses port 80 (HTTP://WWW.), and other proposed network designs use transport layer ports such as 22 (SSH), IPSEC, SMTP, ICMP, or POP3. Some have argued that the Chinese government would be unwilling to block a port such as SSL, since it forms the basis for e-commerce. At the current time, however, very few people in China have credit cards and therefore the demand for secure online transactions is still manageably small.

Countermeasure three: packet sniffing

The transactions of many P2P nets have distinct packet/encryption signatures that could be included in a filter program and blocked. This issue is also especially important in the new networks that attempt to hide their traffic in common ports such as SSL, where care must be taken to make the P2P traffic look like authentic SSL traffic, using the same SSL negotiation type and parameters as common HTTPS servers. As one knowledgeable network engineer points out:

> P2P traffic patterns are very different from HTTP://WWW. traffic patterns, so if you just plop a P2P network on top of an SSL transport layer, on standard SSL ports, it will stick out like a sore thumb. Possibly better alternatives include IPSEC (which is commonly used for commercial VPN deployments, and thus has a more P2P-like traffic pattern), bundling content as S/MIME attachments over SMTP, steganographic stealthing over some of the ICMP protocols with forged headers (which would be really inefficient, and not practical for a "mass market" application where the mechanism is public knowledge, but very stealthy amongst a small, closed group).
>
> (E-mail interview, Beijing-based
> network engineer, July 10, 2002)

Another contentious issue is the relative drain on network resources to conduct packet sniffing on a large scale. While some may believe that the sheer volume of traffic flowing through Chinese routers would preclude this sort of activity, Chinese servers now employ differential routing, allowing them to ignore the vast majority of "trusted" network activity and focus on the much smaller amount of traffic at the ends of the bell curve. This system, which is already being used to hunt down traditional proxy servers and add them to the block list, can easily be adapted to find and block P2P connections.

Countermeasure four: virus attacks against the network

In April 2002, Freenet China received numerous virus-infected email messages, many of which originated in the PRC. Falun Gong, DynaWeb, and the Voice of America also suffered similar attacks at around the same time. Since the attacks coincided with the anniversary of the first major Falungong demonstration, it is tempting to speculate that the Ministry of Public Security (MPS) or another Chinese government organization may have been responsible. Based on available evidence, however, it is not possible to determine whether the Chinese government sponsored the attacks.

Countermeasure five: "If you can't beat 'em, join 'em"

Perhaps the more interesting countermeasures, however, are on the surveillance side. First, there is what one might call the "rogue node" problem. Since you cannot personally vouch for all members of a network once it grows beyond a certain N (nor would you want to if the network is supposed to be a cellular, anti-government operation where everyone has plausible deniability and no one can be coerced to betray the others), then there is nothing to stop the Beijing authorities from simply joining the network. If public key encryption is used, then the rogue node will be given a copy of the network's public key. If digital certificates are used, then the rogue node will be certified. As a result, all content will be at the authorities' disposal. Then the challenge is identifying the location and identity of the other members. Once the authorities set up fake peer servers, they can then trace the IP addresses of people attempting to use the service. This is more difficult if there is an anonymizer aspect to the operation, but effective social engineering will probably make it possible to work out the IDs of the other players. If the operation is based abroad (almost always true), the use of Chinese students in the US as rogue nodes would permit infiltration of the host organization in the US. Being part of a "trusted group" would also make it easier to distribute "spyware" to other members of the group, aiding the ID and sabotage effort.

It would also be relatively easy for the MPS or Ministry of State Security (MSS) to use their infiltration of a P2P network for the purpose of spreading propaganda and disinformation. This is a method that both the MPS and the MSS have reportedly employed both online and off to exploit the fractiousness of the overseas pro-democracy movement. The architecture of many P2P systems would make it easy for the MPS and MSS to distribute propaganda and disinformation disguised as other types of files. It would even be possible for the security services to use P2P networks to distribute messages intended to intimidate selected users. For example, the security services could create a file that contains a message such as, "the MSS knows you are trying to read Falungong materials – don't try it again!" and name it "Falundafanotice.doc" so that Falungong members would retrieve it when searching for legitimate Falungong materials.

This type of rogue node operation would also allow the authorities to develop a clear picture of the content and client software that might be found on a confiscated computer in China, and thus validate the participation of a given individual in this conspiracy. The tried and true strategy is "punishing one to frighten one hundred," so the authorities would very likely seek to promote deterrence by arresting someone and making an example of them for their "subversive" use of P2P technology. Even if they only discovered that a dissident was using P2P applications after the fact (e.g., they might arrest someone for another reason and then confiscate and examine their computer), the police or security services might imply that they had uncovered the use of P2P technology through technical surveillance.

Finally, P2P presents a fundamental dilemma for users, particularly those participating in systems where their computers may be funneling content from one place to another that they cannot themselves examine, usually via encryption. While users may volunteer for idealistic reasons, believing that they are facilitating access to human rights material, they may, in fact, be unknowing co-conspirators in the transmission of non-political but nonetheless illegal or objectionable material, such as child pornography or communications between terrorists. The authorities are unlikely to care if a particular user is capable of decrypting a message for which they are serving as a relay client, but instead will punish them for things well beyond their control. The only antidote for this is cautious and careful assessment of risk. As Cult of the Dead Cow member Drunken Master recently commented on the potential negative consequences of use of their P2P application known as "Peekabooty": "If the user cannot accept a certain level of risk, they should not use it" (Greene 2001).

Potential social and political implications of P2P in China

Technology alone is unlikely to motivate political change in China. At most, information technology can be a medium, and perhaps a catalyst, for political movements. In China today, despite rising disgust with official corruption and discontent on the part of the economically disenfranchised, there is not a huge groundswell of support for radical political change. Moreover, there is little organized opposition to the ruling Communist Party. Thus, in the short term, neither the Internet nor P2P technology in particular will lead to profound shifts in political power in China. In the long term, however, it is not difficult to imagine a situation in which the spread of information technology, including P2P, will contribute to gradual pluralization of the system.

If this happens, the Communist Party and the Chinese government will, to some extent, be the authors of their own demise. The Chinese government has poured billions of dollars into IT infrastructure, and encouraged limited competition among private IT providers. As a result, Internet penetration has continued to grow at remarkable rates since 1995, and the Chinese user base has become increasingly sophisticated. Along with this growth, the use of P2P applications is likely to become more widespread. P2P computing technology is "developing rapidly and gaining prominence," and the market for P2P applications in China is expanding, according to a Chinese software company executive, although the failure of Napster and other companies in the West to find an effective and legal business model for P2P should temper this prediction. Nonetheless, it seems clear that the market popularization of P2P could have implications far beyond the downloading of MP3 music files. Indeed, this report considered it a real possibility that P2P will become a major factor in the online struggle between government censors and Internet activists based in China and abroad.

At the moment, the authorities seem to have the upper hand in the struggle between the government and Chinese Internet users seeking access to websites or other online material deemed "sensitive" or "subversive" by Beijing, much to the surprise and chagrin of those who naively believed that the authoritarian regimes would quickly fold in the face of progressive technologies. "The authorities have become much better at finding and blocking proxies in China," said an activist who recently visited the mainland. "I was there for eight days and experienced eight days of 'Internet blackout'." Advocates of P2P applications assert that as P2P networks become more widely used in China, the advantage now enjoyed by the authorities may shift back to those Chinese Internet users who are interested in viewing banned websites, such as those of Falun Gong, dissident groups, and Western news organizations.

The preliminary conclusions we have drawn from our research, however, are that the Chinese government has once again responded nimbly to a new technical challenge, employing a sophisticated set of equipment and software to exploit architectural flaws in various P2P-based network efforts. Moreover, the Beijing government has also continued with the leverage of significant non-technical countermeasures, relying primarily on traditional, non-technical Leninist methods ranging from surveillance and arrest to effective regulations that encourage users and ISPs to engage in self-censorship and self-deterrence. These trends suggest that activists who would seek to use P2P technology will face a protracted, uphill struggle against a determined opponent, and that the balance of technical skills alone will not determine the outcome of the contest. Thus, the future picture for P2P as a tool of political change in China is decidedly mixed, and will likely be marked by a continuing inconclusive seesaw between new and innovative technical measures by advocates of openness and the technical, political, bureaucratic, and economic countermeasures implemented by Beijing.

Notes

1 The research for this chapter was conducted in 2001–02 when all the websites noted were accessed. While the situation has changed somewhat since then, we believe that the basic conclusions of the chapter remain sound.

2 Ironically, P2P is actually more reminiscent of the original utopian vision of the Net – a world of individuals sharing information free of authority and artificial boundaries. At the same time, it must be pointed out that the content and mechanisms of P2P nets are value-neutral, and can be exploited by both the forces of good (e.g., dissidents) and evil (e.g., child pornographers and terrorists) (see, for example, Schwartz 2001).

3 The most famous struggle over P2P technology involved Napster, pitting a small technology company and the millions of people who adopted its technology to share billions of music files each month against the might of the recording industry and the institutional defenders of copyright law. While Napster lost in court, the story of music sharing is far from over. Newer technologies, even more difficult to control, have sprung up and are quickly spreading. Morpheus, which as of February 2002 had been downloaded 51 million times and KaZaA, 37 million times, are examples (Borland 2002).

4 CNNIC 7/2002 and other previous CNNIC reports; the number of users had reached 87 million by July 2004 (CNNIC 7/2004). The CNNIC was established in June 1997 and operates under the leadership of the MII and CAS. Located in the Haidian district of Beijing, its responsibilities include registering domain names, distributing IP addresses, and conducting statistical surveys on the development of the Internet in China. The first two reports were issued in October 1997 and July 1998. Since then, the CNNIC has issued reports twice annually, every January and July. The reports are available online (all the reports are available in English translation) at the CNNIC website: http://www.cnnic.net.cn/en/ index. CNNIC reports also provide information on topics such as total bandwidth, Internet user demographics, number and geographical distribution on domain names and websites, access locations and expenditure, and user views regarding online advertising and e-commerce. It should be noted that industry experts have questioned the methodology employed by the CNNIC to count Internet users and to tabulate some of the other statistics contained in its reports. It is also worth noting that account sharing is another factor that complicates attempts to accurately estimate the number of people in China who are "wired."

5 See CNNIC 7/2002. More than half of all Chinese Internet users access the Internet at their homes or offices, according to the July 2001 report, while around 18 percent access the Internet at school, and 15 percent at Internet cafés (January 2000 statistics are from CNNIC 1/2000).

6 In the words of an article by a commentator in the *People's Daily*: "The degree of development of information networking technology has become an important yardstick for measuring a country's modernization level and its comprehensive national strength" (*People's Daily*, July 12, 2001).

7 This section borrows very heavily from Anderson and Baer 2001.

8 One working definition suggested by Clay Shirky, a venture capitalist and P2P expert, is that P2P networks use addressing schemes other than the Domain Name Service (DNS) that is a core element of today's Internet (see *The Economist*, 2001a).

9 Groove Networks, http://www.groove.net, founded by Lotus Notes developer Ray Ozzie, appears to be the current leader in developing P2P collaborative workspaces. Its capabilities, as listed on the Groove website, include: "communication tools – live voice over the Internet, instant messaging, text-based chat, and threaded discussion; content sharing tools – shared files, shared pictures, shared contacts; and joint activity tools – co-Web browsing, multiple user drawing and editing, group calendar."

10 For a short, readable introduction to distributed computing concepts, see, *The Economist* 2001b. Interest in P2P distributed computing starts from the fact that most PCs use very little of their processing power most of the time. Utilizing even a small fraction of this idle capacity via the Internet could, in principle, provide enormous processing resources at low cost to work on computation-intensive problems such as designing new drugs, conducting aerodynamic simulations, or assessing global climate change models. One of the early, and still best, examples of distributed computing uses spare PC processing power to analyze signals from the Arecibo radio telescope as part of the Search for Extra-Terrestrial Intelligence (SETI). Since 1998, more than 2.4 million volunteers have downloaded a SETI@home screen saver which retrieves SETI data from the Internet, processes it while the PC is otherwise inactive, and sends the processed results back over the Internet to the SETI distribution server. As of October 2000, SETI@home had received 200 million results with a total of $4 \times 1,020$ floating-point operations, leading the project's director to call it "the largest computation ever performed" (Anderson 2002: 67–76).

11 Computers that act both as servers and clients are sometimes called "servents" in P2P jargon. In this document, however, we shall refer to them as "peers."

12 Many of the P2P networks such as Napster have quite short life spans; Napster, for example, was closed in 2002.

13 Taken from http://duende.uoregon.edu/~hsu/SW_talk/PIMCO_talk.htm. On October 15, 2003, Symantec Corporation acquired the technology and interests of SafeWeb, Inc.

14 Diagram: http://duende.uoregon.edu/~hsu/SW_talk/SW.pdf.

15 Taken from http://duende.uoregon.edu/~hsu/SW_talk/Tboy_diag.pdf.

16 AOL Time Warner pulled the software Triangle Boy off the Web a day later, but it had already been widely downloaded and copied. The Gnutella P2P technology has subsequently been improved and made freely available by a group of software developers working collaboratively. Links to the Gnutella search protocol and free downloads of Gnutella applications could be found during the research period at http://gnutella.wego.com, see also http://www.gnutellanet.com.

17 http://www.musiccity.com/home.htm; see also the more recent URL address http://www.morpheus.com.

18 http://www.kazaa.com.

19 http://www.fasttrack.nu; this URL is no longer accessible.

20 For an introduction to the history, capabilities, and potential uses of Freenet, see: http://www.freenetproject.org/cgi-bin/twiki/view/Main/WhatIs. See also Abreu 2000.

21 http://www.freenetproject.org.

22 Freenet's home page can be found at http://www.freenetproject.org.

23 One suggested approach is to develop an XML-like set of standards for indexing content, with the original publisher responsible for entering identifying information (such as the Dublin core for books).

24 The Publius website was http://publius.cdt.org, see also http://cs1.cs.nyu.edu/~waldman/publius/. Publius is not a P2P system in the strictest sense of the term, according to its developers, but is similar to a P2P system in some respects. For more information on Publius, see Waldman *et al.* 2002: 145–58, Sorid 2000, Schwartz 2000.

25 See http://publius.cdt.org/use_publius.html.

26 The same could be said, of course, for almost any technology that enables communication.

27 The introduction to installing and using the Chinese version of Freenet, available on the group's website at http://freenet-china.org/freenet/freenet4all.htm, is ten pages long. While not overly technical, it is perhaps enough to intimidate casual Internet users.

28 http://freenet-china.org/freenet/freenet4all.htm: 9.

29 For the Chinese-language version of the Openext webpage, see http://www.openext.com; the former, English version http://www.openext.com/english.htm is no longer available.

30 http://www.openext.com/english.htm.

31 For a listing of these sites, see http://www.openext.com/bbs.

32 We were unable to verify this claim independently. It is worth noting that although Workslink touts itself as the most used P2P software specifically designed for Chinese platforms, one interviewee familiar with Workslink said that "traffic is much less than on Bearshare and the total volume being shared is very small."

33 More information is available on the Workslink Chinese-language website, http://www.workslink.com. Relatively limited information, including an introduction to the company that produces Workslink and a brief description of the software, is also available in English at http://www.workslink.com/english/index.asp.

34 An informal poll on the Workslink website indicates that more than half of Workslink users have high-speed Internet connections. This is interesting in that the percentage of respondents in the Workslink poll who have DSL or cable modem access is significantly higher than in the general population of Chinese Internet users.

35 The website of Openext, a Chinese P2P company, hosts more than a dozen P2P discussion boards, see http://www.openext.com/bbs. The Chinese P2P Alliance also hosts a P2P discussion board, http://www.cnp2p.org/bbs.

36 *Weidiannao shijie* (*PC World China*), 2000, Issue 27. See http://www.pcworld.com.cn/2000/back_issues/2027/2721q.asp.

37 This is not meant to imply that the trading of music files online is an action that is always inherently lacking in political implications. It is possible, for example, that some Chinese Internet users are exchanging music with subversive lyrics.

38 The survey was conducted in early 2001 in the cities of Beijing, Shanghai, Guangzhou, Chengdu, and Changsha. For the complete text of the report in Chinese, see http://www.chinace.org/ce/itre. It is only available in Chinese at the above website, but an English translation of the report was also produced.

39 This account is based primarily on discussions with Chinese students and academics.

40 See *Da cankao* May 5, 2001. The article thanks an anonymous Internet user for uploading the Chinese text of *The Tiananmen Papers* to Freenet.

41 The report was also available at http://www.go.openflows.org.
42 According to Freenet China members, a ranking of the most popular sites is not available.
43 On June 4, 2002, for example, http://www.chinesenewsnet.com carried headlines on subjects as diverse as the Chinese soccer team losing to Costa Rica in the World Cup, Tiananmen victims' advocate Ding Zilin's statement on the 13th anniversary of the June 4, 1989 crackdown, and questions surrounding the performance of the US intelligence community prior to the September 11 terrorist attacks.
44 http://www.wenxuecity.com/about_us.htm.
45 Pirated CDs of various types are ubiquitous in China. They are sold openly in small shops in major cities and even from baskets on the backs of bicycles at universities. In some areas it is difficult to find legitimate CDs. The most inexpensive pirated CDs are very basic. They often come in a re-sealable plastic bag with nothing more than a color copy of the cover art and cost about 4 or 5 RMB, the equivalent of about 50 or 60 US cents. Higher quality pirated CDs are also widely available throughout China. These are packaged, typically, in a plastic jewel case and often include good color copies of cover art, lyrics, and liner notes. These usually cost 8 to 10 RMB, or about US$ 1.00 to US$ 1.25. For a recent report on pirated CDs in China, see "China Seizes Record Haul of Pirated CDs" (*South China Morning Post*, 4 March 2002), which cites a story published by the official newspaper *Legal Daily* about the impounding by customs officials of more than four million counterfeit CDs.
46 It is interesting to note that while most sources identify connection speed as the major impediment, this activist contends that language is "the number one barrier."
47 In June 2001, Chinese police in Guangzhou detained Li Hongmin for disseminating copies of the Chinese-language version of *The Tiananmen Papers* on the Internet. It is believed that Li emailed the documents to several other Chinese Internet users, but it is not clear whether the authorities learned of Li's activities through technical surveillance or more traditional means, such as the use of informants.
48 More than two dozen other activists and Internet users have been jailed for distributing officially banned materials online. See Digital Freedom Network, "Attacks on the Internet in China: Chinese individuals currently detained for online political or religious activity," available on the DFN website at http://www.dfn.org/focus/china/netattack.htm. See also Digital Freedom Network, "Attacks on the Internet in China: Internet-related legal actions and site shutdowns since January 2000," available at http://www.dfn.org/focus/china/shutdown.htm.
49 For a more detailed discussion of Beijing's national information security strategy for the Internet, see Chase and Mulvenon 2002.

References

Abreu, Elinor (2000) "Peer-to-peer – we've only begun," *The Standard*, August 21, 2000. Online. Available HTTP: http://www.thestandard.com/article/0,1902,17757,00.html (accessed March 2002).

Adar, Eytan and Huberman, Bernardo A. (2000) "Free riding on Gnutella," *First Monday*, October 2000. Online. Available HTTP: http://www.firstmonday.dk/issues/issue5_10/adar/index.html (accessed December 12, 2004).

Anderson, David (2002) "SETI@home," in Andy Oram (ed.) *Peer to Peer: Harnessing the Power of Disruptive Technology*, New York: O'Reilly & Associates, pp. 67–76.

Anderson, Robert H. and Baer, Walter (2001) "Potential military applications of peer-to-peer computer networks," unpublished RAND report, November.

Anonymous (July 11, 2002) "Peekabooty open-sourced." Online Posting. Available HTTP: http://www.peek-a-booty.org (accessed July 2002).

Anonymous (2002) "Wenjian jiaohuan fuwu keneng hui xielu yonghu geren ziliao" (Document exchange services may divulge the personal information of users). Online posting. Available HTTP: http://www.openext.com/bbs/dispbbs.asp?board ID=5&RootID=187&ID=187 (accessed March 2002).

Baranowski, Paul (2002) "The cost of Peekabooty" (April 9, 2002). Online posting. Available HTTP: http://www.peek-a-booty.org/pbhtml/index.php (accessed April 2002).

Black, Jane (August 1, 2001) "The Beat goes on," *Business Week.*

Bloomberg News (March 27, 2001) "China cracks down on file-swapping sites," *Bloomberg News.*

Borland, John (2001) "Freenet: surfing without a name," *ZDNet News*, June 18, 2001.

Borland, John (2002) "Morpheus looks to Gnutella for help," *CNET News.com*, 27 February. Online. Available HTTP: http://news.com.com/2100-1023-846944.html (accessed March 2002).

Chase, Michael S. and Mulvenon, James C. (2002) *You've Got Dissent: Chinese Dissident Use of the Internet and Beijing's Counter-Strategies*, Santa Monica, CA: RAND (MR-1543).

Clarke, Ian (1999) "A distributed decentralised information storage and retrieval system," unpublished report, Division of Informatics, University of Edinburgh.

Clarke, Ian, Miller, Scott G., Wong, Theodore W., Sanderg, Oskar, and Wiley, Brandon (2002) "Protecting free expression online with Freenet," *IEEE Internet Computing*, January/February 2002, pp. 40–9.

Da cankao (*VIP Reference*) (May 5, 2001), No. 1196.

Digital Freedom Network (n.d. a) "Attacks on the Internet in China: Chinese individuals currently detained for online political or religious activity," *Digital Freedom Network*. Online. Available HTTP: http://www.dfn.org/focus/china/net attack.htm (accessed March 2003).

Digital Freedom Network (n.d. b) "Attacks on the Internet in China: Internet-related legal actions and site shutdowns since January 2000," *Digital Freedom Network*. Online. Available HTTP: http://www.dfn.org/focus/china/shutdown.htm (accessed March 2003).

Freenet (December 11, 2001) "Guanyu Ziyouwang" [About Freenet]. Online. Available HTTP: http://www.Internetfreedom.org/gb/articles/1042.html (accessed January 3, 2005).

FT Asia Intelligence Wire Business Daily Update (July 4, 2001) "China: free music on Internet illegal."

Greene, Thomas C. (July 19, 2001) "Will cDc privacy app Peekabooty put users at risk?" *The Register.*

Guo, Liang and Bu, Wei (2001) *Hulianwang shiyong zhuangkuang ji yingxiang de diaocha baogao* [Survey report on Internet usage and impact], Beijing: Chinese Academy of Social Sciences, April 2001: 14. Online. Available HTTP: http://www.chinace.org/ce/itre/index.htm (accessed January 5, 2005).

Hachigian, Nina (2002) "The Internet and power in one-party East Asian States," *Washington Quarterly* (Summer), pp. 51–8.

Hsu, Stephen (January 18, 2002) "Written testimony of Stephen Hsu, CEO, Safeweb, before the U.S. China Commission."

iDEFENSE iALERT White Paper (March 25, 2002) "A peek at Peekabooty." Online. Available HTTP: http://www.idefense.com/idpapers/PeekP.pdf (accessed April 2002).

Internetfreedom.org (December 11, 2001) "Guanyu ziyouwang" [Concerning Freenet]. Online posting. Available HTTP: http://www.Internetfreedom.org/gb/articles/1042.html (accessed January 5, 2005).

Internetfreedom.org (October 24, 2001) "Yong jiami fangshi anquan shiyong dianzi youjian" [Using encryption for email security]. Online. Available HTTP: http://www.Internetfreedom.org/gb/articles/987.html (accessed January 5, 2005).

Internetfreedom.org (October 31, 2001) "Zhongguo dui wangluo de zhuyao jiankong fangfa he duice" [China's main methods of supervising and controlling the Net and countermeasures]. Online. Available HTTP: http://www.Internetfreedom.org/gb/articles/1012.html (accessed January 5, 2005).

Internetfreedom.org (October 4, 2001) "Wangba shangwang de yixie anquan wenti" [Some security problems of going online at Internet cafés]. Online. Available HTTP: http://www.Internetfreedom.org/gb/articles/979.html (accessed January 5, 2005).

Kan, Gene (2002) "Gnutella," in Andy Oram (ed.) *Peer to Peer: Harnessing the Power of Disruptive Technology*, New York: O'Reilly & Associates, p. 94.

Kennedy, Andy (January 17, 1999) "For China, the tighter the grip, the weaker the hand," *Washington Post*.

Langley, Adam (2002) "Freenet," in Andy Oram (ed.) *Peer to Peer: Harnessing the Power of Disruptive Technology*, New York: O'Reilly & Associates, pp. 123–32.

Lee, Jennifer 8 (August 30, 2001) "U.S. may help Chinese evade net censorship," *New York Times*.

Luman, Stuart and Cook, Jason (2001) "Knocking off Napster," *Wired*, January.

McDonald, Tim (May 7, 2001) "Hackers unleash no-limits Internet browser," *NewsFactor Network*. Online. Available HTTP: http://www.newsfactor.com/perl/printer/9521 (accessed July 5, 2002).

McLaughlin, Kevin (August 14, 2000) "China's two-faced Internet policies (and the people who skirt them)," *Business2.0*. Online. Available HTTP: http://www.business2.com/articles/web/print/0,1650,16088,FF.html.

Minar, Nelson and Hedlund, Marc (2002) "A network of peers," in Andy Oram (ed.) *Peer to Peer: Harnessing the Power of Disruptive Technology*, New York: O'Reilly & Associates, p. 4.

Peekabooty (n.d.) "About the Peekabooty project: the concept and the code". Online. Available HTTP: http://www.peek-a-booty.org/pbhtml/modules.php?name=Content&pa=showpage&pid=1 (accessed January 5, 2005).

People's Daily (July 12, 2001) "Using legal means to guarantee and promote sound development of information network," in FBIS (Foreign Broadcast Information Service).

Ripeanu, Matei (July 24, 2001) "Peer-to-peer architecture case study: Gnutella network." Online. Available HTTP: http://www.cs.uchicago.edu/research/publications/techreports/TR-2001-26 (accessed January 5, 2005).

SafeWeb (2002) *White Paper: Triangle Boy Network*.

SafeWeb press release (March 13, 2001) "Chinese government attempts to block access to SafeWeb; Silicon Valley startup answers with triangle boy technology in effort to combat Internet censorship."

Salkever, Alex (July 23, 2002) "Skirting the Great Firewall of China," *BusinessWeek Online*.

Schwartz, John (June 30, 2000) "Online and unidentifiable? AT&T Labs' 'Publius' system aims to return anonymity to posters," *Washington Post*.

Schwartz, John (July 28, 2001) "File-swapping is new route for Internet pornography," *New York Times*.

Shi, Lei (August 31, 2001) "Xinxi bailinqiang: tupo Zhonggong feng wang de jishu duice tantao" [The information Berlin Wall: discussion of technological measures for breaking the CCP's net blockade]. Online. HTTP: http://www.cdjp.org/01/archives/00000043.htm.

Sorid, Daniel (July 26, 2000) "Divided data can elude the censor," *New York Times*.

South China Morning Post (March 4, 2002) "China seizes record haul of pirated CDs."

South China Morning Post (June 6, 2002) "Beijing punishes Net portals."

The Economist (June 21, 2001) "Computing power on tap."

The Economist (June 21, 2001) "Profit from peer-to-peer."

Truelove, Kelly and Chasin, Andrew (March 27, 2001) "Morpheus out of the underworld," *O'Reilly Network*. Online. Available HTTP: http://www.openP2P.com/lpt/a//P2P/2001/07/02/morpheus.html (accessed January 5, 2005).

Waldman, Marc, Cranor, Lorrie Faith, and Rubin, Avi (2002) "Publius," in Andy Oram (ed.) *Peer to Peer: Harnessing the Power of Disruptive Technology*, New York: O'Reilly & Associates, pp. 145–58.

Weidiannao shijie [*PC World China*] (2001a) "Duideng wangluo jishu de yingyong" [The uses of peer-to-peer technology], Issue 14. Online. Available HTTP: http://www.pcworld.com.cn/2001/back_issues/2114/1403.asp.

Weidiannao shijie [*PC World China*] (2001b) "P2P gei ni geng ziyou de Internet" [P2P brings you a freer Internet], Issue 6. Online. Available HTTP: http://www.pcworld.com.cn/2001/back_issues/2106/0604a.asp (accessed January 5, 2005).

Weidiannao shijie [*PC World China*] (2002a) "2002 nian PC he Internet jishu redian yuce" [Forecast of hot trends in PC and Internet technology for 2002], Issue 1. Online. Available HTTP: http://www.pcworld.com.cn/2002/back_issues/2201/0111.asp (accessed January 5, 2005).

Weidiannao shijie [*PC World China*] (2002b) "Zhongguo P2P lianmeng chengli" [China P2P alliance founded]. Online. Available HTTP: http://www.pcworld.com.cn/2002/online/news/0004/0405_09.asp (accessed January 5, 2005).

Yatsko, Pamela (December 24, 2001) "China's web censors win one – for now," *Fortune*.

5 China's e-policy

Examples of local e-government in Guangdong and Fujian

Jens Damm

This chapter proceeds from a discussion of the definitions and main features of e-government and e-governance in China as a whole, to consider from a micro-perspective examples of local e-government drawn from field work in the two relatively wealthy provinces of Fujian and Guangdong with a focus on Taijiang, a district of Fuzhou. With information obtained from interviews with researchers from local universities and government agencies in charge of e-government, it has been possible to gain a clear picture of the two major functional aspects of local e-government in China. First, it has a government service orientation and offers easier access to information for the public. Informatization and local e-government are seen as an integral part of the government reforms that are required to increase efficiency and speed. Second, local websites offering a comprehensive range of information have been set up by the government. The websites of the sample cities can be described as "local portals," and they provide links to the relevant information and government agencies. This goes some of the way towards resolving the conflict produced by the government's struggle to control the Internet while also taking full advantage of the benefits of economic development which can be achieved through technological modernization in the fields of information and communication. The vast and comprehensive information network offered by local e-government websites, including government information, business opportunities, shopping places, chat rooms, leisure activities, games and news within a "safe sandbox," helps to offset the "danger" that citizens will be tempted to leave the local information network.

Electronic government, abbreviated to e-government, is a slogan that spread throughout the globalized world in the 1990s, becoming one of the most important features of China's administrative and governmental reform at various levels. These developments have to be seen both in relation to the resumption and acceleration of the "reform and opening policy," which started after Deng Xiaoping's famous "southern tour" (*nanxun*) in 1992,[1] and to China's eventual success in being admitted to the WTO in 2001. These events were clearly a historical step for China in her long process of "entering the world" (*ru shi*) (Zhao 2003: 33) and the rapid growth in

ICT (information and communication technology) is now also contributing to China's increasing embeddedness in a globalizing world.

Administrative and governmental reforms in China have been instituted with the goal of bestowing new legitimacy on the rule of the CCP, which even after moving away from a planned to a market economy has still officially continued to uphold the principles of Marxism-Leninism. These reforms, which implement new forms of governance to promote participation and efficiency, have been described as aiming to strengthen the legitimacy of CCP rule, while at the same time preventing any formal opposition from emerging (see Dittmer 2003, Goodman 1998).

The CCP started to develop the e-government system in China at the end of the 1990s, but while international definitions of e-government as proposed by the World Bank or UNESCO were accepted and implemented to some extent, a China-specific definition has also emerged. Attempts to find a globally acceptable definition of e-government, however, have not yet met with any real success and a specific definition is still lacking today. "E-government," sometimes called "government online,"[2] has been given a wider meaning by the new term "e-governance" and, in addition, there is often a local component within the definition which allows different political systems to interpret the term in a variety of ways.[3]

"E-government" usually refers to the electronic delivery of information from the government to citizens and between different government agencies, but some authors also link "e-government" with "digital democracy" which "offers the potential of more efficient public sector service delivery that enhances citizen accountability and governmental responsiveness" (West 2001).

The World Bank,[4] like the Chinese authorities, has chosen to define e-government in terms of "good governance," describing it as:

> The use by government agencies of information technologies (such as Wide Area Networks, the Internet, and mobile computing) that have the ability to transform relations with citizens, businesses, and other arms of government. These technologies can serve a variety of different ends: better delivery of government services to citizens, improved interactions with business and industry, citizen empowerment through access to information, and more efficient government management. The resulting benefits can be less corruption, increased transparency, greater convenience, revenue growth, and cost reductions.
>
> (Center for Democracy and Technology and infoDev 2002: 2)

Elsewhere, e-democracy is presented as consisting of more than just voting via the net or increased opportunities for political parties; it has sometimes been suggested that even in authoritarian and semi-authoritarian states, the introduction of e-government has the potential to "increase governments' efficiency, transparency, and accountability while limiting the scope for arbitrary decisions and abuses of power" (Drake 2001). Other observers, however, remain unable to see a "third way" of achieving more transparency within authoritarian regimes without the transformation of these systems through democratizing processes, and seem to seek to polarize the argument by pointing out that "the information revolution has assisted pro-democracy activists to progressively chip away at authoritarian regimes' grip on power," while at the same time commenting on "the ability of those same regimes both to disseminate propaganda and monitor their own citizens' behavior" (International Institute for Democracy and Electoral Assistance 2001).[5]

In the English-language press of China, however, there has been some speculation about more e-democracy emerging as a result of e-government. Thus, the *China Daily* quoted Zhao Xiaofan, director of the State Council Informatization Office (*Guowuyuan zixunhua bangongshi*) saying that "the e-government initiative would promote democracy by providing residents with more digital connections, such as e-mail, and simplifying election procedures by, for example, allowing voting online" (*China Daily*, April 5, 2004).

Another point frequently mentioned is that e-government can be implemented as an efficient tool to overcome the digital divide:

> The direct effects of e-government include cost-effectiveness in government and public operations, significant savings in areas such as public procurement, tax collection and customs operations, with better and continuous contacts with citizens, especially those living in remote or less densely populated areas.
>
> (Center for Democracy and Technology and infoDev 2002: 2)

Karsten Giese was not convinced that the optimism expressed in the statements quoted above was justified, and he came to the following conclusion:

> Rather than expecting Internet access to speed up development in the backward areas, therefore, it is more realistic to expect its geographical distribution to follow the patterns of general economic development, improvements in income and educational levels, and the process of urbanization. [. . .] Ultimately, therefore, the Chinese government faces a paradoxical situation when it comes to using the Internet as a tool for overcoming the digital divide: the level of connectivity that it wants to achieve in the western regions can only be achieved when a commercially attractive situation has already been created there.
>
> (Giese 2003: 52–3)

In general, the establishment of e-government has to be seen as a process involving different phases, such as "publish," "interact" and "transact" (Jupp 2000, Center for Democracy and Technology and infoDev 2002:

10–12). "Publish" refers to the first phase, when information is placed online: "Governments generate huge volumes of information, much of it potentially useful to individuals and businesses. The Internet and other advanced communications technologies can bring this information quickly and more directly to citizens" (Center for Democracy and Technology and infoDev 2002: 3). This is believed to lead to less bureaucracy and to improved transparency, while at the same time discouraging the widespread custom of paying bribes to officials in order to gain relevant data.

The next phase is "interact": "E-government has the potential to involve citizens in the governance process by engaging them in interaction with policymakers throughout the policy cycle and at all levels of government. Strengthening civic engagement contributes to building public trust in government." This ranges from e-mails, to feedback forms and forums "where people can exchange ideas, broaden public awareness of issues, and establish new opportunities for activism not constrained by distance. [. . .] E-government is not just a cost cutting or efficiency initiative, but rather is directed at bettering the lives of ordinary people" (ibid.).

The final phase is "transact," which describes the creation of websites by the government that allow users to conduct transactions online.

> Just as the private sector in developing countries is beginning to make use of the Internet to offer e-commerce services, governments will be expected to do the same with their services. Potential cost savings, accountability through information logs and productivity improve-ments will be important drivers.
>
> (Center for Democracy and Technology and infoDev 2002: 4)

It is therefore often assumed that the introduction of e-government will lead to quite a number of improvements and will support administrative reforms "by helping to better measure performance, facilitate outsourcing and contestability of public functions, reduce transaction costs, better enforce rules, reduce discretion, and increase transparency" (Wescott 2002: 122).

E-governmentization in China

In China, the introduction of e-government was regarded as part of the general "building of government informatization in China" (*wo guo zhengfu xinxihua jianshe*) (Dianzi zhengfu yanjiu wang, November 3, 2003).[6] In this model, the first phase was office automatization, introduced as early as the end of the 1980s, when "Party and Government on the central and local level started to develop the process of office automatization" (*bangong zidong hua gongcheng*) (ibid.). The second phase began with the announcement of the "Three Golden Projects" (*san jin gongcheng*) in 1993, which were described as "laying the foundation for informatization."

The "government online project" (*zhengfu shangwang gongcheng*) was presented as the third phase (ibid.).

Other authors wrote of a four-phase process: "publicization" (*gong-zhonghua*) of government information; "pre-e-governance" (*zhun dianzi zhengwu*); "local e-government" (*quyu dianzi zhengfu*) and, finally, unified (national) e-government, also called "Great Net Government" (*dawangluo zhengfu*) (Fortuneage, September 28, 2002). Obviously, e-government was seen as a central tool within an all-inclusive e-policy system, which also included the attempts of local and provincial governments to establish a broad-based e-government system.

Since the dawning of the new millennium, the concept of e-government (*dianzi zhengfu*) has gradually expanded to e-governance (*dianzi zhengwu*). The definitions of e-government and e-governance as given by international organizations and the Chinese government differ widely. According to UNESCO (2005) "e-governance" refers to "the process by which society steers itself:"

> In this process, the interactions among the State, Private Enterprise and Civil Society are being increasingly conditioned and modified through the influence of information and communication technologies (ICTs), constituting the phenomenon of e-Governance [. . .] e-Governance is the public sector's use of information and communication technologies with the aim of improving information and service delivery, encouraging citizen participation in the decision-making process and making government more accountable, transparent and effective.
>
> (ibid.)

The Chinese definition of e-governance (*dianzi zhengwu*) focuses specifically on the aspect of government and disregards civil society, NGOs and professional associations:

> E-governance is the system solution scenario whereby the release of government information, and the government functions of management, services and communication are transferred to the Internet against a background of national economy and societal informatization in order to increase the efficiency of the handling of affairs by the government and to improve decision-making, investments and the environment. [. . .] E-governance refers to an applied information system designed to fulfill the demands of concrete affairs, operation and matters of government at every level by implementing information technology.
>
> (Zhongguo dianzi zhengwu wang, February 5, 2005)

In addition, the internal aspect of e-government/e-governance, that is, the optimization of internal processes within government and administration is also emphasized:

E-governance also offers the opportunity to revitalize the two-way flow of government management; it establishes and optimizes the government internal management system, the support system for decision-making, and the automatization system for handling office affairs; it offers solid technological support [. . .] in order to enhance the handling of governmental information and the quality of service.

(ibid.)

It is further pointed out that many Chinese use *dianzi zhengwu* to translate the term "e-government" and thus the difference between these two expressions remains unclear (ibid.).

E-government and e-governance have also been linked with the launch of another project in 1998: the "Governmental Restructuring Plan" (*1998 nian guowuyuan jigou gaige fang'an* (*People's Daily*, Online, October 10, 2000, *Renmin Wang* March 6 2003)). As a result of this, e-government has become a central tool for the modernization of the Chinese administration at every level and the role of government has changed in the newly established market economy (ibid.). The government is no longer seen as being in charge of "handling everything," but as "a supervisor or guide who controls the macro-economy through legal and economic means" (ibid.). Another major feature of the restructuring process has been "a reduction in the over-abundance of departments and staff," which has often translated into younger, more professionally trained staff being hired and older, computer-illiterate employees being laid off, a point that was mentioned several times during the interviews carried out at the People's Government Office in Nanhai City in Spring 2002.

The Chinese government has been promoting e-government since the year 1998. Even when discussing e-government at provincial and local level, it should be kept in mind that e-government has been promoted by the central state as an important tool for providing better services for its citizens and also as a means of gaining "technical legitimacy":

Technical legitimacy aims to promote economic growth in order to improve living standards or to maintain an acceptable living standard for the majority of citizens. In modern times, the material aspect of social prosperity is considered to be so important that even in a democratic country, the populace takes it for granted that the political elite should be judged not only on their political performance, i.e. in terms of their moral legitimacy, but also in terms of their technical legitimacy. A politically stable system cannot endure in the long run if it does not pay sufficient attention to its technical legitimacy. In a democratic system, periodic elections act as a form of guarantee, keeping the two types of legitimacy in equilibrium.

(Zhang 2002, see also Zhang 2001)

E-government was introduced with the aim of reforming the administrative structure and strengthening the economic transformation: "The very intention of the project lies not just in developing e-government itself, but rather in pushing e-commerce to the forefront and encouraging entrepreneurs and inhabitants to go online" (Zhang 2002).

At the end of 1998, it was decided that in addition to the central agencies and ministries, the state agencies at provincial level and even at local level would eventually be online (ibid.). There were, however, no clear criteria to regulate the ways in which local agencies should go online, the kinds of services that should be offered, nor what the relationship should be between front-office and back-office applications.[7]

E-government at local level

In order to examine the gap between "theory and practice," a closer look was taken at the implementation of e-government at micro-level. One of the basic assumptions before the research was carried out – and which was also confirmed in interviews with local academics and government officials – was that although the central government has been trying to keep firm control of the provinces in general and has issued some very detailed instructions related to e-government, localized elements of e-government do exist. Its implementation is very much dependent on regional particularities, ranging from the personnel in charge to the economic situation, to the embeddedness of the region within a wider trading network, to the proximity of universities, and e-readiness in general. Many provinces, particularly the economically well-developed provinces in Southern China, could be regarded (and regard themselves) more as "federal states within a state" and their implementation of a localized version of e-government could thus possibly differ from the central plan or at least interpret the central plan according to local need, which is to say that localization has taken place.[8]

The following questions formed the basis of the research:

- Is there a coherent e-government strategy at local level and what are the characteristics of an e-government strategy at provincial level? What is the relationship between the local, provincial and central levels of government in implementing e-government and how is e-government strategy implemented in practice?
- How is the population (the user/citizen/customer) involved? Are there any special programs to improve e-literacy? Is accessibility a problem? Is there a special program for the disabled? Are there special e-government training sessions? Are there "citizen service centers" and how do they function? What are the features of the regional education system?
- How are websites for local e-government organized/constructed, which elements dominate local e-government sites and what conclusions

may be drawn from this for an evaluation of the aims of Chinese e-government?

- What is the relationship between "back office" and "front office"?
- Will e-government help to overcome *guanxi*-structures (nepotism) and if so, how? Have local governments been successful in overcoming the digital divide or is e-government intensifying the general division between developed and undeveloped regions? Is there any kind of evaluation system? If so, how does it work?

The research: local e-government at provincial and district level

With regard to "e-government" (*dianzi zhengfu*) and "e-governance" (*dianzi zhengwu*), a great deal of research has focused on the two cities of Beijing and Shanghai, where great advances have been made in the use of information technology and informatization, but it could be argued that these cities are very special cases and therefore do not provide appropriate examples of the development in China as a whole (*Renmin Wang*, December 26, 2001). Beijing is very much influenced by the decision-making of the central government and illustrates the ways in which the central plan has been implemented rather than how regional development has unfolded. The digital city of Zhongguancun (a district of Beijing), in particular, is regarded as a highly prestigious project that is being developed in connection with Beijing hosting the Olympic Games in 2008 (Hachigian *et al.* 2001, see also the official website of Zhongguancun, http://www.zhongguancun.com.cn). In official statistics, Beijing and Shanghai as municipalities are treated in a similar way to the other provinces and autonomous regions, despite the fact that they largely consist of urban areas that offer ready support for the implementation of informatization strategies.

For the purposes of analyzing local e-government, attention was focused on Fujian as a rather typical example of the more developed Chinese provinces, where the less advanced infrastructure in rural areas could prove to be a hindrance to efficient and rapid informatization. Another obstacle for the larger provinces is the unequal distribution of educational qualifications among city dwellers and those in rural areas.

Fujian is a heterogeneous province with developed coastal regions, but it also has a vast hinterland and high mountains. Fujian also shows how the spill over effects can lead to a bridging of the digital divide.[9] It is a relatively wealthy province in the South of China with a fairly well-developed e-infrastructure and higher than average e-readiness. Although Guangdong is similar to Fujian in some respects, it is not as representative of the heterogeneous South-Eastern provinces, where urban areas with a high population density and an above-average income can be found alongside regions with a less developed infrastructure and an under-average income. There are some under-developed regions in Guangdong but, on the whole, it could be argued that the province is less heterogeneous and that, in particular, its proximity to Hong Kong, and the special zone of Shenzhen as a "Chinese copy of Hong Kong," are signs that Guangdong is an atypical example of the South-East provinces. On the other hand, neither of the two provinces belongs to the "forerunners," such as Beijing, which, as the national capital, was much more dependent on national decisions when establishing e-government. Despite the fact that Guangdong's examples of e-government (Shenzhen, Foshan, Nanhai, Guangzhou) are better known, the province of Fujian has also created its own digital cities as model projects (Zeng 2001: 102–10). In addition, China's first "B2G (business-to-government) website" was established in Xiamen prior to the implementation of the central Government Online project, whereby government purchases began to be processed online (Lovelock and Ure 2002).

Approaches used in the research

The research combines two different approaches: first, interviews with local academics in the two provinces and with officials in charge of e-government linked with the analysis of published material, and second, a content analysis of selected e-government websites combined with an analysis of selected articles on e-government as found in the Chinese state-owned media.[10]

The content analysis covers those local government agency websites that are aimed directly at a more general audience, that is, citizens and customers, including enterprises seen as potential investors, and small local companies, but not other government agencies. This means, the back-office processes could not be taken into consideration because, for obvious reasons, a government is not usually willing to dispense much information on this subject. From an analysis of the front-office, however, conclusions can be drawn as to the effectiveness of these websites. Since many different kinds of websites (depending on the government agency in charge) were analyzed, no standardized method such as a questionnaire was used. Certain features were grouped together as "interactive," "informative" and "communicative" elements (Bordewijk and van Kaam 1986)[11] in order to clarify the particular aspects of e-government which were being subjected to examination.

Province-level interviews were carried out in Fujian and in Guangdong in order to obtain a general overview of e-development; staff in charge of implementing e-government at local level were also interviewed. These interviews all took place during March and April 2002. These non-standard interviews were carried out with researchers from local universities in both provinces and government agencies in charge of local e-government. While the academics were interviewed about their opinions on e-government in the particular area, on financial questions, political support, future plans and known hindrances and obstacles, the government agencies were asked to present the specific ideas behind their e-government projects, to place them within the larger context of the local government strategy, and also to give examples of successes and failures.

In the case of Fujian, the "Digital Fujian" (*Shuzi Fujian*) strategy is explained in greater detail; sources, in addition to the interviews, were the official webpages of "Digital Fujian," http://www.szfj.gov.cn and the more informative official website of Fujian, http://www.fuijian.gov.cn.

Digital Fujian

Fujian is a coastal province, ranking in the first third of the more developed regions, which had a population of approximately 34 million in 2002 and 35 million in 2004. The Gross National Product (GNP) of Fujian, in 2004, was approximately RMB 17,218 per capita. Even in 2002, teledensity was already relatively high: there were 6.2 million mobile phones, that is, 18 per 100 persons, and a slightly higher rate of 7.5 million fixed lines, that is, 22 per 100 persons. Over the next two years, there was a dramatic increase in the number of telephones, up to 11.3 million mobile (32.4 percent) and 12.7 million fixed lines (36.3 percent), and one third of the 2.85 million Internet accesses are broadband.[12]

Fujian is made up of a prosperous coastal region with Xiamen designated as a Special Economic Zone (SEZ) and Fuzhou as the province capital.[13] Although Fujian has this prosperous coastal region, much of the province is mountainous and has an under-developed infrastructure. Most of the population is therefore crowded into the small coastal area. Fujian's economy is shaped by small and middle-sized enterprises, with the exception of Xiamen, where there are some multi-national companies. There are two prestigious universities, one in Xiamen and one in Fuzhou; Xiamen University is the better known of the two, but regarding e-government and information technology, Fuzhou university has established a "Fujian Province Spatial Information Center" (*Fujian sheng kongjian xinxi gongcheng yanjiu zhongxin*) which serves as the primary location for training and research into the informatization of Fujian (Interview, Fujian Province Spatial Information Center, February 2002).

In 2001, Fujian decided to implement a province-wide strategy called "digital province" (*shuzi sheng*). A "digital province" refers to various combinations of e-commerce, e-government and e-society (*Renmin Wang*, July 3, 2001a). In order to speed up the whole process of Digital Fujian, a Leading Group for the Construction of Digital Fujian (*"Shuzi Fujian" jianshe lingdao xiaozu*), with more than 30 members led by Chairman Xi Jinping, the province governor of Fujian, was established in 2001. Under the supervision of the Leading Group, an office was established that was responsible for the coordination and involvement of the province information industry. Members of the group included Huang Xiaojing, the vice governor of the province, serving as chairman; Su Zengtian, director of the provincial planning department; Zhuang Songwen, assistant director of the provincial planning department; Shao Yu, deputy head of the provincial information industry department; Huang Guomin, director of the provincial economic information center; Wang Qinmin, Vice President of Fuzhou University, Head of the College of Information Science and Technology (*Fuzhou daxue xinxi keji xueyuan yuanzhang*), and President of the Digital Fujian Expert Committee (*Shuzi Fujian zhuanjia weiyuanhui zhuren*).

In 2001, the People's Government of Fujian published a statement regarding the foundation of this group which was directed to each People's Government Office in the cities, counties, and districts, to every provincial government department, to every county organ (*jigou*), to all large enterprises, and to all institutions of higher education (http://www.szfj.gov.cn/shuoming/index.htm, accessed June 12, 2002).[14] The goals for establishing a Digital Fujian are defined in terms of aiming to "strengthen the national economy" and to "informatize the whole of society" (*Renmin Wang*, July 3, 2001a)·. The entire information technology of the province and all the resources must be used for the realization of a "web-based network of intelligence and knowledge" (*wangluohua zhinenghua xinxi gongxiang*) (ibid.). Digital Fujian was set up according to basic guidelines: the individual areas covered by the project must all conform to the general strategy of "Digital Fujian," that is, a "unified standard with homogeneous unification criteria must be developed to avoid the low level repetition that occurs when a standard is lacking" (ibid.). The project is designed to lead to an increase in informatization development and to give an impetus by playing exemplary roles. The applications used must have a high development potential, and one specific group must be placed in charge of the whole project, regarding management, coordination and fund raising (see the website at http://www.szfj.gov.cn/zheng/gonggao.htm). According to the plans, "Digital Fujian" should have become operational in the entire province by 2005 (*Renmin Wang*, July 3, 2001a), but by January 2005, still only part of Fujian was "online" – see Table 5.1.

The website of Digital Fujian can be found at http://www.szfj.gov.cn; it is interesting to note that until 2001, an English name (http://www.digitalfj.gov.cn) was used, but in 2001 the name was changed to "szfj," an abbreviation for "Shuzi Fujian," that is to say, Pinyin started to be used instead of English.[15]

The concept of a "Digital Fujian" involves a very broad definition of informatization (*xinxihua*). Informatization is generally only defined in terms of a particular infrastructure, that is, ADSL (Asymmetric Digital Subscriber Line), but such a narrow and simplistic interpretation is inadequate when applied to the complex phenomenon of informatization in Fujian. As Wang Qinmin said, "building a perfect ADSL infrastructure without taking the users into account is like building a motorway without cars" (Interview at Fujian Province Spatial Information Center, February

Table 5.1 Cases of "advanced" e-government websites in Fujian (2003–04)

Government and party organizations	
25 departments at provincial level	
Organization Department, Provincial Communist Party Committee of Fujian	Zhonggong Fujian sheng wei zuzhibu
United Front Work Department of the Provincial Communist Party Committee of Fujian	Zhonggong Fujian sheng wei tongyi zhanxian gongzuobu
Provincial Office of the People's Government in Fujian	Fujian sheng renmin zhengfu bangongting
Fujian Provincial Committee of Development and Reform	Fujian sheng fazhan he gaige weiyuanhui
Fujian Provincial Department of Science and Technology	Fujian sheng kexue jishuting
Fujian Provincial Department of Justice	Fujian sheng sifating
Fujian Provincial Office of Finance	Fujian sheng caizheng ting
Fujian Provincial Office of Personnel	Fujian sheng renshi ting
Fujian Provincial Office for Land Resources	Fujian sheng guotu ziyuan ting
Fujian Provincial Office of Construction	Fujian sheng jiansheting
Fujian Provincial Office of Foreign Trade and Economic Cooperation	Fujian sheng duiwai maoyi jingji hezuo ting
Fujian Provincial Statistics Bureau	Fujian sheng tongjiju
Fujian Provincial Price Control Bureau	Fujian sheng wujiaju
Fujian Provincial Administration Office of Industry and Commerce	Fujian sheng gongshang xingzheng guanliju
Fujian Provincial Office of Quality and Technical Supervision	Fujian sheng ziliang jishu jianduju
Fujian Provincial Grain Administration Office	Fujian sheng liangshiju
Fujian Provincial Office of the Chinese People's Political Consultative Conference	Fujian sheng zhengxie bangongting
Spatial Information Research Center, Fujian Province	Fujian sheng kongjian xinxi gongcheng yanjiu zhongxin
Fujian TV	Fujian dianshetai
Fujian Provincial State Administration Office of Taxation	Fujian sheng guojia shuiwuu
Fujian Provincial Meteorological Administration Office	Fujian sheng qixiangju
Fuzhou University	Fuzhou daxue
Industrial and Commercial Bank of China, Fujian Provincial Branch	Zhongguo gongshang yinhang Fujian sheng fenhang
Agricultural Bank of China, Fujian Provincial Branch	Zhongguo nongye yinhang Fujian sheng fenhang
Fujian Expressway Company Limited	Fujian sheng gaosu gong lu you xian zeren gongsi

Table 5.1 (Continued)

Government and party organizations

7 departments at municipal level under Fujian Province

Governance Information Center, City of Xiamen	Xiamen shi zhengwu xinxi zhongxin
Information Center, City of Zhangzhou	Zhangzhou shi xinxi zhongxin
Economic Information Center, City of Quanzhou	Quanzhou shi jingji xinxi zhongxin
Information Center, City of Sanming	Sanming shi xinxi zhongxin
Information Center, City of Putian	Putian shi xinxi zhongxin
Economic Information Center, City of Nanping	Nanping shi jingji xinxi zhongxin
Economic Information Center, City of Longyan	Longyan shi jingji xinxi zhongxin

13 departments at county (xian) (town shi/district qu) level

People's Government Bureau, Lianjiang County	Lianjiang xian renmin zhengfu bangongshi
Bureau of the Leading Group for Informatization at Longwen District, City of Zhangzhou	Zhangzhou shi Longwen qu xinxihua jianshe lingdao xiaozu bangongshi
Governance Information Net Administration Center, Zhangpu County	Zhangpu xian zhengwu xinxi wangluo guanli zhongxin
Information Net Administration Center, Changtai County	Changtai xian xinxi wangluo guanli zhongxin
E-governance Net Administration Center, City of Jinjiang	Jinjiang shi dianzi zhengwu wangluo guanli zhongxin
Net Control Center of Yong'an City	Yong'an shi wangkong zhongxin
Governance Information Center, Taining County	Taining xian zhengwu xinxi zhongxin
Bureau of the People's Government of Xianyou County	Xianyou xian renmin zhengfu bangongshi
Information Center, Hanjiang District, City of Putian	Putian shi Hanjiang qu xinxi zhongxin
People's Government Bureau, City of Shaowu	Shaowu shi renmin zhengfu bangong shi
Digital Wuyi Information Center, City of Wuyishan	Wuyishan shi shuzi Wuyi xinxi zhongxin
People's Government Bureau, City of Jianyang	Jianyang shi renmin zhengfu bangongshi
Information Center of the Xinluo District, City of Longyan	Longyan shi Xinluo qu xinxi zhongxin

Source: Author's own compilation based on: Fujian sheng shuzi Fujian 2005.

2002). In more detail, he explained that the creation of a broadband ADSL infrastructure is only the first stage in establishing a "digital province." Important features to be included are human resources, with reference to both the training of personnel within universities and the training of staff in government agencies and companies. Another important aspect is the involvement of the "man on the street," who needs to become accustomed to the new informatization strategy and recognize the potential benefits it offers.

He also pointed out that a glance at the wide-ranging plans and standardized methods of Europe shows quite clearly that China is still lagging behind, even if the more developed provinces of Guangdong and Fujian are taken into account. This is not with reference to the building of an infrastructure, which is easier in China where there are fewer regulations than in Europe. The problem in China is how to develop a general strategy for the use of informatization for social and political development. It is important to distinguish between an infrastructure in a narrow sense, that is, ADSL for the government and individually used PCs, and a broad informatization infrastructure. The comprehensive measures taken by European Online, http://europa.eu.int/, could serve as a suitable model for China, since these take into consideration the differences and particularities of European regions. Such an approach would be essential in China, where enormous differences exist not only between the provinces, but also within them. Up to now, the central problem for China's informatization Policy has been the lack of a standard. In more detail, the following points are seen as crucial for China and for Fujian Province in particular: the need to clarify the data policy, the involvement of the media and the unification of laws and regulations. With regard to the construction of a "digital province," Fujian (and a number of other coastal provinces) could be described as being at the forefront of developments. The most important issue that Digital Fujian has to deal with – according to Wang Qinmin – is the compiling of the data resources. Digital Fujian is a very special project, since it involves cooperation between many different administration units and departments; the general concept, however, is still in a preparatory phase and has not yet been satisfactorily completed.

The plan is to start with the "digital province" (*shuzi sheng*), to move on to the "digital city" (*shuzi shi*), then to the "digital county" (*shuzi xian*) and finally to establish the "digital district" (*shuzi qu*) (see Figure 5.1). One should consider "Digital Fujian" more in terms of a national plan than a provincial project. The problem is that for many people involved in creating a "Digital Province," it is easier to copy the models of other provinces and to ignore regional particularities.

In Fujian, attributing responsibility has become much clearer, as the involvement of the deputy provincial governor, Huang Xiaojing, shows. During the interviews at Fujian Province Spatial Information Center, it became obvious that persons and inter-personal relationships are still of

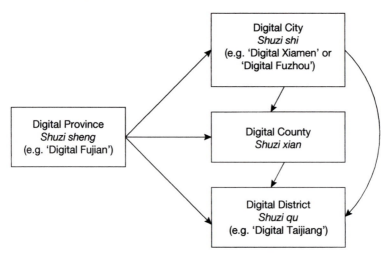

Figure 5.1 Structure of Digital Fujian (author's creation)

much greater importance in China than any structure ordered by law and the formal involvement of high-ranking officials is necessary in wide-ranging plans for there to be any chance of success in establishing a "digital province". This is illustrated by the way in which economic reforms were carried out by the former leader, Deng Xiaoping. Regarding financial resources, Fujian is second only to Guangdong. The first steps toward better basic training and personnel training have been introduced in Fujian, and there is excellent cooperation with scholars from Beijing and also with international scholars. One of the most important issues for setting up a digital province is the involvement of the "ordinary people" (*lao baixing*), who have to recognize the importance of a "Digital Fujian." One step towards achieving this goal is establishing citizen service centers (*shimin fuwu zhongxin*) – as, for example, in Taijiang.

The Fujian provincial government also developed plans for other cities, such as Quanzhou, but during interviews in February 2002 with experts at Xiamen University, Quanzhou was described as a place where a very ambitious project was initiated but finally failed for several reasons, such as poorly trained personnel and lack of support after the initial phase (see also *Renmin Wang*, August 2, 2000). This analysis of the underlying reasons for the failure of the project finds confirmation in a more global context:

> Even in areas where access to technological infrastructure is nearly ubiquitous, there are still marginalized groups who are unable to make use of information and communication technologies because they are not "e-literate." E-government programs will have to take special steps to include people who are not e-literate.
>
> (Center for Democracy and Technology and infoDev 2002: 13)

Digital Taijiang

Taijiang District is part of Fuzhou City, the capital of Fujian Province. It is a well-known commercial area, and has a history going back more than 2,000 years as a trading port. More than 70 percent of the GNP derives from trade; it is an area without an agricultural industry and with only a very limited manufacturing industry. It has a population of about 300,000, not including the "floating people" (*liudong renkou*), e.g. inhabitants without legal registration (*hukou*) who are estimated at more than 150,000. Taijiang covers an area of about 18 sq km, and has, therefore, a very high population density (http://www.taijiang.gov.cn, accessed May 2, 2002).[16]

Taijiang has a well-known reputation for trading in agricultural and subsidiary products in Fujian Province. The government of Fujian intends to establish Taijiang as the commercial center for the whole province. In 1999 alone, the sum of RMB 469 million was invested in the construction of the commercial center, together with the building of a science park (Ta'xi-Park) (see http://www.taijiang.gov.cn/tjgk.htm, accessed May 5, 2002).

The e-government concept in Taijiang is often described as a "government supermarket" (*zhengfu chaoshi*), a newly coined expression that describes a citizen service center, where every branch of the local government is brought together in one place.[17] Its function is to "improve quality in order to serve the people" (*Renmin Wang*, July 3, 2001b, see also *Renmin Wang*, July 24, 2002). It is a model project and has thus been the subject of a nation-wide media report.

In 2001, for the first time, the People's Government of Taijiang opened a citizen service center, which offered an all-in-one center for administrative functions such as the registration of residents (*hukou*), applications for identity cards and passports and the payment of local taxes. Police, registry office and planning office services were also made available at this center. The setting up of this service center was accompanied by the Digital Taijiang project, which consisted of four basic components: "e-society" (*dianzi shequ*), "e-government" (*dianzi zhengfu*), "e-commerce" (*dianzi shangwu*) and "e-family" (*dianzi jiating*). E-society refers to the infrastructure, the administration of the net, "the administration of the fee-oriented service net" (*shequ zengzhi [fufei] fuwu xinxi*) and to "e-governance news" (*zhengwu deng zonghe xinxi*). E-government refers to an "online administration service" (*wangshang gongzhong xingzheng fuwu xitong*), to an "automated internal information system" (*jiguan neibu bangong zidonghua xitong*), the "administration system of the city government" (*shizheng guanli xitong*) and an "administration system for social welfare" (*shehui zhi'an zonghe guanli xitong*). E-commerce refers to an "online virtual market" (*wangshang xuni shichang*), to the project "enterprises online" (*qiye shangwang gongcheng*), to an "online pay- and banking system" (*wangshang zhifu xitong, wangshang yinhang*) and to a "digital signature system" (*wangshang zonghe xinyong renzheng xitong*). E-family refers to the "digitalization of the family" (*jiating shuzihua*), "netization" (*wangluohua*) and "intelligentization" (*zhinenghua*). Most of the above-mentioned services are available via the World Wide Web, but the three internal features of e-government "the automated internal information system," "the administration system of the city government" (*shizheng guanli xitong*) and "the administration system for social welfare" are only available via Intranet.[18]

The portal, umbrella-like website of Taijiang, www.taijiang.gov.cn, is maintained by the People's Government of Taijiang (Government of Taijiang) which bears full responsibility for the project. The web portal covers different sectors such as administration, economic development and communication services.

Administration is composed of three features: "New government business of Taijiang" (*xin Taijiang zhengwu*), "Official publications of Taijiang" (*banbu Taijiang qu ji ban*) and "How to deal with the authorities" (*ban shi zhinan*).

Economic development (*jingji dongtai*) includes a link to the integrated but separately managed commercial net, http://www.86market.com. Communication services cover two main links, one to "Taijiang forum" (*Taijiang luntan*) and one that is called "Dialog with the people" (*yu min duihua*). Another interesting feature of Taijiang's e-strategy is the combining of e-government and e-governance with e-commerce and e-entertainment. E-entertainment has not yet been fully implemented, but this is envisioned as part of the next phase in conjunction with the introduction of e-learning, as was mentioned several times during the interviews.

The Taijiang Forum (*Taijiang qu zhengfu luntan*), http://www.taijiang. gov.cn/tjilt/sub.asp, offers discussions on various topics, ranging from the last soccer results, to the development of Taijiang and problems concerning residents' rights (*hukou*). Another aspect of direct communication is the opportunity offered to communicate with the official in charge of the district "Would you like to talk to the district leader?" (*Ni xiang he quzhang duihua ma?*). Users are, however, warned to abide by the legal regulations of the PRC: "Here you may write in Chinese or in English. But keep this in mind: do not say anything which violates the present laws of the PRC!" http://www.taijiang.gov.cn/tjchat/ltshi.htm (accessed July 5, 2002). It is not necessary to register for this chat, in contrast to the chats offered by the big portals such as *Netease* or *Sohu*.[19]

"Information" does not play an important role; most items on the website are found under "consultation" and "registration." The participative aspect is of minor importance, but there are some items relating to "conversation" (direct e-mail and forum). The citizen service center is often described using the old slogan "Serving the People" (*wei renmin fuwu*). While, however, during the rule of Mao Zedong, the expression *renmin* ("the people") referred to the "masses" (*dazhong*) in a Communist sense, today the expression *renmin* ("the people") refers to "citizens" (*shimin*), or, to be more precise, to "consumers of government products" (*xiaofeizhe*) (see CMS 2002). The greater part of the website is devoted to "How to deal with the authorities" (*banshi zhinan*). It offers the opportunity to obtain information easily from several administration units, such as the civil administration office (*minzhengju*), the birth control office (*jishengju*), the housing office (*fangguanju*), the education office (*jiaoyuju*), the environmental office (*huanjingju*), the labor office (*laodongju*), the justice office (*sifaju*) and the public health office (*weishengju*). The service orientation becomes obvious when examining, for example, the websites of the civil administration office. The services offered include detailed information on marriage registration, forms for marriages involving citizens of Hong Kong or Macao, information on marriage involving foreign Chinese peoples, information on divorce by mutual consent, information on divorce contested by one party, regulations concerning adoption, information on requirements that need to be fulfilled in order to apply for basic welfare benefits, and an introduction to senior citizen accommodation in Taijiang. In addition, contact addresses are provided for each of the 161 work units in the district.

Extensive descriptions of business and shopping opportunities can be found on the "district service pages" (*shequ fuwu*). There are, however, few illustrations (http://www.taijiang.gov.cn/sqfw/streetyz1.htm), and the webpages resemble a Yellow Pages directory with the names of contact persons and their telephone numbers. It is not clear who is responsible for updating the pages or how often this is carried out. The website works more like an "annotated telephone-directory" than an interactive website. There are no downloadable forms or interactive forms so that citizens still have to consult the local authorities in person.

All the authorities, however, are now located in one place, and citizens can find out via the Internet how, for example, to apply for social welfare or for a state-subsidized apartment. The service orientation is illustrated on the "family planning page" by the slogan "taking mankind as the basis for serving the family" (*yi ren wei ben, fuwu jiating*).

One frequent criticism of the government online project (*zhengfu shang wang gongcheng*) in general, is that the websites lack "real" and up-to-date content ("*liang xiang*") (*Renmin Wang*, March 17, 2000). The e-government service pages are too bureaucratic, with many legal regulations given in detail. The multi-media opportunities offered by the World Wide Web are not fully exploited. One example of this is found on the website of the "Fujian Province Prevention and Control Center for Skin Diseases and Venereal Diseases" (http://www.taijiang.gov.cn/bszn/weis. htm, accessed July 25, 2002). In addition to information on contact addresses (telephone numbers, but not e-mail addresses), there is an extended piece of text containing information on the history of the center, the employees, and the different diseases treated at the hospital. The language of the text is complex and there is wide use of specialist terms.

There is an almost complete lack of interactive features: no pictures or videos, no e-mail addresses, no forms, no chats or forums; no elements of "communication" or "registration" are available, and only a simple form of consultation is provided.

In contrast to most other government agencies, the local tax office website (*dishuiju*) (http://www.taijiang.gov.cn/bszn/dis.htm, accessed November 7, 2002, and Interview at the local tax office in February 2002) is the only website that has a few interactive features and offers transaction opportunities. On this website, the taxpayer can find a detailed description of the documents required to open a "local tax account" (business license, ID card); after opening the account at the citizen service center, further transactions can be carried out online.

Conclusion: "To serve the people?"

The Communist Party has been seeking to legitimize its rule by applying the concept of good governance, which is based less on participative and democratic elements than on a higher degree of efficiency and a strong service-attitude. This service-attitude is often referred to under the slogan "to serve the people" (*wei renmin fuwu*) which was one of the most widely used slogans during the Mao era. This slogan has been revitalized and is now used to describe the modern service-attitude of the government within the previously mentioned government restructuring process: "The government is the public servant, the people are the master" (*zhengfu shi gongpu, renmin shi zhuren*) (Yang Liangmin 2001).

An evaluation of the introduction and use of e-government in one local community, in Taijiang, in the province of Fujian, has shown how central, provincial and local government have worked together with local enterprises and other groups to establish local e-government. Although it might be difficult to draw general conclusions regarding the effectiveness of e-government in other parts of China from so few examples, it could be argued that many obstacles that do not become apparent through analyzing central strategies for e-government can be illustrated much more clearly from a micro-perspective. This approach, however, to be fully effective, requires examination of a more typical example of Chinese e-government, such as Taijiang, rather than a well-known "model" of a "digital city" such as Nanhai in Southern Guangdong (Xu 2002, Yang and Sheng 2002, Hachigian and Wu 2003: 80, China Internet Information Center, March 10, 2003).

It could also be argued that e-government has become the central feature of Chinese e-policy because the government agencies are, in this case, "by definition" in control of the content, and e-government is regarded as a central tool for the desired governmental reform. In addition, e-government is regarded by the Party as an efficient means of overcoming the digital divide even at provincial or local level. Nonetheless, gaps and inconsistencies can be detected between the state government's wide-ranging plans and strategic considerations for e-government on the one hand, and the practical implementation of e-government on the other, so that some e-government goals may only be partially achieved and, in some cases, the introduction of e-government might even be counterproductive to the publicly announced goals of the Chinese government.[20]

Fujian has, however, been able to establish a broad e-government system and this can be regarded as an important step, since many problems that arise in implementing a functioning e-government have to do with "archaic laws, old regulatory regimes, overlapping and conflicting authorities" which "can all greatly complicate or altogether halt a project" (Center for Democracy and Technology and infoDev 2002: 13).

Local e-government is an attempt by the Chinese government to increase efficiency and to offer citizens better service with the aim of strengthening technical legitimacy. Good governance, therefore, serves to strengthen the legitimacy of the Party state. This will be achieved by offering local all-inclusive web portals with a varied content (hosted by local governments) which will serve as a tool for the creation of a "safe sandbox" (Hartford 2001) for Chinese citizens so that they remain within the framework of "legal sites" provided by the government or other state-approved organizations.[21] Different social groups, such as publishers and local enterprise associations, are integrated within e-government so that for the population of certain areas it is unnecessary to venture outside the framework offered by local government. It has become obvious that it is less the censorship of foreign pages (frequently mentioned in Western/US media) than the "positive content" of more localized websites which allows the Party and the government to retain control of the media content. Local government has been able to keep control of the content, and the offer of a "positive content" in the Chinese language has shown itself to be much more effective than the blocking of content perceived as harmful.[22] This phenomenon is coherent with the development of Chinese media in general, which, although it is becoming more profit-oriented, still offers a content that does not undermine the legitimacy of the CCP (Lynch 1999, Fischer 2001, Goh 2003).

Today, the local government portals are intended to serve as a primary source for the spread of local information to a wider audience and it is characteristic of local e-government strategy that having a service orientation is widely understood as offering information to the public. E-government is seen as an effective tool for overcoming *guanxi*-structures and fighting corruption, because public information is made more easily accessible and transactions become more transparent. These views were expressed during the interviews by mostly young technocrats who seemed to be convinced that the successful implementation of e-government (in particular regarding transactions) would help to overcome the *guanxi*-system and thus the importance of inter-personal relationships.

This is essential since *guanxi*, the Chinese term for interpersonal relations, has been the central element of Chinese culture and society since Confucian times. Bell and Avenarius (1999: 5) argue that the "traditional Chinese social system was not defined in terms of individuals but in terms of dyadic ties between individuals, reflecting the teachings of Confucius." These *guanxi*-relationships still form the basis of many Chinese societies, but in a market-oriented society, it becomes more difficult to differentiate between *guanxi*, nepotism and bribery, so that *guanxi*-relationships are now frequently the target of criticism. Personal relationships are also of much greater importance in rural areas, where the old *danwei* structures can still be found; in the urban areas, however, a new middle class has emerged that often finds employment with private and foreign companies. This middle class expects the local government to act as a "service center" for "citizens" (*shimin*) and not as a ruler of the "people" (*renmin*). The case of Taijiang shows that "normal citizens" are involved in the process. Citizen service centers help to encourage people to use the new technology, and visits for administration purposes can be combined with a form of computer training.

The case of Taijiang demonstrates the following: it seems that a coherent e-government strategy could be developed at local level if the administration and local e-government were committed to making these changes. Economic considerations play an important role; Taijiang wishes to attract foreign customers and investors and trade is one of the most important features of Digital Taijiang.

The provincial level (Digital Fujian) works as the basis for establishing digital cities and e-governments. As was emphasized in the interviews, the personal involvement of high-ranking cadres is of the highest importance. The funding of e-government could become a problem after the initial phase. Many programs have been launched at provincial level to support cities and counties in establishing e-government, but after the first phase, when money and specialists are provided from outside, the web pages are often not updated. There are many reasons for this: a lack of specialists within the local administration, the relatively low income of citizens in remote areas, which means a proportionally low rate of PC and Internet users, and limited Internet literacy. In addition, at local level, there is a higher rate of "old cadres," that is, a lower number of "young urban professionals."

The successful implementation of e-government depends on the e-readiness of the population; even in highly developed regions such as Fujian, it is difficult (if not impossible) to narrow the digital divide by means of e-government. Other measures to improve education and infrastructure must be implemented during the initial phase and e-government can only be employed during a secondary phase. Wealthy regions such as Taijiang, which do not have a developed IT industry, but a rather "old fashioned" textile or commercial economy, can use e-government and government-sponsored e-commerce to attract new customers and improve the "old economy."

E-government as an all-in-one shop (or "government supermarket," as it is called) has many advantages both for the citizens and for the government administration as well. The fact that interactive elements are often lacking might be counterproductive to the idea of involving many "normal citizens," so that the information now available on the websites (and presented in a rather bureaucratic style) is more suitable for smaller companies or other government units than for the "normal citizens."

In China, e-government often has to be seen in conjunction with governmental reform: at local level, even in the "model cities," the possibilities and opportunities offered by the new technology and the high rate of ADSL infrastructure in the new housing areas have not yet been fully implemented, and to achieve this, there is a need to drive forward governmental reform. The Chinese government hopes that e-government will serve as an efficient tool for much wider governmental reforms, which are intended to "modernize" the country by using fewer, but better-trained personnel, and by overcoming *guanxi*-structures.

The outsourcing of services, although possible now, is still blocked by the old personnel within the administration and there is an ongoing power struggle between the old bureaucrats and young urban professionals (technocrats), even if – pro forma – the latter are supported by high-ranking cadres at central and provincial level.

A look at the situation two years after the field research was concluded, reveals that the wide-ranging plans have only been partially fulfilled and many of the problems remain; for example, the digital divide, websites without updated content and interactive features. A study of the State Council Informatization Office showed that only 5.2 percent of China's government websites are used frequently; this study reported furthermore that "nearly half of the 11,764 sites are simply one-way mirrors [. . .] and more interaction is badly needed" (*China Daily*, April 5, 2004). In January 2005, the Leading Group for the Construction of Digital Fujian named several administrative units as "advanced units"; in other words, not all the ambitious plans have been carried out, and the quality of e-government still varies considerably.

As a result of adopting the term e-governance and attributing a very narrow definition focused on government alone, insufficient attention has been given to the much wider implications of e-governance, that is, the inclusion of business, commerce and civil society has been disregarded. It is thus obvious that the Chinese government at different levels, despite a few references to e-participation and e-democracy, has still not fully exploited the opportunities offered by the new information and communication technologies.

Notes

1 In 1992 Deng Xiaoping went on his famous "southern tour" to promote the resumption of the reform and opening policy which had come to a standstill after the suppression of the large-scale protests in 1989 at Beijing's Tiananmen Square.

2 The central government's enthusiastic support for e-government and the use of the new communication technologies for promoting economic growth and administrative reforms can be identified in the "Government Online Project" (GOP) three-stage initiative: stage one focused on connecting selected government offices and agencies to the Internet; stage two focused on having government offices and agencies move their information systems into – more or less compatible – electronic form; and stage three aimed at government offices and agencies becoming paperless (Lovelock and Ure 2002). Since the formal launch of the Government Online Project, http://www.gov.cn, on January 22, 1999, the provision of basic e-government features on local government websites has more and more frequently been combined with several other features such as e-commerce, e-society, e-entertainment and e-news.

3 The ranking of e-government has been attempted several times, but the results differ widely: "The World Markets Research Center," http://www.worldmarket-sanalysis.com/e_gov_report.html, lists as "Top Ten" for 2001: US, Taiwan, Australia, Canada, UK, Ireland, Israel, Singapore, Germany and Finland; the methodology used, however, was questioned by Di Maio and Kreizman (2001). UNPAN, for example, saw Singapore as ranking third, http://www.unpan.org/e-government/global%20leaders%20index.htm (Taiwan, ranked number three by the World Markets Research, was not included as it is not recognized by the UN). In 2004, the United Nations published the *Global E-government Readiness Report 2004: Towards Access for Opportunity*, which also dealt with the Chinese situation. This report distinguished between service orientation such as "government service portals and/or one-stop-shops" and "e-participation" (United Nations 2004: x). This report focused on the Access-for-Opportunity model which:

> maintains that physical access to ICT is only the first step towards building real access which leads to opportunity. Access must be blended with relevant and culturally appropriate content for onward transmuting into knowledge. The blended knowledge is processed and utilized to create opportunity for economic and social empowerment.
>
> (United Nations 2004: xi)

4 infoDev: The Information for Development Program consists of an international consortium of official bilateral and multilateral development agencies and other key partners, facilitated by an expert Secretariat housed at the World Bank. Its mission is:

> to help developing countries and their partners in the international community use information and communication technologies (ICT) effectively and strategically as tools to combat poverty, promote sustainable economic growth, and empower individuals and communities to participate more fully and creatively in their societies and economies.

See also the website of infoDev at http://www.infodev.org/section/aboutus (accessed March 3, 2005).

5 Meyers and Ruge (2002) also claimed that e-government and the Internet itself would "encourage democracy and challenge authoritarian regimes"; see also, Hacker and van Dijk 2000, Hague and Loader 1999, Norris 2001, Kaiser 2001.

6 The term "e-governmentization" (*dianzi zhengfu hua*) is frequently used in China; this is also true of the term "informatization" (*xinxihua*), which is used in China, even in its English translation, more than in English-speaking countries.

7 There are several definitions of "front vs. back office:" basically "front office" is associated with offering direct contact to citizens, for example, a German "citizens' office" (*Bürgerbüro*), a "One Stop Shop" (in the case of Taijiang, the "Government supermarket" (*zhengfu chaoshi*), and the related websites, while "back office" is related to the part of e-government which does not offer direct contact to citizens (see Lenk and Klee-Kruse 2000: 83f, see also Off 2004.).

8 Interview with Wang Qinmin, Principal of Fuzhou University, February 2002.

9 For a detailed debate on digital divide in China, see Giese 2003.

10 More specifically, interviews were conducted with the following researchers: Prof. Wang Qinmin from the Spatial Information Center at Fuzhou University; Prof. Luo Shisheng, Department of Information & Systems Management, Zhongshan University, Guangzhou; Prof. Xie Kang, Department of Business Management, School of Business, Zhongshan University; Prof. Xiao Xiaofeng, School of Business, Zhongshan University, Research Center for New Economy; Prof. Li Wenpu, Xiamen University; Prof. Zhuo Yue, Xiamen University. In Fujian, government agencies were visited in Fuzhou and in Xiamen; in Guangdong, government agencies were visited in Guangzhou and in Nanhai; these were, for example, the Guangdong Province Information Center; the Xiamen Government Website Administration Center; the Xiamen Economic Information Center; the Guangzhou Informatization Center Leading Group; the Guangzhou Informatization Center; the Office for Science, Technology and Informatization, Nanhai; the Office of People's Government of Nanhai City; the Nanhai City Administration Service Center; the Digital Taijiang – Citizen Service Center; the Xiamen Fine Network Engineering Co. Ltd; the Local Taxation Bureau of Xiamen; Guangdong Nanfang Technical Innovation Center; Nanhai City, Xijiao District, Local government of the "Mountain and Tourist District."

11 With regard to the content analysis of websites, the model developed by Bordewijk and van Kaam in the 1990s is used. The model focuses on the relation between the information center and the recipient: "Information" in this model describes the allocation of information from a center to all members of a group simultaneously. Although found very often in traditional means of communication (everything from a lecture, a presentation or sermon to a radio or television broadcast), it is seldom found on the Internet; the center here is usually not in control of time and place, which are more often determined by the recipient. Exceptions are real-time broadcasting via the Internet or the passive reception of a chat. "Consultation," however, with reference "to all those communication situations in which an individual seeks information in a central place (database, library, book, CD-ROM)" (van Riet 2001) has become a major feature of the Internet and also of e-government. The online publication of laws, rules, and information and news offers the citizen an important tool for obtaining information more appropriate to his needs, and thus enables him to become more independent of government action. "Registration," the opposite of consultation, refers to requests from the center. It receives information from (all) individual(s). "This is applicable to all situations in which data about individuals is stored and processed. Security systems, viewing and listening investigations, registration of participants" (van Riet 2001). In the new media, log files and cookies are used, that is, information is left via visited websites on the visitor's hard disk. Regarding e-government, however, the visible and voluntary part of registration might be viewed as evidence of interactivity and of a communication being sent from the citizen to the information center, for example, registration forms, opinion polls, guest books that offer the opportunity to leave messages, or

subscriptions to newsletters. Although registration might, therefore, refer to the more interactive and participative aspects of e-government, it is also related to questions of control, such as, when participants in BBSs and chats have to register with their actual ID number. The last feature, "conversation," refers to individuals or groups in a communication network who interact directly with each other. There is no need for control by a center, but a conversation with the center is possible. This is applicable to many situations in the Internet such as chats and e-mail. Conversation, therefore, also contains many interactive elements; this kind of conversation might be synchronous (chat) or asynchronous (e-mail), and it could be argued that chat plays an important role for the emergence of a civil society, where citizens are able to discuss controversial topics freely. However, it is also possible to trace the users involved, and a chat moderator might interrupt and disturb a chat if he/she thinks that inappropriate things are being said and users might even be banned from taking part in chats. From the existence of these three features on a website, we can draw conclusions as to which e-government features are of special importance for local Chinese government. In e-government literature, one often finds a strong link between democratic potential and the type of government: a "truly" democratic government should therefore offer mostly interactive features (Jensen 1999).

12 All figures taken from National Bureau of China (Zhonghua Renmin Gongheguo guojia tongju ju), http://www.stats.gov.cn (accessed December 2, 2002 and March 5, 2005).

13 From 1980 onwards, China began to establish special economic zones (SEZ). These rely on attracting foreign capital, are primarily product-oriented and also serve as a forerunner model for the introduction of market economy. The best-known and first-established SEZs are Shenzhen, Zhuhai and Shantou in Guangdong province, Xiamen in Fujian and Hainan province.

14 Information on the current status of local e-government – mostly press releases – can be found on the website of "Digital Fujian," http://www.szfj.gov.cn/ – for example, Fuzhou, Putian, Quanzhou, Xiamen, Zhangzhou, Sanming, Nanping and Ningde.

15 A recent research report on China's e-government (Zhongguo dianzi zhengwu yanjiu baogao 2005) drew similar conclusions. This seems to be a general problem: domain names are often not standardized, the design is described as unprofessional, there is not enough information, there are many implementation problems, a lack of interactivity, the content is not updated and the expectations of users are not fulfilled. This report concluded that the e-governance rate (*dianzi zhengwu du*) of China is only 22.6 percent by analyzing 196 governmental websites and their content, functions, usability and problems.

16 The website of Taijiang was online by the end of 2004. It was not possible, however, to access the site in the first months of 2005.

17 Similar terms such as "Government supermarket" are used in other countries; the expression "One-Stop-eGovernment-Shop" is fairly common, used for example in German government publications in the English language (see, "Federal Government procurement goes online." Online. Available HTTP: http://www. bescha.bund.de/media/files/publikationen/englisch_online.pdf, and also in the State of Idaho (see "Digital Government Day 2003". Online. Available HTTP: http://www2.state.id.us/itrmc/events/digitalgovtday/2003/boothsheet.pdf).

18 The information was obtained during an interview with the administration of Digital Taijiang in February 2002; in addition the website http://www. taijiang.gov.cn was consulted and a leaflet (Shuzi Taijiang: Jianshe lingdao xiaozu bangongshi 2001) was evaluated.

19 On March 20, 2003, a check showed that the interactive communication parts, such as dialogue and forum, had disappeared from the first page; the forum now

seems to have disappeared altogether but the "dialogue" page is still available under the former URL.

20 Although no large-scale survey has been carried out to evaluate the number of local governments actually online, some recent detailed research shows that except for the large conurbations and some more "advanced" provinces, e-government on a provincial and local level is still under-developed. A 2005 survey on 12 districts in the Zhengzhou area in Henan showed that there were 91 websites, but 14 of these did not exist or were inaccessible and 61.5 percent were inadequate, although the local governments in charge had been alerted to the problems six months before the survey had been carried out, see Xi 2005.
21 For a general discussion of China's media policy, see Lynch 1999, Fischer 2001.
22 This filtering of foreign news, Taiwanese websites, religious groups and pornographic sites has often been the focus of political scientists, particularly in the US. For an extensive list of blocked sites, see Zittrain and Edelman 2002. These authors show that the Chinese government claims to be taking action against pornography and gambling, but in reality politically oriented sites are subject to much more blocking: taboo themes, such as Taiwan independence or direct criticism of the Chinese leadership, are two of the main reasons for websites being blocked.

References

Bell, Duran and Avenarius, Christine (1999) "Guanxi, bribery and ideological hegemony." Online. Available HTTP: http://orion.oac.uci.edu/~dbell/bribery.pdf (accessed August 6, 2003).

Bordewijk, L. Jan and van Kaam, Ben (1986) "Towards a new classification of tele-information services," *Inter Media*, 14, pp. 16–21.

Center for Democracy and Technology and infoDev (2002) *The E-Government Handbook for Developing Countries*. Online. Available HTTP: http://www.cdt.org/egov/handbook/2002-11-14egovhandbook.pdf (accessed March 5, 2003).

China Daily (February 13, 2003) "Digital divide between urban and rural China." Online. Available HTPP: http://www.china.org.cn/english/2003/Feb/55753.htm (accessed November 12, 2004).

China Internet Information Center (March 10, 2003) "Nanhai jiangyan: shuzihua zhengfu zaizao" [The experience of Nanhai: reform of a digital government]. Online. Available HTTP: http://www.china.org.cn/chinese/zhuanti/290013.htm (accessed August 5, 2003). Originally in *Jingji guancha bao*, March 10, 2003.

CMS (Zhonghua mishu wang) (2002) "Dianzi zhengwu yu zhengfu shangwang" [E-governance and the government going online]. Online. Available HTTP: http://www.china-mishu.com/p8/p82/p82007.htm (accessed July 2, 2002).

Di Maio, Andrea and Kreizman, Gregg (October 22, 2001) "E-government ranking survey is meaningless." Online. Available HTTP: http://www3.gartner.com/resources/101800/101888/101888.pdf (accessed February 26, 2003).

Dianzi zhengfu yanjiu wang [Research net on e-government] (November 3, 2003) "Fenxi: Zhongguo li dianzi zhengwu chenggong zhi lu hai you duo yuan?" [Analysis: How far away from success is China's e-government?]. Online. Available HTTP: http://e-gov.nsa.gov.cn/search.asp?articleid=49 (accessed February 2, 2005). Originally in *Xin lang keji*, March 14, 2003.

Digital Fujian (February 21, 2001) "Zhongguo xinxihua de jige jiben wenti" [Some basic problems related to the informatization of China]. Online. Available

HTTP: http://www.digitalfj.gov.cn/news/guoneixw/2002221103548.htm (accessed January 10, 2003).

Dittmer, Lowell (2003) "Three visions of Chinese political reform," *Journal of Asian and African Studies*, 38: 4–5, (August), pp. 347–76.

Drake, William J. (2001) "Conference background paper democracy forum 2001, Stockholm 27–29 June 2001." Online. Available HTTP: http://www.idea.int/2001_forum/policy_paper.htm (accessed January 5, 2002).

Fischer, Doris (2001) "Rückzug des Staates aus dem chinesischen Mediensektor? Neue institutionelle Arrangements am Beispiel des Zeitungsmarktes," *Asien*, 80, July, pp. 5–24.

Fortuneage (September 28, 2002) "Zhongguo dianzi zhengwu yanjiu baogao" [Research report on China's e-governance]. Online. Available HTTP: http://www.fortuneage.com/webnews/view.asp?id=200209281005177236 (accessed February 2, 2004). Originally in: *Tianqi keji* April 19, 2004.

Fujian sheng shuzi Fujian jianshe lingdao xiaozu bangongshi [Fujian Province, office of the leading group for the construction of a Digital Fujian] (January 20, 2005) "'Shuzi Fujian' dongtai 2005/2" [Developments in "Digital Fujian" 2005/2]. Online. Available HTTP: http://www.szfj.gov.cn/ReadNews.asp?NewsID=6457 (accessed February 3, 2005).

Giese, Karsten (2003) "Internet growth and the digital divide: implications for spatial development," in Christopher R. Hughes and Gudrun Wacker (eds) *China and the Internet: Politics of the Digital Leap Forward*, London and New York: RoutledgeCurzon, pp. 30–57.

Goh, Sui Noi (2003) "State-run newspapers in for major shake-up," *The Straits Times*, August 8, 2003. Online. Available HTTP: http://straitstimes.asia1.com.sg/asia/story/0,4386,203782,00.html (accessed May 9, 2003).

Goodman, David S. (1998) "Continental China: the social and political consequences of reform and openness," in Eberhard Sandschneider (ed.) *The Study of Modern China*, London: Hurst, pp. 52–78.

Hachigian, Nina (2001) "China's cyber-strategy," *Foreign Affairs*, March/April. Online. Available HTTP: http://www.foreignaffairs.org/20010301faessay4267/nina-hachigian/china-s-cyber-strategy.html (accessed June 11, 2001).

Hachigian, Nina and Wu, Lily (2003) *The Information Revolution in Asia*, Santa Monica, CA: RAND. Online. Available HTTP: http://www.rand.org/publications/MR/MR1719/ (accessed July 17, 2003).

Hachigian, Nina, Lin Ma and Zhu, Rapheal (2001) "Case study of a Beijing pilot project on e-government for the World Bank," May 23, 2001, Santa Monica, CA: RAND. Online. Available HTTP: http://www.rand.org/nsrd/capp/pubs/egovernment.html (accessed June 4, 2002).

Hacker, Kenneth L. and van Dijk, Jan (eds) (2000) *Digital Democracy: Issues of Theory and Practice*, London: Sage.

Hague, Barry N. and Loader, Brian D. (1999) *Digital Democracy: Discourse and Decision Making in the Information Age*, London: Routledge.

Hartford, Kathleen (2001) "Cyberspace with Chinese characteristics." Online. Available HTTP: http://www.pollycyber.com/pubs/ch/home.htm (accessed June 11, 2001).

Harwit, Eric and Clark, Duncan (2001) "Shaping the Internet in China: evolution of political control over network infrastructure and content," *Asian Survey*, 41: 3, pp. 378–408.

International Institute for Democracy and Electoral Assistance (International IDEA) (2001) "Democracy and the information revolution: values, opportunities and threats, democracy forum 2001 report." Online. Available HTTP: http://www.idea.int/2001_forum/Democracy_Forum_2001_Report.pdf (accessed January 5, 2003).

Jensen, Jens F. (1999) "Interactivity: tracking a new concept in media and communication studies," in Paul. A. Mayer (ed.) *Computer Media Communication: A Reader*, Oxford: Oxford University Press, pp. 160–87.

Jupp, Vivienne (2000) "Implementing eGovernment – rhetoric and reality," *Accenture – Insights*, June 21, 2000. Online. Available HTTP: http://www.accenture.com/xdoc/en/industries/government/insightsissue2.pdf (accessed June 3, 2003).

Kaiser, Karl (2001) "Wie das Internet die Weltpolitik verändert," *Deutschland: Forum for Politics, Culture, Economy and Science*, 3, pp. 40–5.

Keji gongguan jihua [Program for tackling science and technology] (August 5, 2003) "Foshan shi Nanhai qu chengwei diyige dianzi zhengfu" [Nanhai district, city of Foshan becomes first e-government]. Online. Available HTTP: http://www.gongguan.most.gov.cn/zxdt/newsitem.asp?ID=1583 (accessed August 5, 2003).

Lenk, Klaus and Klee-Kruse, Gudrun (2000) *Multifunktionale Serviceläden Ein Modellkonzept für die öffentliche Verwaltung im Internet-Zeitalter. Modernisierung des öffentlichen Sektors*, Berlin: edition sigma rainer bohn.

Lovelock, Peter and Ure, John (2002) "E-Government in China," in Zhang Junhua and Martin Woesler (eds) *China's Digital Dream – The Impact of the Internet on the Chinese Society*, Bochum: The University Press Bochum, pp. 149–74.

Lynch, Daniel C. (1999) *After the Propaganda State: Media, Politics and "Thought Work" in Reformed China*, Stanford, CA: Stanford University Press.

Meyers, Neville and Ruge, Mark (2002) "IT and E-democracy: a report commissioned for the Australian computer society." Online. Available HTTP: http://www.bbc.qld.edu.au/resource/files/ITN330Report.pdf (accessed January 5, 2003).

Norris, Pippa (2001) *Digital Divide: Civic Engagement, Information Poverty, and the Internet World Wide*, Cambridge: Cambridge University Press.

Off, Thomas (2004) "Über die Beliebigkeit des Begriffspaares Back Office/Front Office." Online. Available HTTP: http://home.arcor.de/thomas_off/sofftwaretechnik2004/download/SWT_Konzepte_eGov_BackFrontOffice_V0_1.pdf (accessed February 8, 2005).

People's Daily. Online (October 10, 2000) "Government reform makes progress." Online. Available HTTP: http://fpeng.peopledaily.com.cn/200010/10/eng20001010_52221.html (accessed January 15, 2003).

Renmin Wang (March 17, 2000) "Zhengfu shangwang gongcheng qi neng yi 'shang' liao zhi" [How can it be government online when the government only steps out onto the stage once?]. Online. Available HTTP: http://202.99.23.245/zdxw/19/20000317/20000317195.html (accessed February 15, 2003).

Renmin Wang (August 2, 2000) "Quanzhou 'dianzi zhengfu' chuju guimo" [Quanzhou's e-government is in its initial phase]. Online. Available HTTP: http://www.peopledaily.com.cn/GB/channel4/964/20000802/169839.html (accessed March 14, 2002).

Renmin Wang (July 3, 2001a) "Fujian sheng shengzhang Xi Jinping, zhuanbian zhengfu zhineng zeng qiang fazhan houjin, jiakuai jianshe haixia xian fanrong dai" [Fujian Province Governor Xi Jinping: transform the government function to enhance the growth potential; speed up the construction of the prosperous west belt]. Online. Available HTTP: http://www.peopledaily.com.cn/GB/shizheng/19/20010703/503107.html (accessed July 3, 2001).

Renmin Wang (July 3, 2001b) "Tigao fuwu zhiliang, jiegui guoji guanli, Fuzhou chuangban 'zhengfu chaoshi,' tuijin shehuihua xingzheng fuwu" [Improve the quality, connect the international conventions/institutions; Fuzhou promotes a "governmental supermarket." Push the societal administration service]. Online. Available HTTP: http://www.peopledaily.com.cn/GB/shizheng/19/20010703/503 107.html (accessed June 5, 2002).

Renmin Wang (December 26, 2001) "Cong Pudong kan 'dianzi zhengfu'" [From Pudong see "e-government"] (2001). Online. Available HTTP: http://www.people daily.com.cn/GB/it/48/297/20011226/635164.html (accessed January 5, 2002).

Renmin Wang (July 24, 2001) "Fuzhou chuangban 'zhengfu chaoshi': Taijiang qu shimin fuwu zhongxin 'yingye'" [Fuzhou creates a "governmental supermarket": the citizen service center of the district Taijiang "goes into business"]. Online. Available HTTP: http://www.peopledaily.com.cn/GB/shizheng/19/20010724/518 462.html (accessed March 14, 2002).

Renmin Wang (March 8, 2003) "1998 nian guowuyuan jigou gaige fang'an" [1998 Reform project of state department organs]. Online. Available HTTP: http://www. people.com.cn/GB/shizheng/252/10434/10435/20030306/937527.html (accessed January 8, 2003).

Shuzi Taijiang: Jianshe lingdao xiaozu bangongshi [Digital Taijiang: bureau of the leading group for the construction] (2001) *Xin shiji de Taijiang: Shuzi Taijiang* [Taijiang of the new century: digital Taijiang]. Shuzi Taijiang.

Shuzihua shehui [Digitalized society] (August 7, 2001) "Nanhai: Zhongguo 'dianzi zhengfu' xiyin shijie muguang" [Nanhai: China's "e-government" attracts the eyes of the world]. Online. Available HTTP: http://www.dengit.com/dits9/CHINAELE. HTM (accessed July 3, 2003). Originally in *Guangzhou Ribao*, August 7, 2001.

UNESCO (2002) *Joint UNESCO and COMNET-It Study of E-governance.* Online. Available HTTP: http://www.comnet.mt/Unesco/CountryProfiles/Project/joint_ unesco_and_comnet.htm (accessed April 20, 2004).

UNESCO (2005) *E-governance Capacity Building.* Online. Available HTTP: http:// www.unesco.org/webworld/e-governance (accessed March 3, 2005).

United Nations (2004) *Global E-government Readiness Report 2004: Towards Access for Opportunity*, New York: United Nations.

UNPAN (2002) *Chinese Information Environment and its Influences on eGovernment Construction.* Online. Available HTTP: http://unpan1.un.org/intradoc/groups/ public/documents/untc/unpan007015.pdf (accessed March 13, 2003).

Van Riet, I. (2001) "The role of new technology in European non-formal adult education," Adult Learning Information Centre Europe. Online. Available HTTP: http://www.kaapeli.fi/~vsy/alice/pub/role4.html (accessed January 15, 2001).

Wescott, Clay (2002) "E-Government: enabling Asia-Pacific governments and citizens to do public business differently?" in Christopher Edmonds and Sara Medina (eds) *Defining an Agenda for Poverty Reduction*, Volume 1, Manila: Asian Development Bank. Online. Available HTTP: http://www.adb.org/Documents/Books/Defining_ Agenda_Poverty_Reduction/Vol_1/chapter_11.pdf (accessed February 9, 2005).

West, Darrell M. (2001) "State and federal e-government in the United States." Online. Available HTTP: http://www.brown.edu/Departments/Taubman_Center/ polreports/egovt01us.html (accessed December 12, 2002).

Xi, Xuchu (2005) "You duoshao zhengfu wangzhan xuyao jiaoxing?" [How many websites have to be awakened?], *Beijing Qingnianbao*, January 29, 2005. Online. Available HTTP: http://www.echinagov.com/article/articleshow.asp?ID=7057 (accessed February 2, 2005).

Xu, Zhibiao (March 26, 2002) "An introduction to the informatization of Guangdong province." Online. Available HTTP: http://www.newsgd.com/business/bizevents/200305140009.htm (accessed March 5, 2003).

Yang, Bo and Sheng, Feng (2002) "E-government: the case study of Nanhai's e-government in practice," *Proceedings of ICEB 2002*, Beijing, 420–4.

Yang, Liangmin (2001) "WTO kuangjia xia de zhengfu xinxi gongkai: yu difang zhengfu guanyuan he Zhongguo shehuikexueyuan zhuanjia duihua WTO" [Within the framework of the WTO, government information is made public: discussions with local authority personnel, officials and specialists from the Chinese Academy of Social Sciences]. Online. Available HTTP: http://www.peopledaily.com.cn/GB/guandian/29/171/20010731/524594.html (accessed January 17, 2003). Originally in *Zhongguo Jingji Shibao*, July 31, 2001.

Zeng, Qiang [Edward Zeng] (2001) *Zhongguo dianzi shangwu lan pi shu: China Electronic Commerce Blue Paper*, Beijing: China Economic Publishing House.

Zhang, Junhua (2001) "China's government online and attempts to gain technical legitimacy," *Asien*, July, pp. 93–115.

Zhang, Junhua (2002) "Chinas Steiniger Weg zum E-Government," in Günther Schucher (ed.) *Asien und das Internet*, Hamburg: Institut für Asienkunde, pp. 97–110.

Zhao, Yuzhi (2003) " 'Enter the World:' Neo-liberal globalization, the dream for a strong Nation and Chinese press discourses on the WTO," in Chin-Chuan Lee (ed.) *Chinese Media, Global Contexts*, London and New York: RoutledgeCurzon, pp. 32–56.

Zhongguo dianzi zhengwu wang [China e-governance net] (February 5, 2005) "Dianzi zhengwu de dingyi shi shenme?" [What is the definition of e-governance?]. Online. Available HTTP: http://www.e-gov.org.cn/ziliao/show.asp?id=29990 (accessed March 5, 2005).

Zittrain, Jonathan and Edelman, Benjamin (2002) "Real-time testing of Internet filtering in China: documentation of Internet filtering worldwide." Online. Available HTTP: http://cyber.law.harvard.edu/filtering/china/test (accessed February 27, 2003).

6 Industrialization supported by informatization

The economic effects of the Internet in China

Xie Kang

Chapter 6 seeks to establish an academic framework to explain the potentially beneficial effects of the Internet on the Chinese economy. Within this framework and using data drawn from investigations and statistics, this chapter discusses the spread of the Internet in China and the growth in Internet investment, analyzing the spill over effects or externalities of the Internet in China on the following areas: on a selection of major industries, on the adjustment of the industrial structure, on the growth of the local economy, on the reform of traditional industries, on employment opportunities and on the transformation of competitive advantages among the companies. Finally, it reviews Chinese informatization policies and their impacts. The author considers that the Internet not only offers a way to shorten the distance between China and the developed countries by improving communication generally, but also provides tools that may be implemented to narrow the digital divide between China and the developed countries. Although there has been a lack of investment in the Internet in some areas, there is a substantial amount of evidence to show that the Internet has made a positive impact on economic growth in China.[1]

The effects of the Internet on the Chinese economy can be considered from very different perspectives. This chapter focuses on the effects of the Internet on the Chinese economy by analyzing the ways in which informatization supports the industrialization process. The term "informatization" (*xinxihua*) was first used in 1967. It was often used by Japanese, Chinese and Russian scholars, but was not so popular with European and American scholars at that time. European and American scholars mainly referred to the concept of the spread or infiltration of information technology.

Chinese scholars began to study informatization from the late 1980s onwards and research on this topic, particularly with regard to business, industry, urban development, the national economy and society, has developed very rapidly as a result of the growing popularity and spread of the Internet in China since the late 1990s. Wu Jiapei *et al.* (1993, 1996, 2002) pointed to some very important contributions to the development of an economy-based informatization theory in China.

The concept of informatization used in this chapter will be contrasted with the concept of industrialization, with reference to the spread, infiltration and growing influence of information technology in every area of society, both within the different industries and enterprises, and in the interaction between them. This chapter is divided into five sections. The first section outlines the academic framework, highlighting the knowledge advantage theory of industrialization supported by informatization. The second section offers a discussion on the spread of the Internet in China and the impacts of Internet investment on the development of the Chinese economy in general. The third section gives a detailed picture of the spill over effects, that is, the economic externalities of the Internet, of industrialization supported by informatization. The fourth section presents an analysis of Chinese informatization policy with comments on its spheres of influence. The fifth section brings together some important conclusions for future research.

Industrialization supported by informatization: the Internet and the knowledge advantage theory

One of the most important effects of the Internet on enterprise informatization is that the enterprises gain the knowledge advantage (Xie 1998). According to this theory, the most important effects of the Internet on enterprises, industries and the national economy can be discussed from the perspective of industrialization supported by informatization. An analysis from this perspective offers one of the most feasible academic frameworks for a consideration of the economic effects of the Internet. The theory of industrialization supported by informatization can be divided into three parts: the knowledge advantage of enterprise informatization, the knowledge advantage of industrial informatization and the knowledge advantage of national economy informatization.

Relationship between industrialization and informatization

In general, industrialization appears first of all during the economic development process, after which informatization gradually comes into being together with the spread and infiltration of information technology in industrial areas. Informatization thus supports the further development of industrialization. This gradual development, however, is not seen in developing countries and areas, where there is co-existence of industrialization and informatization right from the beginning. This co-existence results from the developments in information technology both world-wide and in less developed regions; the spread and infiltration of information technology does not stop to wait for the process of industrialization to catch up. Nowadays, economic and technological developments are not restricted by the rules that used to apply to the historical process of industrialization.

Thus, finding an effective means of supporting the industrialization process by informatization and leap-frogging early stages of development in industrial structure and technological standards has become a frequent topic of discussion in developing countries and regions.

Spill over effects of informatization – mechanisms that support industrialization

In economic theory, the externalities of technological pervasion are described as the "spill over effect." For example, a multinational enterprise sets up a subsidiary in a host country. This leads to an influx of technology and management experience from the enterprise, which supports technology and productivity in the host country. The benefits of the resultant income do not accrue to the multinational enterprise alone; the host country is also able to benefit from the "spill over effect," that is, from the improved technological productivity of the region. As far as the multinational company is concerned, however, these improvements are not generally planned.

In this chapter, the term "spill over effect" will be used more frequently than "externality" to describe the actual effects of information technology and enterprise informatization that are not completely under the control of the economic agent. The spill over effect of information technology is only one of the spill over effects of technological development. It refers to the effects on the development of enterprise technology and productivity resulting from the spread of information technology. Similarly, the term "spill over effect" with regard to enterprise informatization may also be applied to describe the situation where enterprises use information technology to restructure the enterprise and its systems; it is not only these enterprises that benefit from the investment in informatization and from the restructuring of the enterprises.

The mechanism of industrialization supported by informatization functions in the following way: the Internet as part of the informatization process has a spill over effect on the economy. This spill over effect supports the productivity of the traditional industries, brings improvements in productivity, changes internal structures in traditional enterprises and gives rise to new industries. The spread and infiltration of information technologies throughout industry has four important consequences: first of all, industrial production and organizational flow gather pace, which results in a more efficient allocation of limited resources within industry and leads to a transformation of company organization. Second, the transaction costs within or among enterprises decrease continuously, which then leads to a reduction in the marginal transaction costs within industry. Third, industrial business opportunities increase and the uninterrupted flow of information creates various new business opportunities, which lead to improvements in trade efficiency within industry. Finally, new business modes are set up resulting from the spread of information technology, which improve the efficiency of processing and distribution of enterprise knowledge within industry, and which form the "industrial knowledge advantage." The four important factors outlined above describe the main characteristics of the industrial informatization spill over effect.

Directions of spill over of informatization

For countries and regions at different stages of economic development, the need for industrialization supported by informatization occurs at different times. For developed countries, informatization occurs during an advanced phase of industrial development as the natural and logical result of the close combination of industrial development and information technology. For developing countries, however, informatization is the key to industrial optimization and upgrade, and is also a key element for achieving industrialization and modernization. It is an important tool for leap-frogging various stages in industrial development.

The main feature of industrialization supported by informatization is that it allows the industrial structures in developing countries and regions to make rapid advances. The internal mechanism that permits the leap-frogging of various stages in industrial development may be described as follows.

Informatization leads to new high-tech industries

Informatization produces a social demand for information technology and its products. Such a demand promotes the development of new high-tech industries such as the information technology industry. The information technology industry (including information products, manufacturing and modern information services) thus lays the foundation for market expansion. The new high-tech industries, such as bio-engineering and new high-tech material production, are closely related. Information products and services become more efficient as a result of developments in the informatization processes. With the spread and infiltration of information technology in the research and development processes and in the production and organization of high-tech industry, some high-tech sectors such as bio-engineering and new high-tech material production have to rely increasingly on information technology, which becomes the most important element of informatization.

Restructuring traditional industries through informatization

With the spread and infiltration of information technology, the traditional industries – for example, the automobile, shipbuilding, iron and steel, architecture and weaving industries – have gradually achieved new standards of productivity. Enterprise informatization supported by information technology has also brought about a number of changes in organizational structure which, in turn, have led to an increase in the enterprise productivity of traditional industries. Yukiko Fukasaku (1998: 19–22) maintained that enterprise computerization and organizational transformation have provided the basis for an increase in productivity in the automobile industry, in the iron and steel industry, in the construction industry and in the weaving industry in 14 OECD countries since the 1980s.

Among these five industries, the productivity of the iron and steel industry has shown the greatest increases since the new smelting technologies together with new forms of management were introduced in 1983; these increases are clearly related to the rapidly expanding use and popularity of computer-assisted management and production tools, such as CAD/CAPP/CAM, CE, LP and JIT in the iron and steel industry.

Informatization supports modern industry

Informatization can lead to increases in technological innovation, to the improvement of technological production processes and to the strengthening of the organizational management of modern industries – such as the fine engineering industry, the petrochemical industry, the medical industry, the metallurgy industry, and the automotive/transport industry. In brief, informatization increases the throughput of modern industries and expands their technological development space.

Informatization strengthens production capability

Informatization does not only increase production capability and improve the organization of industrial production processes, but also strengthens the service capability of production services that are closely related to the production and organization of industrial products. In fact, it offers solid support for industrialization in general. Production services, that is, those related to the processes of production, such as industrial product design, arts and crafts design, packaging design, computer technology services, advertisement and management consultation, are able to increase productivity through the spread and infiltration of information technology.

Informatization leads to the expansion of industry and the blurring of boundaries between agriculture, industry and services

As a result of informatization, the traditional boundaries between agriculture, industry and services become increasingly difficult to define. The mutual amalgamation, investment and cooperation of modern agriculture, modern industry and modern services based on informatization result in the continuous expansion of the borders of the three industries. This results in the redefinition of the business spheres of the three industries and illustrates the trend toward expansion among industries.

Industrial investment supported by informatization: the infiltration of the Internet and the growth of investment

Growth and infiltration of the Internet in China

By the end of June, 2004, the number of computers connected to the Internet in China had reached 36.30 million, 6.52 million (18 percent) of which were using DDN (Digital Data Network) (see Table 6.1), while 20.97 million (58 percent) were using a dial-up connection service. The number using other connections was 8.81 million (24 percent). At the same time, there were 87 million users on-line.

First of all, the number of Internet users is continually increasing. From July 1998 to July 2000, the annual growth rate of Internet users was more than 50 percent; it reached a peak in January 2000 and then gradually began to decrease. It began to increase again rapidly after January 2002. The total number of Internet users rose from 33.7 million in December 2001 to 87 million in June 2004. Although the number of Internet users in China reached a new high in June 2004, the popularization rate of the Internet in China is still rather low, and the Internet has, therefore, great development potential.

The percentage rate of users is usually regarded as the main indicator of the Internet infiltration level. There are obvious differences in infiltra-

Table 6.1 Computers connected to the Internet in China (1997–2004)

	Number of computers connected to the Internet	Number of computers using DDN	Number of computers using a dial-up connection	Number of computers connected to the Internet using other connections
1997.10	0.299	0.049	0.25	n.a.
1998.7	0.542	0.082	0.46	n.a.
1999.1	0.747	0.117	0.63	n.a.
1999.7	1.460	0.250	1.21	n.a.
2000.1	3.500	0.410	3.09	n.a.
2000.7	6.500	1.010	5.49	n.a.
2001.1	8.920	1.410	7.51	n.a.
2001.7	10.020	1.630	8.39	n.a.
2002.1	12.540	2.340	10.20	n.a.
2002.7	16.130	3.070	12.00	1.06
2003.1	20.830	4.030	14.80	2.00
2003.7	25.720	5.150	17.39	3.18
2004.1	30.890	5.950	19.45	5.49
2004.7	36.300	6.520	20.97	8.81

Sources: Author's own compilation based on data from CNNIC reports, various years 1997–2004.

Note: 1 unit: 1 million

tion levels in the different regions. The municipalities of Beijing and Shanghai have the highest Internet infiltration level; the second highest level is found in the municipality of Tianjin; the provinces of Zhejiang, Guangdong, Jiangsu, Fujian and Liaoning make up the third highest level; the six provinces of Heilongjiang, Hubei, Xinjiang, Jilin, Hainan and Sichuan are in the fourth group; the other 17 provinces are in the fifth.

In China, the communication industry has developed very rapidly: by July 2002, the number of telephone users became the highest in the world by reaching 380 million and exceeded the number in the US. This popularization rate, however, was only 30.22 percent, and the demand remained very high. Furthermore, according to the research of the WebSideStory Company published in June 2002, the total bandwidth of information transmitted via Internet in China amounted to 6.63 percent of the data transmitted worldwide, which is second only to that transmitted in the US (WebSideStory, July 31, 2002).[2]

Impacts of enterprise investment in the Internet on the development of the Chinese economy

From 1996 to 2000, the Chinese government went to great lengths to promote the use of CAD and CAM systems. Between 2001 and 2005, a special fund of RMB 800 million (approximately US$ 105 million) has been allocated for the organization of key technical research into the informatization of manufacturing industries and model application projects for information support technology with the aim of penetrating traditional industries.

According to research on a sample of 638 large and medium-sized enterprises conducted by the State Economic and Trade Commission (Zhongguo guojia qiye wang, February 10, 2002), investment in enterprise informatization showed a steady increase from 1999 to 2000. The growth rates of investment in informatization and the planned investment are 8.27 percent and 13.16 percent respectively. The average growth rate is more than 10 percent. From 2001 to 2005, these 638 enterprises plan to invest RMB 9.75 billion (US$ 1.25 billion) in enterprise informatization, which is 12 percent less than the actual investment of RMB 109.1 billion (US$ 14.3 billion) during the last five years (ibid.). One reason for this is probably that large quantities of IT equipment have now been procured so that the construction of the network infrastructure has been completed. Another possible reason is that there have been reductions in the price of IT equipment. On the other hand, it perhaps indicates that investment by Chinese enterprises in informatization has reached a new stage, where, step by step, investment in hardware is giving way to investment in software and management.

The research carried out by the State Economic and Trade Commission also showed that from 1999 to 2001 there were 22 industries/business sectors where the growth rate of investment in informatization was higher than that averaged among all 32 industries/business sectors in China (Zhongguo guojia qiye wang, February 10, 2002). Only the growth rate of the engineering industry was less than 10 percent; in the other 21 industries it was over 10 percent. From 1995 to 2000, the top five industries were: domestic trade (RMB 2.03 billion/US$ 0.26 billion), the petrochemical industry (RMB 1.85 billion/US$ 242 million), the metallurgy industry (RMB 0.85 billion/US$ 0.24 billion), the electronics industry (RMB 0.7 billion/US$ 91.8 million) and foreign trade (RMB 0.57 billion/US$ 74 million) (ibid.).

If we take a look at the development of 34 different regions in China between 1999 and 2001, it can be seen that there were 27 areas where the annual average growth rate of investment in enterprise informatization was positive; in only eight of these 27 regions was the growth rate below 10 percent, while in the other 19 regions, it was over 10 percent; the top five areas were Ningxia (125.78 percent), Hubei (119.03 percent), Yunnan (115.07 percent), Liaoning (82.01 percent), Ningbo (73.93 percent). During 1995–2000, the top five regions for total investment in enterprise informatization were: Beijing (RMB 5.85 billion/US$ 767 million), Shanghai (RMB 0.6 billion/US$ 78.75 million), Hebei (RMB 0.58 billion/US$ 76 million), Heilongjiang (RMB 0.35 billion/US$ 46 million) and Guangdong (RMB 0.32 billion/US$ 42 million) (ibid.).

The following conclusions can be drawn from the data outlined above: from the perspective of the development of informatization in every industry and from the perspective of investment growth in enterprise informatization, it is clear that there have been very rapid developments in the informatization of China, especially in intranet construction and in the connection of enterprises to the Internet. Although the level of informatization cannot be compared with that of the developed countries,[3] the process of informatization in China is taking place at a very rapid rate. Investment in enterprise informatization has not only increased domestic demand, especially regarding the consumption of information, but has also promoted the development of the Chinese information industry and information market. According to research conducted by the Guangdong Statistics Bureau in January 2002, there are 42.7 personal computers and 114.6 mobile telephones per 100 families among Guangzhou citizens (http://www.gdstats. gov.cn). The total expenditure on informatization every month amounts to RMB 1.8 billion (US$ 236 million), that is, RMB 38 (US$ 5) per person. Thus, information consumption is becoming one of the most important areas of expenditure for the Chinese people. On the other hand, investment in enterprise informatization has hastened the pace of industrialization and improved standards of management. What is more, it has led to an increase in productivity in traditional industries and also in other industries that still have development potential (see also, Guangdong tongji xinxi wang, May 20, 2004).

Industrialization enhanced by informatization: the spill over effects of the Internet

With Internet investment increasing and Internet services flourishing, investment in the development of e-commerce in China is also increasing rapidly. The development of e-commerce may be regarded as one of most important spill over effects of the Internet and, at the same time, as one of the major forces driving both industrialization and the business environment.

According to a survey carried out by the State Economic and Trade Commission in 2001 on 638 large and medium-sized enterprises, 24 percent (156 enterprises) of these have installed a basic or partial e-commerce system, amounting to a total investment figure of RMB 280 million (US$ 33 million); 54 percent (350 enterprises), however, have not yet started to install an e-commerce system (Table 6.2) (Zhongguo guojia qiye wang, February 10, 2002). E-commerce in foreign trade, agriculture and the electronics industry is developing more rapidly than in other sectors, and the total investment of 23 enterprises in these three sectors stands at RMB 34.36 million (US$ 4.1 million). By 2000, of the 156 enterprises which had a basic or partial e-commerce system, only 138 enterprises had put e-commerce activities into practice, accounting for 21.6 percent of all enterprises included in the survey. The total transaction figures for 138 enterprises amount to RMB 4.98 billion (US$ 0.6 billion), which includes RMB 0.57 billion (US$ 70 million) from procurement and RMB 4.41 billion (US$ 530 million) from sales. The average figure for procurement is RMB 4.13 million US$ 500,000) and the average for sales is RMB 31.96 million (US$ 3.9 million) (ibid.).

The reasons for the limited development of e-commerce in Chinese enterprises may be traced to the social environment; for example, there is a very low popularization rate: by the end of 2000, computer ownership stood at only 9.72 for every 100 families. Furthermore, there are wide regional variations in China as a whole. In developed regions, such as the city of Guangzhou in Guangdong Province, the popularization rate for computers was 60.8 percent in June 2002, while the popularization rate in

Table 6.2 Enterprise investment in e-commerce systems

Total investment	Present situation			
	Basic system	*Partial system*	*System not yet being installed*	*No information available*
RMB 278.6877 million	8 enterprises	148 enterprises	350 enterprises	132 enterprises

Source: Author's own compilation based on data from a survey conducted by State Economic and Trade Commission 2001.

Anhui Province was less than 1 percent. The uneven regional development of the Chinese economy and infrastructure will inevitably lead to a great "digital divide" in China. It may be concluded that since the popularization rate for computers in Beijing, Shanghai and Guangdong (Table 6.3) is higher than in other regions, these three regions will be in the forefront of e-commerce development in China. Similarly, these three regions will be the first to employ a strategy of industrialization supported by informatization and the restructuring of traditional industries by the application of information technology will also progress more rapidly. The efforts of the government to promote changes in traditional industries by means of informatization have been most successful in these three regions.

An examination of the informatization process in China shows that informatization drives industrialization forward in five important ways: first, informatization promotes the information industry itself, making it one of the pillars of Chinese industry. Today, there are already three information industry clusters in existence: (1) the information industry cluster of the Zhujiang Delta (Pearl River Delta) which extends around the Guangdong information industry corridor connecting Guangzhou, Dongguan, Huizhou and Shenzhen with each other; (2) the information industry cluster of the Changiiang Delta together with the Hu-Ning information industry corridor (Shanghai Nanjing Corridor) which connect Shanghai, Kunshan, Suzhou, Wujiang and Nanjing with each other; (3) the Beijing-Tianjin information industry corridor that connects Zhongguancun in Beijing with the Tianjin high-tech zone, and which links up with the

Table 6.3 Computer ownership (per 100 families) in different regions of China (2000)

Region	Quantity	Region	Quantity
Beijing	32.10	Anhui	6.72
Guangdong	25.78	Shanxi	6.23
Shanghai	25.60	Liaoning	5.79
Tianjin	16.40	Guizhou	5.74
Zhejiang	14.02	Henan	5.72
Chongqing	13.67	Xinjiang	5.68
Fujian	11.47	Gansu	5.39
Hunan	10.73	Heilongjiang	4.79
Jiangsu	10.65	Jilin	4.62
Shandong	9.53	Jiangxi	4.56
Guangxi	9.36	Hainan	4.33
Hubei	8.36	Ningxia	3.78
Yunnan	7.89	Neimeng	3.47
Sichuan	7.69	Qinghai	2.36
Hebei	7.43	Xizang	1.00
Shaanxi	7.03		

Source: Author's own compilation based on data from *China Statistical Year Book* 2001.

information industry cluster of Northern China. The growth of the information industry in these areas has supported the development of local
industrialization, leading, in particular, to the rapid expansion of other sepa-
rate enterprises that have close relationships with the information industry.
    Second, informatization leads to the upgrading of local economic struc-
tures. For example, local government authorities in China are, today,
investing more widely in the information industry; between 2001 and 2005,
Shenzhen city in Guangdong Province is planning to invest RMB 36 billion
(US$ 4.4 billion) to promote the informatization process, so that by 2005,
the level of informatization in Shenzhen city will have reached that of the
central cities in the most developed regions of the country (Shenzhen
guomin jingji he shehui xinxihua gongzuo huiyi, January 8, 2004).
    Third, informatization leads to the restructuring of traditional industries,
forcing them to reduce operating costs and improve productivity. The
textile industry of Xijiao in Nanhai city in Guangdong Province, for
example, employs CAD to develop new products and carries out purchasing
and distribution worldwide via the Internet; this integration of a local
industry within the world market also leads to improvements in quality
(Interview, June 2001; Wu Di, October 11, 2001).
    Fourth, the constant restructuring of industry by informatization creates
a wide variety of employment opportunities, the new technologies give
birth to new professions and the demand for labor increases. According to
the survey by 51job.com in 2001 (Xiao Nan, February 9, 2002), the demand
for labor created by information technology and the Internet industry is
the highest in all industries as Table 6.4 shows.
    Finally, informatization can strengthen the competitive capabilities of
enterprises and transform traditional competitive advantage to knowledge
advantage by restructuring the internal technology framework and the
management of enterprises. Enterprise informatization and e-commerce

Table 6.4 Regional labor demand in the Top Ten sectors of industry in China
(2001)

Industry	Demand for jobs
Information technology and Internet	13,564
Electronics	4,609
Manufacturing industry	3,380
Durable consumer products	2,909
Consulting services	2,829
Bio-technology/pharmacy/health care/medicine	2,676
Perishable consumer products	2,347
Real estate	2,209
Architecture/designing/home styling	1,605
Advertising	1,600

Source: Author's own compilation based on data from 51job.com.

activity bring not only direct material benefits, by increasing labor productivity, but also enhanced business opportunities together with other indirect benefits. The survey conducted by the State Economic and Trade Commission on 638 enterprises shows that e-commerce activities can assist enterprises to gain information more rapidly and also improve their profiles (Table 6.5).

Informatization policy

The spread and infiltration of the Internet in China has made it easier for the Chinese government to implement informatization-promoted strategies. The Chinese government is determined to seize the opportunities offered by the Internet boom to strengthen economic growth in China. An evaluation of the Chinese government's strategies for industrialization supported by informatization shows that if developing countries plan to carry out a policy of informatization, they should first combine informatization with high-tech industries, in particular with information technology industries. The next steps should be to restructure the production and the organizational efficiency of traditional industries by means of informatization, and the production capability of modern industries should then also be improved by means of informatization technology. Finally the information and knowledge gaps between the three industries should be narrowed.

On the one hand, the traditional and modern industrial systems should be restructured by implementing a development strategy for the informatization of the national economy and society; on the other hand, modern high-tech production and service systems must be established. At the same time, it is necessary to facilitate the flow of information and knowledge among the three industries and form the industrial knowledge advantage. This should be one of the important strategic objectives of informatization.

Table 6.5 Changes in enterprises as a result of e-commerce activities

Changes in enterprises	Number of enterprises
More rapid gaining of information	116
Improved performance	115
Increase in innovative measures	99
Improved efficiency in business transactions	90
Increased sales	90
Cost reductions	84
Consolidation of management	60
Streamlining of decision-making processes	45

Source: Author's own compilation based on data from a survey conducted by the State Economic and Trade Commission 2001.

Industrialization promoted by informatization should not be regarded as a general tool for general use in all industries at all times nor as a specific tool for specific applications only; the mode of application should, rather, be according to the industry, to the stage of development in a particular industry, and to the management level in a particular enterprise at a particular stage of development, since informatization is ruled by both "rigid" and "flexible" restrictions. If this does not occur, the strategy of industrialization promoted by informatization may lead to blind investment in information technology, may fail to promote industrialization and also lead to the waste of precious capital that could be better used to bring about industrialization. These are the main issues China should take into consideration when implementing a strategy of industrialization supported by informatization.

Informatization is one of the most efficient means by which a country can achieve industrialization, gain economic benefits and increase production efficiency. This, however, is not the ultimate goal of industrialization. The industrial policy of industrialization promoted by informatization should not only settle for the spread and infiltration of information technology in industry, but also focus on investment in the management areas of information technology and establish management and supervisory structures from a macro-perspective.

Investment in informatization at management level must be increased, in particular with regard to post-supervision and performance evaluation of investment in informatization. This is essential to guarantee the realization of economic benefits from the strategy of industrialization promoted by informatization.

The informatization of human resources is the basis of all the industrialization processes. Each individual human being is a complex information system. Finding a way to combine a "human" information system effectively with the "computer" information system of the Internet is another important consideration when carrying out policies leading to industrialization supported by informatization. The human–computer system with its interfaces for dealing with information is one of the keys to realizing the economic benefits offered by informatization. Similarly, the "informatization of families" is the key to the social human–computer system and its interfaces for dealing with information in the informatization processes for the national economy and society.

Only the informatization of families can increase the stock of human capital required for the complete informatization of society. Thus, the industrial policy of industrialization promoted by informatization must include human capital, which is necessarily related to the informatization of families. An example of this can be found in Sweden: in 1998, the Swedish government started to promote the informatization of families by permitting ordinary employees to use communication facilities and later to purchase communication facilities at low prices (Nagy *et al.* 1995). As a result, the Swedish government has gained obvious social and economic benefits from informatization through the spill over effects of enterprise and industry informatization. This indicates that research into industrialization promoted by informatization should not be limited to the framework of industrial policy. It must also take into consideration policies related to enterprise informatization, and policies related to the national economy and society informatization. Society informatization includes informatization of families, informatization of government, informatization of medical treatment and informatization of cities.

Conclusion

The spread and infiltration of the Internet in China has greatly expanded the potential of the consumer market for information in China. In addition, enterprises confronted with the challenges of new technology are investing more heavily in informatization. The demands of the consumer market for information and enterprise informatization has led to rapid growth in the Chinese information technology industry. The development of the information technology industry supports informatization, and vice versa. Informatization in China has now reached a historical point in the process of change. Thus, informatization programs and the required investment in informatization are now subjects of great interest for all governmental agencies ranging from the central government down to the various levels of regional government. A national strategy of industrialization promoted by informatization has been established. It is hoped that the innovative information technology will support the Chinese economic reforms and lead to continued economic growth.

The basic logic of the strategy of informatization is that informatization is the inevitable trend in the world information economy in the twenty-first century for developing countries. Informatization is necessarily accompanied by globalization, and globalization can only be achieved by means of informatization. During this process, informatization will deeply influence international trade, international finance and the flow of international capital. It will also affect the modern patterns of the world economy, politics and diplomacy. Whether developing countries can gain benefits from the flow of world information depends not only on how well they prepare for informatization, but also on the efficiency level regarding the management of informatization. However, the efficiency level regarding the management of informatization is closely related to the achievement of the knowledge advantage from information technology. This is one of the decisive factors concerning the economic benefits that can be gained from informatization. The Internet offers one of the most effective ways to narrow the digital divide between the developed countries and China. This chapter shows that although there is still a lack of investment and a generally inefficient standard of management in China, the Internet is a critical multiplier in China's drive toward achieving an advanced level of economic development.

Notes

1 This work was supported by the National Social Science Foundation and the National Natural Science Foundation (79800014) at Sun Yat-Sen University in China.
2 The countries ranked third to sixth for data transmission are: Japan (5.24 percent), UK (3.94 percent), Canada (3.93 percent) and Germany (3.64 percent).
3 According to the investigation, during 1995–2000, the investments of the Chinese enterprises in enterprise informatization occupied 0.22 percent of the enterprises' total assets. Comparatively, that of the large enterprises in developed countries is more than 5 percent.

References

CNNIC (7/2004) *14th Statistical Survey Report on the Development on Internet in China*. Online. Available HTTP: http://www.cnnic.net.cn (accessed August 21, 2004).

CNNIC (1/2004) *13th Statistical Survey on the Internet Development in China (2004/1)*. Online. Available HTTP: http://www.cnnic.net.cn (accessed March 23, 2004).

CNNIC (7/2003) *12th Statistical Survey on the Internet Development in China (2003/7)*. Online. Available HTTP: http://www.cnnic.net.cn (accessed February 15, 2003).

CNNIC (1/2003) *Statistical Survey Report on the Development of Internet in China (Jan. 2003)*. Online. Available HTTP: http://www.cnnic.net.cn (accessed February 15, 2003).

CNNIC (7/2002) *Statistical Survey Report on the Development of Internet in China (July 2002)*. Online. Available HTTP: http://www.cnnic.net.cn (accessed February 15, 2003).

CNNIC (1/2002) *Statistical Survey Report on the Development of Internet in China, January 2002*. Online. Available HTTP: http://www.cnnic.net.cn (accessed September 15, 2002).

CNNIC (7/2001) *Semiannual Survey Report on the Development of China's Internet (2001/7)*. Online. Available HTTP: http://www.cnnic.net.cn (accessed September 15, 2002).

CNNIC (1/2001) *Semiannual Survey Report on the Development of China's Internet (Jan. 2001)*. Online. Available HTTP: http://www.cnnic.net.cn (accessed September 15, 2002).

E-Works.net.cn (April 16, 2004) "Baijia qiye xinxihua diaochao baogao" [Investigation report on informatization of one hundred enterprises]. Online. Available HTTP: http://www.e-works.net.cn/zt72/2002416/36621_2.htm (accessed September 20, 2002).

Fukasaku, Yukiko (1998) "Revitalising mature industries," *Organisation for Economic Cooperation and Development, The OECD Observer*. August/September 1998.

Guangdong tongji xinxi wang [Guangdong statistical information net] (May 20, 2004) "2003 nian Guangdong dianxin ye zai jilie jingzheng zhong kuaisu fazhan"

[Guangdong's telecommunication industry in a fast development within heavy competition]. Online. Available HTTP: http://www.gdstats.gov.cn/tjfx/t20040520_10681.htm (accessed December 12, 2004).

Nagy, Hanna, Ken, Guy and Arnold, Erik (eds) (1995) *The Diffusion of Information Technology. Experience of Industrial Countries and Lessons for Developing Countries*, Washington, DC: World Bank (Discussion Papers, 281).

Saidi Consultant (August 1, 2001) "Wo guo gaosu gonglu xinxihua jianshe zhuangkuang diaocha" [Investigation on constructive status of informatization of highway in China]. Online. Available: HTTP: http://www.e-works.net.cn/ewk Articles/Category15/Article3885.htm (accessed February 3, 2002).

Shenzhen guomin jingji he shehui xinxihua gongzuo huiyi [Working conference on Shenzhen's national economic and societal informatization] (January 8, 2004) "Shenzhen shi guomin jingji he shehui xinxihua 'shi wu' guihua (2001–2005)" [The Tenth National 5 year Plan for Shenzhen's national economic and societal informatization (2001–2005)]. Online. Available HTTP: http://www.shenzhen.net. cn/jujiao/zhuanti/zt6/200401080861.htm (accessed March 26, 2002).

WebSideStory (July 31, 2002) "China's online population second only to U.S., according to WebSideStory's StatMarket." Online. Available HTTP: http://www. websidestory.com/news-events/press/release.html?id=163 (accessed June 24, 2002).

Wu, Di (October 11, 2001) "Fangzhi qiye xinxihua xianzhuang diaocha he fenxi" [Investigation and analysis on the status of informatization of textile enterprises]. Online. Available HTTP: http://www.e-works.net.cn/zt114/20011011/39754.htm (accessed November 11, 2001).

Wu, Jiapei (1993) *Xinxi yu jingji* [Information and economy], Beijing: Qinghua daxue chubanshe.

Wu, Jiapei (1996) *Jingji, xinxi, xinxihua* [Economy, information, informatization], Dalian: Dongbei caijing daxue chubanshe.

Wu, Jiapei, Xie, Kang and Wang, Mingming (eds) (2002) *Xinxi jingji xue* [Economics of information theory], Beijing: Gaodeng jiaoyu chubanshe.

Xiao, Nan (February 9, 2002) "Wuyou zhishu cai shi pian" [Carefree index: chapter human resources market, November12–18]. Online. Available HTTP: http://www. 51job.com/arts/05/131539.html (accessed March 14, 2002).

Xie, Kang (1998) *Xinxi jingji xueyuanli* [The principle of the economics of information], Changsha: zhongnan gongye daxue chubanshe.

Zhongguo guojia qiye wang [China State Enterprise Network] (February 10, 2002) "Guojia jingmao wei xinxi zhongxin; quanguo qiye xinxihua jianshe xianzhuang he 'shi wu' guihua qingkuang diaocha baogao" [The national economy and trade as the focus for information: Investigation report on constructive status of enterprise informatization of China and the blue-print of the tenth five-year plan]. Online. Available HTTP: http://www.chinabbc.com.cn/anli/view.asp?newsid=20041211167835&classid= (accessed March 3, 2003).

Zhonghua renmin gongheguo guojia tongji ju [Chinese National Bureau of Statistics] (2002) *Zhongguo renkou tongji nianjian 2002* [Statistical Yearbook for the Population of China 2002], Beijing: Zhongguo tongji chubanshe.

7 Net business

China's potential for a global market change

Simona Thomas

Developments in China's e-commerce have expanded exponentially during the last decade. While many observers merely assume that Internet usage may have a positive effect on China's overall economic performance, the research presented here is focused on a more specific set of questions regarding the roles of the different protagonists involved with China's Internet: what are the major driving forces behind e-commerce in China? How do the protagonists of e-commerce in China meet in Cyberspace? Are new business models emerging? Who are the economic beneficiaries of the technical innovations and Internet revolution? Are the opportunities for e-commerce in China exploited to the full? What are the expected impacts for foreign companies active in the PRC? These questions were discussed during interviews conducted in Beijing and Shanghai with two main groups: foreign companies from different industrial sectors (information technology, systems and applications, transportation, interactive advertising, law consultancy) and intermediate players, such as the German Chamber of Commerce and an e-commerce lobby group.[1]

In 2001, a large billboard advertising campaign in Beijing was launched by the pharmaceutical company, Sanjiu, to promote its website. It showed an image of a Chinese People's Liberation Army Soldier dressed in the style of the Cultural Revolution, with the sun in the background. The underlying caption read "*Yi ren shangwang, quan jia jiankang*" – "One person starts surfing the net and the whole family gets healthier." Although this was intended as an advertisement for health products, it also shows one predominant characteristic of the Internet in China: the connection between business and government.

The main protagonists of the Internet in China, those responsible for its economic thrust, still come from the state sector: the Ministry of Information Industry (MII), the former Ministry of Foreign Trade and Technological Co-operation (MOFTEC) (replaced by and incorporated into the newly set up Ministry of Trade in March 2003), the State Council Informatization Leading Group Office, and Provincial and Municipal Administrations.[2] On the industrial side, also highly regulated and often owned by the state, there are the telecommunications industry and corporations belonging to the IT sector. The *Xinhua News Agency* Group and the *People's Daily* Group also have to be mentioned in this context, since they represent the leading state-driven online media industry involved in the portal/ISP business.

The situation in China tends to present some very contradictory features: in terms of GDP per capita, it still belongs to the group of developing countries but, on the other hand, China is about to become a global IT player. Describing the impact of IT and China's competitive capability in the IT industry, Peter Nolan (2001: 172) points out:

> Most analysts believe that, unlike the "old technology", the IT sector offers a true "global level playing field" in which "everyone is starting at the ground floor" [...] The IT sector offers China an opportunity to "leapfrog the Second Technological Revolution", which dominated the twentieth century, and rapidly become a leader in the new technologies of the Third Technological Revolution in the early twenty-first century. This view presents deep problems. These problems are especially significant in view of the central role of information technology in the negotiations for China to join the WTO.[3]

For a deeper understanding of China's performance in the global information economy and society, it is necessary to analyze the role of the Internet and its commercial applications in order to show how information and communication technology (ICT) has contributed towards preparing the country for a possible global market change. First of all, the share of ICT attributed to China's GDP almost doubled, from 2.9 percent in 1995 to 5.7 percent in 2001 (World Bank 2002, 2003). The growth of the ICT sector is regarded as a key pillar for the general approach to China's development, with respect to achieving "e-readiness." According to the outline proposed by the authors of the *Global Information Tech Report 2002–2003*, certain criteria are taken into consideration to measure the e-readiness of a nation, such as network access (information infrastructure), network policy (ICT policy, business and economic environment), networked society (networked learning, ICT opportunities, social capital), and the networked economy (e-commerce, e-government, general infrastructure) (Dutta and Jain 2003: 8).

One of the earliest starting points in the formulation of a coherent Internet policy by the PRC was their use of the new technologies to support economic development. The bridging of the digital divide[4] between different regions and social groups by new technologies, the re-structuring of governmental spheres of responsibility such as the establishment of e-commerce and e-government institutions, the construction of web-portals by MOFTEC and the creation of a new ministry, the MII, and the concepts concerned with the implementation of technology within companies and government agencies are all co-determinants of such an Internet policy on the agenda of the Chinese state.

In the early 1990s, the foundations for the informatization attempt were laid with the announcement of the first three so-called "Golden Projects" (*san jin gongcheng*). These projects were started in 1993 as "an ambitious information infrastructure initiative aimed at simultaneously developing an information economy and building administrative capabilities" (Cartlege and Lovelock 1999: 24). The "overarching goals" of these projects, first "to build a national information highway as a path to modernization and economic development," second "to drive development of information technology in China," and third "to unify the country by tying the centre to the provinces and by allowing the government to act across ministerial and industrial demarcation lines" were described as follows:

> These three goals overlap but are significantly different in nature. The first is concrete – an information infrastructure over which data can flow. The second is emotional – a cry for the country to become a modern nation. The third is a combination of goals one and two: it is clearly the most important, and the driver of the other two. Realising it will allow the central government to reacquire administrative control by being able to act as an information gatekeeper for the country.
>
> (Cartlege and Lovelock 1999: 24)

The first projects were the Golden Bridge Project (*jinqiao*), the Golden Card Project (*jinka*), and the Golden Customs Project (*jinguan*). Meanwhile, 13 projects have been established either by ministries or other high-level administrative bodies of the Chinese state (ibid.). The importance of the projects for enterprises and customers should not be overlooked. The structural framework of China's e-commerce practice has been set, for example, by enabling new payment methods using ATMs, debit and credit cards according to the scope of the Golden Card Project (*jinka*), introducing surveillance mechanisms for banking, customs and revenue offices according to the Golden Audit Project (*jinsheng*), and digitalizing the invoice and tax revenue system according to the Golden Tax Project (*jinshui*). The Golden Trade Project (*jinmao*) aims to connect over 100,000 companies country-wide according to the Ninth Five-Year-Plan (for this and a further, more up-to-date assessment of the other Golden Projects, see also Wang 2003: 216–66).

After the bursting of the "new economy bubble" at the turn of the millennium, the overall governmental direction shifted towards building a networked economy, in order to obtain a coherent concept for the Chinese economic development. Li Yuxiao, an official from the Internet Society in China, a non-profit organization that was established in Beijing in 2001 and has a membership of 150 (including IT companies, universities and research institutions), said that "the Internet must play a larger role in building electronic government and management information systems as well as in upgrading the overall competitiveness of many traditional trades." In an interview published by *Xinhua News Agency* on November 22, 2002, he pointed out that "the potential and value of the Internet in China are far from fully exploited. [...] It's high time for us to concentrate on the application aspect." At the same time, at the highest level of the Chinese leadership, the scope of this concept was made very clear in Jiang Zemin's speech on November 8, 2002 at the 16th Party Congress Meeting:

> IT application is a logical choice if the industrialization and modernization of our country are to be accelerated. It is, therefore, necessary to persist in using IT to propel industrialization, which will, in turn, stimulate IT application, blazing a new trail to industrialization featuring high scientific and technological content, good economic returns, low resources consumption, little environmental pollution and a full display of advantages in human resources.
>
> (Xinhuanet, November 18, 2002)

Jiang Zemin also pointed out that the development of the IT industry laid the foundations for achieving economic growth by "transforming traditional industries with high technology" as well as "invigorating the equipment manufacturing industry" (ibid.). He went on to emphasize that in order to prevent any imbalance in the "ICT for industrialization and modernization" objective:

> We must correctly handle the relationships of development between the high and new technology industries and traditional industries, between capital-and-technology-intensive industries and labor-intensive industries and between virtual economy and real economy.
>
> (ibid.)

Towards a concept for e-commerce in China

By July 2004, the development of the Internet in China had advanced so far that in terms of infrastructure, the eight operating networks had reached over 50,000 Mbps of the total bandwidth of leased international connections (CNNIC 7/2004). Worldwide, by 1994, the number of commercial domains of the World Wide Web had exceeded the number of educational and network domains. China joined this international trend in 1997. Since then, commercial domains in China have reached an average share of about 80 percent. Chinese dot-com websites are identified as enterprise (77.8 percent) and business websites (5.4 percent) by the Chinese Internet Network Information Center (CNNIC 2001). They follow sorting standards by the Forrester Research: business websites are described as "fictitious network-like websites e.g. such '.com' companies as sina and sohu." Enterprise websites are "founded by enterprises whose operations are mainly off-line" (ibid.).

One problem in research regarding the use of the Internet for economic purposes is the lack of any universal definition of the term "electronic commerce." Although not standardized, most of them can be summarized in two main categories: a narrow definition describes e-commerce as a "commercial transaction, whereby the order for goods or a service is made using some form of Internet based communication" (UNCTAD 2003a). According to this definition, the act of delivery and payment may be settled in the off-line sphere. A broad definition includes the "use of Internet and non-Internet communication systems, such as telephone ordering, interactive television and electronic messaging" (ibid.), but in this case, it is important that the buyer and seller do not meet physically during the order placement. Some definitions go even further, making a distinction between a narrow definition of e-commerce where "everything must be settled on-line" (only possible for example, when downloading software and paying for it by credit card), and e-commerce in a very broad sense as "any information via the Internet that will lead to a potential purchase," which is described as e-business.

The rapid developments in this field sometimes also lead to rapid changes at the analytical level; for example, in February 2005, the Information Society Portal of the European Union stated: "The e-business concept goes well beyond e-commerce (buying and selling on-line) as it also encompasses the integration of ICT into the business processes of enterprises. In this context, managerial innovation and entrepreneurial spirit are as important as technological breakthroughs" (EUROPA 2005).[5]

An examination of literature of Chinese origin reveals a different methodological challenge: both terms, "e-commerce" and "e-business," are covered by only one singular term in Chinese: *dianzi shangwu*. When e-commerce gained more importance at national level at the end of the 1990s, it was seen by the researchers of the "China E-Commerce Challenge Group"[6] as a kind of a new commercial model (*quan xin de shangwu moshi*) with potential for a new industrial revolution (*xin de chanye geming de dongli*) (Zheng *et al.* 1999: 3–22, 109–24). The group's report *Zhongguo dianzi shangwu de fazhan yu juece* (*China E-Commerce Development and Policy Decision*) states: "Generally, E-Commerce is a kind of commercial style taking advantage of the advanced information technology." E-commerce characteristics are listed as follows: "it is a global commerce," "it is more suitable and quickly," "it costs lower than traditional one" and "it is more efficient and has more selection" (Zheng *et al.* 1999: 109–10). Of course, nowadays, such characteristics have to be seen in context with the parallel "hype" of the so-called new economy at the time this report was written, but it still clearly reflects the attempts to arrive at a definition of e-commerce for the Chinese market.

The official meaning of *dianzi shangwu* is stated in the "Circular of the Beijing municipal administration for industry and commerce concerning e-commerce activities registration" of March 28, 2000, which offers a definition of e-commerce that places an emphasis on Internet-related "profit making activities [. . .] by commercial dealers and organizations" (Wong and Nah 2001: 55). The definition presented in the circular is outlined as follows:

> The Circular defines e-commerce to include using the Internet to sign contracts and conduct business, disseminate commercial advertising, promote products, provide Internet access, network technology services, graphic design or e-commerce or information services, or undertake any other profit-making activity.
>
> (McKenzie 2000)[7]

This chapter will employ both terms, e-commerce and e-business. For measuring the role of ICT and the new media applications it will define e-commerce as "any marketplace transaction," and e-business as "electronic communication to re-engineer the internal and external value chains, everything from procurement to sales, from production to warehousing, from supply chain management to customer relations management, from finances to human relations, etc." (Ure 2001). For the enhancement of communication and transactions with all of an organization's stakeholders, including customers, suppliers, government regulators, financial institutions, managers, employees, and the public at large (Watson *et al.* 2000: 1), both B2B (business-to-business) and B2C (business-to-consumer, often meaning online shopping) can be put into practice.

For the measurement of worldwide e-commerce, Table 7.1 shows that, due to differences in methodology, there are wide variations in the statistical data.

Table 7.1 Worldwide e-commerce: some estimates and forecasts (US$ billions), compared to worldwide Internet users (millions)

	Forrester: *worldwide* *e-commerce*	*IDC:* *worldwide* *e-commerce*	*Emarketer:* *worldwide* *e-commerce* *(B2B only)*	*ITU:* *Internet* *users* *worldwide*
2000	n.a.	354.90	278.19	399
2001	n.a.	615.30	474.32	495
2002	2,293.50	n.a.	823.48	622
2003	3,878.80	n.a.	1,408.57	688
2004	6,201.10	n.a.	2,367.47	n.a.
2005	9,240.60	4,600.00	n.a.	n.a.
2006	12,837.30	n.a.	n.a.	n.a.

Source: Adapted and compiled based on data from UNCTAD 2003b: xix, ITU, various years, http://www.itu.int/ITU-D/ict/statistics/ (accessed March 22, 2005).

These figures have to be compared with the overall worldwide B2B and retail transactions. According to the *E-Commerce and Development Report 2002* by UNCTAD (2003b: xix), the most optimistic forecast suggests that e-commerce will represent about 18 percent of global transactions by 2006. Even if the total amount of e-commerce is difficult to forecast, the ratio of around 95 percent B2B to 5 percent B2C e-commerce will remain constant. In the late 1990s, during the rise of the dot-com industry, B2C was the engine that moved commerce onto the Internet, while EDI (electronic data interchange) was the only e-commerce modality before B2B (UNCTAD 2003b: 8).

In its 2004 report, UNCTAD basically stopped making predictions about global e-commerce and presented only data from the US, "which represents by far the largest share of all e-commerce in the world and continues to set the trends which e-commerce and e-business follow" (UNCTAD 2004: 12).[8] In 2003, B2C e-commerce represented 1.65 percent of the US total retail sales. Figures provided by the US Census Bureau in 2004 show that B2C sales in the United States reached US\$ 55.996 million, representing an annual growth rate of about 26 percent since 2000 (ibid.).

In China, e-commerce has expanded exponentially over the past five years and is widely expected to continue its rapid development. The forecasts for B2B e-commerce in China diverge significantly. Table 7.2 shows some of the estimates for B2B e-commerce in China predicted by leading global e-commerce research and consulting firms. The figures assembled in this table show extreme variations. This, as mentioned earlier, is due to differences in methodology, for example counting only online processed transactions or including offline settlements as well.

The research – from the perspective of foreign companies

This analysis of the potential contribution of the Internet and the presumed effects of its commercial applications within the PRC is based on field research conducted in Beijing and Shanghai which took the perspective of foreign companies as a starting point. The reason for choosing this perspective derives from the special role of such companies. Their statements reflect, first of all, their experience with new technological developments

Table 7.2 Estimates for B2B e-commerce in China (US\$)

	eMarketer (2001)	Forrester (2001)
2002	6 billion	600 million
2004	22 billion	n.a.
2006	n.a.	9.6 billion

Source: Author's own compilation based on data from UNCTAD 2003b: 13.

at a global level but they also show how the local situation forces them to develop business strategies suitable for dealing with the Chinese market environment. The interviews were held with two main groups: foreign companies from different industries, in the fields of IT (systems and applications), transportation, interactive advertising and law consultancy. The other group consisted of intermediate protagonists, in particular, the Chamber of Commerce and an e-commerce lobby group.[9] These interviews all took place during February and March 2002.

The research focused on various aspects of e-commerce in the PRC as detailed below:

- general questions relating to concepts;
- performance of foreign companies in the field of e-commerce in the PRC;
- major trends, future plans and future outlook;
- legal/governmental framework for e-commerce in China;
- hindrances and barriers to development.

These issues were considered from the perspective of foreign companies in China, and their specific roles in China's e-commerce development, so that the following questions emerged:

- What are the major driving forces behind e-commerce in China?
- How is their role defined?
- How do the protagonists of e-commerce in China meet in Cyberspace (Platforms, One-to-One Marketing)?
- What is the response of the users?
- Are new business models emerging?
- Who are the economic beneficiaries of the technical innovations and the Internet revolution?
- Are the opportunities for e-commerce in China exploited to the full?
- What are the expected impacts especially for foreign companies active in the PRC?

The role of e-commerce for foreign companies in China

Since the reform and opening policy was introduced in 1978, China has become a "global hot spot" for foreign economic engagement. It has attracted an increasing amount of foreign direct investment every year, and this reached US\$ 52.7 billion in 2002 (*China Statistical Yearbook* 2003: 671). Many publications in recent years have focused on China's position in the world economy and the development of China's domestic market since joining the WTO. The following section of this chapter will discuss the special usage of new and emerging technology by foreign enterprises for matters related to e-commerce.

Strategy, size, infrastructure, and security

Foreign companies active in any field of e-commerce in China are confronted with the impact of emerging technology for their industry's business, general e-commerce trends, and the special market characteristics prevailing in China. To begin with, the formulation of a corporate e-commerce strategy is determined by the enterprises' overall organizational structure and the decision-making processes within this structure, between, respectively, the corporate centers/head offices abroad and their subsidiaries in China. In the field of e-commerce, this – of course – differs widely depending on the strategies used in different industries. In very standardized businesses, the same methods are applied worldwide. Take, for example, as being representative of the transportation sector, the German airline, Lufthansa: Lufthansa's e-commerce strategy is formulated in the head office in Frankfurt, Germany, and the translation of this strategy into the Chinese market follows the centralized integration into the overall company network structure via fixed lines to carry out the business; the systems and applications are also provided by Germany (Interview with Lufthansa, March 21, 2002). Another aspect, besides such a strategic centralization concept that includes the provision of technology by a head office, is the size of the company. In the interview with representatives from SAP China, one of the global leading companies in the IT systems and applications market, it was pointed out that:

> small and medium-sized enterprises with a total investment of, for example, one million euros simply cannot afford to spend three quarters of that on IT. For these enterprises, IT is not the "number one" priority. Instead, the big multinationals see their e-commerce activities as part of their global e-commerce rollout.
>
> (Interview with SAP, March 4, 2002)

SAP clients in China are eager to adopt e-commerce solutions for their businesses. First of all, they demand enterprise resource planning (ERP) solutions, starting with basic financial accounting tools. Developments in the field of customer relationship management (CRM) are relatively new. The overall trend is towards an integration of suppliers, manufacturing and customers, towards supply chain management (SCM). Problems in connection with technical solutions are high development costs and the need for long-term investments (ibid.).

One common fact emerging from the statements of all the interviewees, which can be considered a very important result of this research, is that the whole telecommunication and network infrastructure within China is no longer seen to be a major problem. Experience with SAP clients shows that for them the Internet has created "a public infrastructure" (ibid.). But enterprises have to face another challenge: "Hosting has to be provided by the system developer, as the clients do not have sufficient capacity" (ibid.). In contrast to the efficient network infrastructure, the general infrastructure was described as having a limiting effect on e-commerce. This limitation leads to a logistical bottleneck in the execution of online business. These findings were confirmed by all the interviewees as applicable to their fields of activity.

E-commerce activity in China also faces a technical challenge. A key factor for success in online business is having the capability to provide secure transmission of any data involved. The IT multinational corporation, Siemens has long maintained a company presence in China, the country that represents their biggest market. During an interview, an Information Security Officer from Siemens stated quite clearly that the performance of e-commerce in China was still lagging behind because:

> any transaction must guarantee privacy, availability and security. That touches, for example, the integration of digital signatures, e-contracts, authentication within invoice systems etc. The biggest problem of enterprises is their lack of awareness of the importance of this area, of guaranteeing trust.
>
> (Interview, March 7, 2002)

B2C – shaping the interface

A presentation entitled "E-volution in China," which was carried out by Roland Berger & Partners in Shanghai in September 2000, formulated the following question as a critical issue for foreign investors and the management of foreign companies: "Could we gain a market/customer advantage with a leading B2C e-solution?" At the time the research was carried out, the volume of foreign company engagement in any B2C e-commerce was perceived as relatively low. A representative of China and Hong Kong of Tribal DDB, the interactive branch of the advertising company DDB, offered two reasons for that:

> E-commerce is not taken seriously by the companies themselves, and it is handled by people who do another job and have taken up the Internet too; even if the corporate office has a vision, it cannot be adopted. In addition, the appearance of companies in China's Internet varies a lot. For B2B, the big companies try to have a global structure strategy, but the field of B2C is not at all standardized. Domestic companies have no strategy at all, they just try out what is cheap and do not know whether it is effective; there is no need to know this while the market is expanding anyway.
>
> (Interview with Tribal DDB, March 13, 2002)

Generally, online B2C business models have become more comprehensive as the Internet has entered a stage of consolidation. Both customers and industry have become more familiar with online activities. Hence, the development of online business models was named by all interviewees as crucial for long-term engagement in China's Internet.

> The business model defines the company's value proposition in the marketplace in relation to its customers, suppliers, competition and even employees. The business model analyzes the company's ability to sustain profitability over the long term in measuring a company's offering versus the provision costs of goods and services. It is an extremely useful tool for predicting a company's ability to survive and generate returns for shareholders, especially for early stage companies where a great deal of uncertainty still exists.
>
> (Li and Wong 2001: 39)

Chinese enterprises in particular are benefiting greatly from the use of new media applications. This result was also confirmed for various industries in China at the interview with a German Chamber of Commerce representative in Beijing (Interview, February 27, 2002). Experience with SAP clients, half of them domestic enterprises, shows that for them the "online business models are becoming as important as their overall strategy" (Interview with SAP, March 4, 2002). Especially for Chinese technology companies, Li and Wong (2001: 40–1) identify seven business models that apply for the Chinese market. These business models are displayed in Table 7.3.

Beyond the specific business models used predominantly by Chinese companies, foreign companies in China mostly integrate B2C in the field of marketing. When Internet use was on the increase as a common information tool, the online presence of companies shifted from offering information towards

Table 7.3 Seven Internet business models in China

Business model	Revenue derived from
Infrastructure/access revenue model	Charging user subscription fees
Technology enabler revenue model	Sale of hardware or software products designed with proprietary intellectual property
Content/portal revenue model	Online advertising
E-retailing revenue model	Principal sale of goods online
Online marketplace revenue model	Commissions, posting fees, success fees or other agency "toll fees"
Service revenue model	Providing consulting, technical support, or sales support services
Investment revenue model	Income and return derived from investment in technology companies

Source: Author's own compilation based on Li and Wong 2001: 40–1.

using it as a marketing channel. This included the field of brand building via the Internet. This, of course, starts with the companies' Chinese-language websites. The expert from the German Chamber of Commerce stressed the importance of Chinese-language content: "Otherwise companies will not reach Chinese users at all" (Interview, February 27, 2002).

Using the company's website in a more comprehensive way, however, does not only mean advertising it on the big Chinese portals to attract more traffic. The role of online advertising was discussed in the interview with Lufthansa China:

> We do not want to simply buy banners or exchange banners. Instead, the Internet is regarded from our side as a "customer information channel" and a "customer care channel." Overall, it has been far quieter about e-commerce compared with two years ago. Now, the shift is towards CRM.
>
> (Interview with Lufthansa, March 21, 2002)

Using the web for customer relationship management purposes means in this case, for example, that customers have the opportunity to apply for Lufthansa's "Miles&More" program, being notified via email about special offers and information about the company. Generally, the concept of CRM is one of the major trends of B2C e-commerce worldwide.[10]

Nevertheless, companies have to be careful about what kind of customer benefit is presented, since any online activity has to meet the requirements set by the Chinese business environment. Online auctions, for example, do not play a large role in China yet. At the time the interviews were conducted, online auctions were seen from the Chinese side as leading to the undermining of prices and the introduction of dumping methods. The experience of Lufthansa China underlined the fact that auctions are case sensitive, since prices in the transportation business are fixed and regulated by the Civil Aviation Administration of China (CAAC – *Zhongguo minyong hangkong zongju*). Lufthansa does not differentiate between online and offline prices for air tickets: "Only in the case of special offers do the prices differ, but we do not do that generally for online" (ibid.).

B2B – creating Chinese marketplaces

MOFTEC, whose responsibilities were incorporated into the newly set up Ministry of Trade in March 2003, has played a crucial role in shaping B2B opportunities for the Chinese market. In 2002, at the Ministry's website, accessible online at http://www.moftec.gov.cn, foreign and domestic companies could access a wide variety of general and specific information regarding trade issues. Furthermore, the site functioned as a starting point for entering various portals run by MOFTEC itself. The conceptual foundation lies back with the government's attempt at promoting the so-called "Golden

Projects," especially the "Golden Trade Project" (*jinmao*). Chinese companies can register on the "Chinamarket" site, accessible online at http://www.chinamarket.com.cn, to promote themselves and their goods and services. Another site is the China Business Guide (CBG) at http://www.cbg.com.cn, which is part of the national information service system for international trade and economic cooperation. As is stated on the website, the "CBG aims to assist Chinese enterprises, small and medium-sized enterprises in particular, to cultivate their overseas markets and increase their exports."

One particular site was mentioned by the interviewees involved in the research: China Bidding. Established in 1998, Chinabidding.com.cn was appointed by the State Development and Planning Commission, on July 1, 2000, as the only official website for announcing the PRC governmental and public tender notices. The company, China Bidding Ltd. (CBL), describes itself as "the bridge linking the huge Chinese bidding market and the overseas suppliers and investors." In 2002, the annual amount involved in the tendering, bidding, and procurement business has reached approximately RMB 3,000 million (US$ 362.37 million). By March 20, 2003, a total of 43,996 tender notice listings had been posted at the site.[11]

On May 1, 2001, the Chinabidding.com site started its operations. It is designated as the sole official website for online operation of international competitive bidding (ICB) for the procurement of machinery and equipment from abroad. Some desk research, carried out by the e-Business Department of Siemens Ltd., China, made a comparison of both portals: it was concluded that Chinabidding.com "is more specialized at international bidding for machinery and electronic products," while Chinabidding.com.cn "provides an online bidding platform in all business areas and mainly deals with domestic biddings" (Zhao 2001).[12] Many Siemens companies in China have registered on these sites as "suppliers" and made successful bids via Chinabidding.com. By November 2001, Siemens companies had won 77 out of 173 bids (ibid.). By March 2002, as a representative of Siemens Ltd., China e-Business Department pointed out in an additional interview, they had already achieved an "increase of around 50 percent" (Interview, March 7, 2002). Furthermore, these portals were seen as representing "an extreme shift in the Chinese governmental practice towards improving efficiency in the process of bidding in China regarding procedure, accessibility, time saving" (Zhao 2001). The portals keep the details of the submitted bids strictly confidential; that is also seen as an advantage, despite the fact that statistics on competitors' bids would certainly be of interest for the purpose of market analyses (Interview, March 7, 2002).

An intermediate approach – the E-Commerce China Forum/the International Informatization Forum

The E-Commerce China Forum (ECCF) was founded in Beijing in 2000. This lobby group aims to work as an industry-based coalition with the

Chinese government on questions regarding e-commerce development in China. The ECCF was officially recognized by the Chinese government as the E-Commerce Working Group (ECWG) under the China Association of Enterprises with Foreign Investment (CAEFI) in September 2000. It tries to help to discuss and develop e-commerce policy and the market in China. At the time the research was carried out, in March 2002, there were nine ECCF-members, mostly from the IT industry: Oracle, Ericsson, Intel, IBM, Hewlett-Packard, Siemens, Gemplus, Nokia, and Standard Chartered Bank.[13] The ECCF Secretariat is located at APCO Associates, Beijing. As the Chairman Gregory Shea (2002) pointed out, the ECCF has become the International Informatization Forum (IIF) which was initiated in September 2002 as the ECWG (E-Commerce Working Group) project.

The general structure has changed considerably over the years. In 2002, as a result of market changes, the ECCF/IIF and its members became active in two working groups, a paperless trading working group and an m-commerce (mobile-commerce) working group. The paperless trading working group has been trying to establish a pilot project for customs procedures, in the field of B2B via fixed lines, making electronic documents "legal," e.g. using technology for electronic seals. The expected benefits are named by the interviewees as follows: increased operational efficiency, savings in time and money, and reductions in inventories. For the Chinese government, this is considered to be very close to e-government, in particular with regard to the efforts of the government to establish a "China e-Port System." The overall responsibility lies with MOFTEC and the State Council. Chinese corporations are benefiting from competitive advantages through improved access to the global market (Interview, March 7, 2002).

All interviewees expressed the conviction that m-commerce will set the next major trend with China as the biggest mobile phone market in the world, enabling Internet access. M-commerce applications will play a large role in the field of B2B e-commerce as well. The ECCF confirmed this view of m-commerce as heralding the next revolution in e-commerce. From their work experience, all foreign and domestic players in the industry believed that China has the potential to leap-frog standards set in this field and, in addition to this, the government is keen on building an environment that will enable a stable mobile market. As a result of these trends, the ECCF has become active in setting up an ECCF mobile commerce working group (ibid.).

The lobbying work of the working groups consisted of compiling papers, such as practical reports, legal analyses and executive summaries, all to be addressed to MOFTEC and/or the State Organization Leading Group Office at the State Council. In addition to these activities, closed-door policy workshops, industry round tables, best practice seminars and private government meetings were organized. The working atmosphere was described as cooperative:

The foreign companies are interested in long-term strategies. In the beginning, it was difficult to attract members. At that time the government was under pressure because of the rise of the dot-com industry, reacting with new regulations every day. Nowadays, there is no longer any time pressure, but a more selective approach on how to incorporate new technology applications into the e-policy framework.

(ibid.)

Whether or not the ECCF/IIF really is becoming a government forum seems to be a matter of doubt for both foreign and domestic industry players. In theory it would like to attract also more Chinese companies as members, but in practice it is clear that Chinese companies are often able to utilize alternative communication channels, attending to official or business matters through personal relationships, usually known as *guanxi* (ibid.).

Legal framework

Since 1999, with the growth in popularity of the dot-com industry, there has been speculation about an e-commerce law for China:[14]

Instead of a comprehensive law there have been regulations incorporated into the existing legal framework, for example for consumer protection and the Chinese Contract Law. Other governance aspects touched on issues of fulfillment, delivery, security, and intellectual property. Meanwhile, the current legal approach mainly addresses China's overall ICT competitiveness instead of focusing on e-commerce.

(Interview with Dr Stucken, March 13, 2002)

And hence, the trend is once again towards the role of the protagonists of China's Internet, the government and the enterprises:

China's preparation and implementation of its WTO commitments could provide the catalyst for China to become a center of innovation, content creation, and research development. On the other hand, the government is facing difficult trade-offs, and enterprises need to redefine their core competencies while constantly assessing and responding to changing market circumstances, including the evolving regulatory framework.

(Lanvin *et al.* 2003: vii, 162–77)

Despite the media discourse and the speculations about an e-commerce law, all the interviewees pointed out that such a law is of little importance. In this context, regional attempts are seen as an extension of the existing law into the Internet sphere. For example, in May 2000, the Beijing

Administration of Industry and Commerce (BAIC) promulgated a notice on Regulations of Internet Advertising Operation Qualifications (including e-commerce), and in 1999, the Office of Shanghai National Economy & Society Informatization Leading Group and the Shanghai Municipal Foreign Investment Working Commission issued "e-licences" (Stucken and Li 2000: 37).

Response from the users

The CNNIC statistical report of July 2004 shows that 626,600 websites meet an audience of 87 million users in China. Internet use is rising at a rapid rate, both at home and at work. The average user is still young, male (59.3 percent), urban, affluent, and well-educated. The largest group are students (31.9 percent), followed by engineering personnel (13.2 percent), enterprise managers (9.6 percent), and business/service workers (8.4 percent) (CNNIC 7/2004).

Retrieving information from the net is the main reason (42 percent) given for going online and one third simply wants to be entertained (ibid.). The use of e-business services by Chinese users is losing acceptance slightly, with 7.3 percent using online purchasing, 4.9 percent using online banking, and even fewer, 3.9 percent, using online trading (CNNIC 7/2004: 13). During the time the research was being carried out, real online shopping was used by only 11.8 percent, followed by online stock trading (5.5 percent), and online banking (3.6 percent) (CNNIC 1/2002). The overall figures are very low even if over two thirds of those asked said that they accessed online shopping websites "frequently/sometimes." In January 2002, nearly 70 percent of online buyers purchased books and magazines (7/2004: nearly 60 percent), and 30 percent purchased computer appliances (7/2004: 33 percent). A closer look at the type of information required and the needs that still cannot be satisfied, shows the large potential for future purchase opportunities, mainly in the field of computer hardware and software, entertainment, e-books, science and education, job hunting, and even automobiles. Interviewees repeatedly mentioned that the Chinese users are regarded as the "future decision makers" and the consumers who will be targeted by companies. And the online audience is aware of this fact. In this context, the awareness of the underlying e-business concepts is stated in the January 2003 CNNIC report: more than 50 percent of users responding to the survey were aware of – and even familiar with – terms like CRM and ERP.[15]

The primary obstacle to online purchasing lies in the field of customer satisfaction. In July 2004, nearly 44 percent of the users complained that "the quality of products, after-service and credit of the producer cannot be guaranteed," 29 percent, that "security cannot be guaranteed," and 7 percent expressed dissatisfaction with, respectively, "unreliable information," "inconvenient payment methods," and "late delivery" (CNNIC 7/2004: 20).

Obviously, the task of turning users into (satisfied) customers is still a long way from being fulfilled.

Conclusion

From the start, the Internet in China was state-driven with huge investments being made in the infrastructure and further applications, such as those introduced by the Golden Projects. Building up an adequate information infrastructure and regulatory framework, however, is only the first step towards establishing functioning e-commerce. The agenda is clearly formulated: all the related governmental departments and enterprises in China follow the societal consensus of contributing to the overall economy in China to overcome the disparities in the country and to develop an information society. How governance aspects impact on the action of foreign companies and China's e-commerce readiness in general, for example, in the field of consumer protection, security, intellectual property, taxes, does not necessarily mean there is a call for a special legal e-commerce framework; interviewees considered this to be of little importance, because many regulations have already been incorporated into existing laws and regulations.

The major results of the research presented here are summarized and discussed as follows: all foreign companies active in the field of e-commerce are present in China and their activities are twofold. First, they follow worldwide (e-)business trends and transfer these into the Chinese market. Parallel to this, they have to conform to certain Chinese market conditions set by the government, the competition, and the customers. B2B e-commerce platforms, actively promoted by the government, are regarded as decisive factors for future changes in business processes in China, for example the bidding-platforms established by former MOFTEC, but the scope and objectives of industries' platforms must be clearly defined in order to ensure gains in efficiency.

The results of the research allow the conclusion to be drawn that there is an overall potential for e-commerce in China because Chinese users are enthusiastically embracing new online features. This will lead to concepts of more sophisticated marketing strategies beyond simple online advertisement by the enterprises and lays a positive foundation for integrated online communications. In the field of B2C e-commerce, the focus is shifting towards customer relationship management systems and brand-building via the Internet. Furthermore, the exploding Chinese mobile market is enabling m-commerce to set a major trend both for B2B and B2C applications, via mobile phones or other hand-held devices.

What about the hindrances and barriers of e-commerce in China? The telecommunication and network infrastructure within China is no longer seen by the interviewees to constitute a major problem. Instead, logistics and payment were widely named by all interviewees as the major weak points. Government and industry should provide solutions on a nationwide scale to overcome such external problems. Internally, technical facilities and networks within the enterprises have to be developed. This applies to both foreign and domestic companies. Hence, internal budgets for establishing and updating suitable e-solutions are becoming a crucial factor for a company's e-commerce realization.

Overall, the "hype" about e-commerce has entered a stage of consolidation and the greatest challenge for foreign companies will be to understand the specifics of the Chinese market. So far, the main beneficiaries are the Chinese companies. It seems that the tremendous investments in the ICT sector within the periods of the ninth and tenth Five-Year-Plans are paying off. Whether these companies really become competitive on a global scale through e-commerce applications remains doubtful at this point in time. A general challenge lies in the methodological approach: while the Internet is consolidating as a comprehensive economic tool, the measurement of revenues and business models are still at an initial stage of standardization. Regarding the competition within the Chinese domestic market, the leading role of foreign companies can no longer continue to derive only from their past advantageous positioning in the capital-intensive fields. If they are not able to accompany that with suitable business models, they will be forced to change by successful companies such as Haier or Lenovo (former company Legend).

> After all, if e-commerce matters for development, it is not because it is a fancier or more convenient way to go shopping: e-commerce matters because it allows enterprises to generate efficiency gains at all the stages of their production and distribution processes. It is these gains, made essentially through the adoption of B2B and e-business practices, that count for development, because they translate into improved competitiveness for enterprises and higher levels of productivity, and hence incomes for the economy as a whole.
>
> (UNCTAD 2002: 9)

Notes

1 These interviews all took place during February and March 2002. The research presented here excludes the field of the automotive industry. A case study on the role of e-commerce for the automotive industry in China is part of the author's PhD research project.
2 Prominent examples at provincial and municipal level are initiatives run by the Beijing and Shanghai city authorities. Furthermore, examples of local-level activities can be found, as presented in the research carried out by Jens Damm: he analyzed the concepts of local e-government in the two relatively wealthy provinces of Fujian and Guangdong with a focus on Taijiang, a district of Fuzhou (see Chapter 5 in this volume).
3 For a further discussion on the impact of the WTO process on China's ICT competitiveness, see also Lanvin *et al.* 2003.

4 For a detailed examination of the problem of digital divide, see Giese 2003.

5 The same source pointed out just three months earlier:

> Transactions are called "electronic," and thus fall into the categories e-business or e-commerce, if at least one step in each phase is pursued electronically. E-business does not only describe external communication and transaction functions, but also relates to flows of information within the company, i.e., between departments, subsidiaries and branches. E-commerce refers to external transactions in goods and services.
>
> (EUROPA 2004)

6 The "China E-Commerce Challenge Group" project directors are Prof. Zheng Youjing, Executive Director of the Center for Information Infrastructure and Economic Development, Chinese Academy of Social Sciences (CASS), and Mr G. Russel Pipe, Deputy Director, Global Information Infrastructure Committee and Senior Advisor, International Communications Studies Program, Center for Strategic and International Studies (CSIS). Other Chinese members come from high-level research institutes at academic, political, and administrative levels, such as CASS, MII, State Council, State Economic and Trade Commission, and MOFTEC, to name but a few. The group's international members are, for example, representatives of multinational corporations such as Intel, Mitsubishi, Coudert Brothers, Hewlett Packard, Oracle, etc. In 1999, delegates of the group visited Silicon Valley in San Jose, USA, and met with eight international information industrial companies to "understand the attitude and measures of the American information industries and American government for E-Commerce according to the firsthand materials" (Zheng *et al.* 1999: 117).

7 Furthermore, the scope outlined in the circular includes that:

> (a)ny entity in Beijing engaging in such activity is to register with the BAIC, and to display a registration seal issued by the BAIC on the home page of its Web site. A registered e-commerce business desiring to alter or terminate its business activities must inform the BAIC.
>
> (McKenzie 2000)

8 As a reason for not continuing to give worldwide predictions, the report states:

> Several chapters in this Report, as well as in Reports of previous years, refer to the rarity of statistically significant measurements of the value of e-commerce transactions in most countries, and particularly on the developing world. [. . .] the situation in this regard has not changed sufficiently to warrant a revision of the remarks made in the introductory chapters of the previous two Reports [. . .] .
>
> (UNCTAD 2004: 12)

9 More specifically, interviews were conducted with the following experts: for SAP China: Vice President of SAP Greater China, Global Key Account Manager China of SAP China; for Lufthansa German Airlines: Head of China Coordination Office; for Tribal DDB (part of Worldwide DDB): Regional Interactive Marketing Director Greater China; for Siemens Ltd China: Executive Manager e-Business, Information Security Officer Information and Knowledge Management; for German Chamber Industry and Commerce Beijing (AHK): Head of Department Marketing/Internet; for E-Commerce China Forum (ECCF): Senior Consultant APCO Public Affairs & Strategic Communications, Project Assistant Association Practice; and Dr Bernd-Uwe Stucken, Chief Representative and Partner of the Shanghai-based law consultancy Haarmann, Hemmelrath & Partners.

10 For the concept of Integrated Marketing, see also Watson *et al.* 2000: 65–6:

Consequently, the Internet offers an excellent basis for a variety of marketing tactics, which permits the development of a model for integrated Internet marketing. The concepts of integrated Internet communication apply to all forms of communication, not just that between seller and buyer.

The process of customer management is formed as a combination of relationship management and opportunity management. The strategic use of CRM combines marketing, sales and services. Electronic CRM includes the Internet as a communication channel.

11 Accessible online at http://www.chinabidding.com.cn, the tender notices by categories are: Agriculture/Forestry/Herd/Fisheries, Commerce, Energy/Chemical, Environment, Irrigation Works/Bridge, Light Industry, Machine/Electronics, Medicine/Health, Metallurgy/Raw Materials, Public Security/Utilities, Real Estate/Architecture, Telecommunication/Computer, Transportation, Sciences/Technology/Education, others (accessed March 20, 2003). In 2005, with a total of 20,995 active notices listed, the English sister website to Chinabidding.com.cn, Chinabidding.org used the following categories: Transportation (1,024), Construction (1,499), Environment (821), Telecommunication/Computer (582), Machine/Electronic (11,266), Medicine/Health (1,554), Printing/Packaging (160), Textile/Apparel (1,451), Sciences/Technology (130), Energy/Chemical (566), Agriculture/Food (142), Irrigation Work/Bridge (359), Metallurgy/Mining (144), Public Utility (267), Education/Training (150), Business and Related Services (620), Materials (18), Others (278) (http://www.chinabidding.org/bids_bank/all/, accessed March 12, 2005).

12 Here, I refer to the desk research carried out by Andrew Zhao Jifeng for the E-Business Department of Siemens Ltd, China, in December 2001. I would like to offer special thanks to the E-Business Department of Siemens Ltd, China, for making the material available for academic use.

13 Past members were also AOL Time Warner, Baker & McKenzie, Cable & Wireless, Digital China, General Motors, Global Sources, Jardine Matheson Group, Ji Tong Communications Company, Legend Technology, Lucent Technologies, Microsoft, Motorola, Nokia, Perkins Coie, Rockwell, Samsung, SAP, Sony, TNT Post Group, United Parcel Service (UPS), Xin De Telecom, Zi Corporation.

14 The State Council, with its sub-department, the State Council Informatization Leading Group Office, is technically in charge of setting up the legal agenda for the Internet in China. Vivienne Bath (2000: 2) points out that although this office holds overall authority, many other parties are involved: "numerous ministries and other governmental bodies have been jockeying for position in order to hold the power, or some power, to regulate the Internet." The field of domain names is handled by the CNNIC and the registration of Chinese character domain names has been accepted since November 2000 (Ermert and Hughes 2003: 127–38).

15 This category was only found in the January 2003 CNNIC report: The users' acquaintance with the term CRM was listed as 46.7 percent, "never know;" 32.1 percent, "heard of it;" 15.6 percent, "understand;" and 15.6 percent "know well." Instead of this category, the July 2004 CNNIC report offers a more extensive set of questions regarding use of online chatting, short message service, and familiarity with online recruitment services.

References

Bath, Vivienne (2000) "E-commerce in China – Is China ready to do e-business?" Seminar in Hong Kong, June 8, 2000. Online. Available HTTP: http://www.china

online.com/commentary_analysis/Internet/currentnews/secure/ecommerce-vb03 22-s.asp (accessed November 22, 2002).

Cartlege, Simon and Lovelock, Peter (1999) "Special subject: e-China," *China Economic Quarterly*, 3: 1 (First quarter), pp. 19–35.

CNNIC (2001) *Survey Report on the Quantity of China's Internet Information Resources, 30.04.2001.* Online. Available HTTP: http://www.cnnic.net.cn (accessed February 15, 2003).

CNNIC (1/2002) *Statistical Survey Report on the Development of Internet in China, January 2002.* Online. Available HTTP: http://www.cnnic.net.cn (accessed February 15 2003).

CNNIC (1/2003) *Statistical Survey Report on the Development of Internet in China (Jan. 2003).* Online. Available HTTP: http://www.cnnic.net.cn (accessed February 15, 2003).

CNNIC (7/2004) *14th Statistical Survey Report on the Development on Internet in China.* Online. Available HTTP: http://www.cnnic.net.cn (accessed August 21, 2004).

China Statistical Yearbook (2003) "Amount of utilization of foreign capital and foreign investment," p. 671. Online. Available HTTP: http://www.stats.gov. cn/English/statisticaldata/yearlydata/yearbook2003_e.pdf (accessed March 18, 2005).

Dutta, Soumitra and Jain, Amit (2003) "The networked readiness of nations," in: World Economic Forum/Inseat *The Global Information Technology Report 2002–2003*, New York and Oxford: Oxford University Press, pp. 2–25. Online. Available HTTP: http://www.weforum.org/site/homepublic.nsf/Content/Global+ Competitiveness+Programme%5CGlobal+Information+Technology+Report (accessed March 15, 2003).

Ermert, Monika and Hughes, Christopher R. (2003) "What's in a name? China and the domain name system," in: Christopher R. Hughes and Gudrun Wacker (eds) *China and the Internet: Politics of the Digital Leap Forward*, London and New York: RoutledgeCurzon, pp. 127–38.

EUROPA (2004) "Making the e-Economy Work," in: Homepage of Europe's Information Society – Thematic Portal "Economy and Work." Online. Available HTTP: http://europa.eu.int/information_society/ecowor/print_en.htm (accessed November 1, 2004).

EUROPA (2005) "A dynamic e-business environment," in: Homepage of Europe's Information Society – Thematic Portal "Economy and Work: eBusiness." Online. Available HTTP: http://europa.eu.int/information_society/ecowor/ebusiness/print_ en.htm (accessed February 21, 2005).

Giese, Karsten (2003) "Internet growth and the digital divide: implications for spatial development," in: Christopher R. Hughes and Gudrun Wacker (eds) *China and the Internet: Politics of the Digital Leap Forward*, London and New York: RoutledgeCurzon, pp. 30–57.

Lanvin, Bruno, Mar, Pamela, Qiang, Christine Zhen-Wei, Richter, Frank-Jürgen (2003) "Born global: the impact of the WTO process on China's ICT competi- tiveness," in: World Economic Forum/Inseat (2003) *The Global Information Technology Report 2002–2003*, New York and Oxford: Oxford University Press, pp. 162–77. Online. Available HTTP: http://www.weforum.org/site/home- public.nsf/Content/Global+Competitiveness+Programme%5CGlobal+Information +Technology+Report (accessed March 15, 2003).

Li, Gabriel and Wong, Edmond (2001) *The Rise of Digital China: Investing in China's New Economy*, San Francisco, CA: China Books and Periodicals.

McKenzie, Paul D. (2000) "Electronic commerce law – People's Republic of China." Online. Available HTTP: http://www.perkinscoie.com/page.cfm?id=68 (accessed March 17, 2005).

Nolan, Peter (2001) *China and the Global Economy*, London and New York: Palgrave.

Roland Berger & Partners (2000) *E-volution in China*, Powerpoint-Presentation, Shanghai, September 9.

Shea, Gregory (Chairman, IIF) (2002) "China's evolving communications industry," Presentation to Silicon Valley Chinese Wireless Association, October 22, 2002. Online. Available HTTP: http://www.svcwireless.org/programs/seminar102302/Oct%202002%20Silicon%20Valley.ppt (accessed March 19, 2003).

Stucken, Bernd-Uwe and Li, Edna (2000) "E-Commerce in China: Rechtliches Umfeld," *China Nachrichten*, 1, pp. 35–7.

UNCTAD (2002) *E-commerce and Development Report, 2002*, New York and Geneva: United Nations.

UNCTAD (2003a) Homepage of UNCTAD Electronic Commerce Branch (ECB). Online. Available HTTP: http://www.unctad.org/ecommerce/ecommerce_en/faq_en.htm (accessed February 25, 2003).

UNCTAD (2003b) *E-commerce and Development Report, 2002*. Online. Available HTTP: http://r0.unctad.org/ecommerce/ecommerce_en/edr02_en.htm (accessed February 25, 2003).

UNCTAD (2004) *E-commerce and Development Report 2004*. Online. Available HTTP: http://www.unctad.org/en/docs/ecdr2004_en.pdf (accessed February 11, 2005).

Ure, John (2001) "Presentation at the workshop on strategic electronic commerce and management," Bangkok, May 23–25, 2001. Online. Available HTTP: http://www.trp.hku.hk/trp_papers.html (accessed February 27, 2002).

Wang, Changsheng (ed.) (2003) *Zhongguo Zhengwu Fazhan Baogao No.1 (China E-Government Development Report No.1). Dianzi Zhengwu Lanpi Shu (Blue Book of Electronic Government)*, Beijing: Shehui kexue wenxian chubanshe.

Watson, Richard T., Berthon, Pierre, Pitt, Lyland F. and Zinkhan, George M. (2000) *Electronic Commerce: The Strategic Perspective*, Fort Worth, TX: The Dryden Press.

Wong, John and Nah, Seok Ling (2001) *China's Emerging New Economy: The Internet and E-Commerce*, Singapore: Singapore University Press.

World Bank (2002) "ICT at a glance China." Online. Available HTTP: http://unpan1.un.org/intradoc/groups/public/documents/APCITY/UNPAN008304.pdf (accessed March 18, 2005).

World Bank (2003) "ICT at a glance China." Online. Available HTTP: http://www.worldbank.org/cgi-bin/sendoff.cgi?page=%2Fdata%2Fcountrydata%2Fict%2Fchn_ict.pdf (accessed March 18, 2005).

Xinhuanet (November 18, 2002) "Build a well-off society in an all-round way and create a new situation in building socialism with Chinese characteristics, full text of Jiang Zemin's report at 16th Party Congress, November 8, 2002." Online. Available HTTP: http://news.xinhuanet.com/english/2002–11/18/content_632532.htm (accessed November 18, 2002).

Xinhuanet (November 22, 2002) "The Internet must play a larger role in China: expert." Online. Available HTTP: http://news.xinhuanet.com/English/2002–11/22/content_637859.htm (accessed November 22, 2002).

Zhao, Andrew Jifeng (2001) "Desk research: www.chinabidding.com," Presentation for the e-Business Department, Siemens Ltd, China, December.

Zheng, Youjing, Russel, Pipe, Wu, Gang and Fan, Xing (1999) *Zhongguo dianzi shangwu de fazhan yu juece (China E-Commerce Development and Policy Decision)*, Beijing: Zhongguo caizheng jingji chubanshe.

Index

Page references in bold indicate figures and tables.